Notes of a Red Guard

★

Notes of a Red Guard

Eduard M. Dune

Translated and edited by
Diane P. Koenker
and S. A. Smith

UNIVERSITY OF ILLINOIS PRESS
Urbana and Chicago

This book is printed on acid-free paper.

Library of Congress Cataloging-in-Publication Data
Dune, Eduard M. (Eduard Martynovich), 1899–1953.
    Notes of a Red Guard / Eduard M. Dune ; translated and edited by
Diane P. Koenker and S. A. Smith.
        p. cm.
    Translated from Russian.
    Includes bibliographical references and index.
    ISBN 0-252-01972-5 (cl) (alk. paper). — ISBN 0-252-06277-9 (pb)
    1. Dune, Eduard M. (Eduard Martynovich), 1899-1953. 2. Soviet
Union—History—Revolution, 1917-1921—Personal narratives.
3. Revolutionaries—Soviet Union—Biography. I. Koenker, Diane,
1947– . II. Smith, S. A. (Stephen Anthony), 1952– .
III. Title.
DK254.D78A3 1993
947.084'1'092—dc20
                                                    92-18937
                                                        CIP

For the descendants of Eduard Martynovich Dune

Contents

Acknowledgments

The Hoover Institution on War, Revolution, and Peace at Stanford University has generously given us permission to publish this translation, and we are indebted to the staffs of the Hoover Institution's archive and library for their help throughout our work on this project. Thanks are also due to the superb Slavic Library of the University of Illinois and especially to Helen Sullivan. The University of Illinois provided financial support in the critical final stages of the manuscript's preparation. Lewis Siegelbaum, William Rosenberg, Andrew Verner, and Ben Eklof read versions of the manuscript and offered their encouragement for our efforts. Kathleen McFarland helped to track down aspects of Dune's biography. A Soviet archivist also provided key information about Dune's career. Chris Ward solved a refractory problem about rifles and discussed encouragingly a text he never got to see. James A. Bier drew the maps. Natalia Pervukhin's careful review of our translation, as well as her knowledge of Chekhov, was extremely helpful in the final stages of our work. Vicki Miller contributed efficient clerical and editorial services. Any errors remain our sole responsibility.

Diane Koenker wishes also to thank Steve Smith, who gave generously of his time, even when conducting his own research in far-flung locations, for his stimulating ideas about the project and for his unflagging enthusiasm. Steve Smith thanks Diane Koenker for making his first experience of collaborative scholarly work entirely enjoyable and for proving that the Atlantic Ocean is no bar to efficiency and effective coordination.

Introduction

The events in Russia in 1917 that toppled the old regime and brought into being the first socialist society continue to provoke controversy and debate. Generations of public figures as well as historians have argued whether the 1917 revolution was a triumph of social justice or a world tragedy of the highest order, whether it represented the aspirations and self-determination of society in the Russian Empire or whether it was a conspiracy engineered by ruthless intellectuals. The conflict of ideals represented by these diverging views has provided much of the motive force of twentieth-century history. Assessments of the revolution differ so widely not only because revolutions are such complex events, inherently difficult to disentangle, but above all because revolutions represent the clash of subjective values. Revolutions happen in part because shared value systems break down or because dominant value systems become challenged by the mobilization of a competing value system.

Well before 1917 the tenets of the Russian autocratic order—hierarchy, patriarchy, and privilege—were already facing severe challenge from many elements in society. But there was no single, uniform "opposition" position. Proponents of civil rights, of women's rights, of economic democracy, of national self-determination, and of political democracy vied for influence among Russia's elite and among society at large. Their political messages sometimes contradicted and sometimes reinforced one another. The clash of values implicit in these contradictory appeals helps explain why contemporary accounts as well as historical ones of the Russian revolution have differed so widely in their perspectives and interpretations.

Eyewitness accounts of the revolution—diaries, letters, and retrospective memoirs—provide a valuable and abundant trove of insight into the revolutionary process, events, and consequences. Such accounts have emanated from all parties in the revolutionary struggle, from partisans of the old regime, from supporters of the liberal revolution, from socialist intellectuals both radical and moderate, from distressed bystanders who professed no political allegiance, and from outside observers such as journalists, diplomats, and foreign visitors of all sympathies. All brought to their memories and their records their own perspectives shaped by their values, their positions in society, and their specific experiences. Inevitably most of those who recorded their memoirs came from educated society, and their perspective on events tended to focus their attention on high politics, on leadership, and on ideas. Some of these accounts have become classics in aid of understanding the dynamics of the revolution and the motivations of the participants.[1]

With one important class of exceptions, fewer usable accounts have emerged from among eyewitnesses in the rank-and-file of the revolutionary movement, from peasants or soldiers, accountants or shop clerks, housewives or schoolteachers. The one exception to this absence of reminiscences "from below" has been an outpouring of memoir writing from factory worker participants in the revolution. These accounts emerged from oral "evenings of reminiscences" starting in the early 1920s and from more formal efforts to provide workers, the official victors of the revolution, with their own history.[2] Their numbers run into the thousands, ranging from one-paragraph anecdotes to several-hundred-page books. The best of them are extraordinarily rich documents of working-class life and values, especially for the portions that deal with prerevolutionary conditions and themes.[3]

Memoirs about 1917, however, with a few exceptions, tend to focus on narrowly formulaic issues and to emphasize the success and legitimacy of Bolshevik party policies and actions. The effort to give workers their history was also one to legitimize their revolution, to refashion retrospective memories into a politically acceptable justification for communist society. These formulas applied even in the 1920s, before Lenin's death, and the genre became progressively more rigid and prescribed with the onset of the Stalinist political mentality of the late 1920s and 1930s. This meant, of course, the elimination of Trotsky and other subsequent opponents of Stalin from the historical record, but also the purging of doubt, of ambiguity, and of conflict within the working class and its parties. It is consequently extremely difficult to use such sources to evaluate popular attitudes and perceptions during the immediate revolutionary period.

This memoir by Eduard Dune is a unique and valuable exception to this pattern. Dune was an enthusiastic participant in the revolutionary events of 1917–21, but also a lifelong opponent of the Stalinist regime. This memoir consequently offers the authentic voice of a fiercely independent thinker, but one who was an equally fierce supporter of the ideals of the 1917 revolution. There is nothing else like this on the revolution and civil war.

Eduard Martynovich Dune was born in Riga, of Latvian parents Martyn and Zila Kristina Dune, on 10 September 1899. His father was a skilled worker at one of Riga's largest factories, the Provodnik rubber plant. Riga at this time was a thriving city of half a million people, the fourth largest city in the Russian Empire. German and Russian influences were strong, as Dune describes, but the native population was Latvian. Riga's political life was circumscribed by Russian autocratic rule, just as in the largest cities of St. Petersburg and Moscow, but Riga's citizens enjoyed substantial freedom to form cultural and civic organizations, and according to Dune's recollections, workers in Riga had extensive access to evening schools, choral societies, temperance societies, and the like. Young Eduard attended school in Riga and developed a voracious appetite for books; his family hoped he would finish school, find employment in the lower echelons of the factory administration, and thus rise above the skilled blue-collar position held by his father. Growing up, Dune absorbed tales of factory life from his father, and the 1905 revolution intensified the family's interest in politics and social questions.

In 1915, the Dune family was uprooted by the transfer of the Provodnik factory to Moscow. The German army threatened to capture Riga and its important armaments production, so the Russian government ordered the city's most important factories to resettle, with their work forces, to locations inside Russia. The Provodnik plant was one of 352 enterprises to be transferred from Riga, among which a third were sent to the Moscow region.

For Dune, the move to Moscow more or less coincided with his entry into the world of work, and his memoir of his revolutionary experiences begins at this point. With the reopening of Provodnik in its new location in Tushino (a northwest suburb of Moscow), Dune was taken on as a machine operator, and with seven years of schooling behind him, an ability to read technical drawings, and a smart head on his shoulders, he was soon transferred to highly specialized work in the ebonite section, carrying out important war orders. At the age of sixteen, therefore, he found himself earning twice the monthly wage of his father and, to his pride, financially independent of his parents.

Dune's continued thirst for books and ideas, combined with his comfortable financial position, took him to downtown Moscow on his Sundays off, where he browsed the second-hand book stalls of the city's street markets. His intellectual interests led him to enroll in evening classes at the Moscow Polytechnic Society, and, ultimately, he moved to a room in the city, attending class at night and commuting to Tushino during the day. By the eve of the February revolution, Dune was a seventeen-year-old adult living and studying on his own and forming his own independent view of the world. The first chapter of the memoir thus describes Dune's transition from the world of his family to the world of work and from unskilled worker to skilled craftsman. It also describes his transition from "mere" worker to an educated "conscious" socialist. Dune was already quite interested in problems of socialism and revolution.

Late in 1916, Dune made the acquaintance of a veteran Bolshevik, Timofei V. Sapronov, then working under a false name as a housepainter at Provodnik. Sapronov had followed a classic trajectory of the worker-turned-professional-revolutionary. Born in 1887 as one of seven children in a poor peasant family in central Russia, he shuttled between village school, work as a shepherd, and domestic service for a noble family in St. Petersburg. A fellow servant introduced him to books and new ideas about justice and the plight of workers. From the age of fifteen, Sapronov supported himself as a housepainter in various construction crews, participated in the infant trade union movement during the 1905 revolution, and continued to organize construction workers despite police harassment. By 1912, his political views led him to join the Bolshevik wing of the Russian Social Democratic party. Throughout the war, Sapronov was prominent in the union movement and active in trying to keep intact the Moscow organization of the Bolsheviks, despite unremitting persecution by the secret police. He arrived illegally at Provodnik in November 1916, where he must have soon met Dune and other radically minded workers.[4] Sapronov remained Dune's political mentor and sponsor, and their political connection survived the arrest of them both in 1928.

Dune was an eyewitness and participant in both the February and October revolutions in Moscow. His account of the February events stresses both the unplanned nature of crowd mobilization and the overwhelming enthusiasm for revolution, even from people such as his chance companion during the first day of demonstrations. This young woman had never previously thought much about politics at all. After the fall of the tsar, Dune evidently quit the technical college and threw himself into work and into organizing the hugely popular Bolshevik club at Provodnik. He joined other young militants from his factory to form a workers' militia to defend and police the factory; later in the year this militia was transformed into a Red Guard unit, whose task was to help defend the revolution. Dune thus spent the months after February as a rank-and-file Bolshevik, probably helping to mobilize others and certainly trying to come to grips personally with the rapidly evolving political crisis in Russia. Provodnik was a strong center of Bolshevik support, but as Dune describes it, this was not a narrow sectarian bolshevism. Workers freely argued and borrowed viewpoints from a number of left socialist positions. But the younger militants like Dune were growing impatient with the level of political discourse in revolutionary Russia. "We were beginning to tire of words. . . . The counterrevolutionary forces were ready, yet the Provisional Government was doing nothing, confining itself to idle chatter from Kerensky." Dune's Red Guard unit from Tushino, armed with antique rifles, joined the battle in the first days of the October revolution in Moscow, and he describes the peculiar military conditions associated with urban street-fighting: barricades, snipers, and the siege of buildings such as the military school and the telephone exchange; he notes also the absence of discipline and the differences in fighting styles among workers and soldiers.

When the street battle was over and the soviet forces victorious,

Dune remained a fighting man. Barely eighteen, he had made yet another transition, from militant worker activist to an armed soldier of the revolution. Only a month after the battles of October, Dune's Red Guard unit was sent south to put down a Cossack rebellion that threatened to cut access to vital supplies of coal from the Donets coal basin. The first phase of Dune's military career ended with the temporary defeat of the Cossacks and the signing of the Brest-Litovsk peace treaty between Russia and Germany, and he returned in the spring of 1918 to help build soviet power. For the time being, armed opposition to soviet rule had diminished but discontent with soviet power was growing in direct proportion to the continuing collapse of normal economic relations. "The working family lived near starvation," writes Dune, and he scraped by only with under-the-table handouts from "young Salmyn'," who ran the kitchen at military headquarters in Moscow. Moscow area peasants openly scorned the workers, but for enthusiasts like Dune, the culprit was not soviet power but the outbreak of armed counterrevolution in Siberia and the south, which drained resources from the regime and blocked food and fuel supplies from reaching the hungry center. In response to a call to mobilize Communists to serve in the new Red Army, Dune volunteered for duty at the front, and in November 1918 he reported to the Ninth Army on the southern front, then deployed in the province of Saratov, along the west bank of the Volga.

The new Red Army was a conscript army led by "military specialists"—officers from the tsarist army. Rank—symbolized by epaulets—was taboo but discipline and procedure were much more closely regulated once full-scale war had begun. Loyalty to the Communist cause on the part of peasant recruits and professional officer-specialists was to be monitored by the revolutionary introduction of political commissars, who were chosen from among loyal Communists. Dune found himself, to his amazement, appointed as assistant political commissar for a regiment of peasant conscripts from the province of Nizhnii Novgorod, or Nizhegorod. Leon Trotsky, the Red Army commander-in-chief, appears in this account as the draconian dispenser of Communist discipline, and Dune's distaste for Trotsky's brand of communism perhaps began at this time.

With the success of the Red Army in early 1919, Dune's division spent less time fighting and more time assimilating the Cossack territories to soviet power. But Dune's peaceful assignment among the peasants and Cossacks of the Don region came to an end with a renewed White Army offensive in mid-1919. Dune's army was ordered to retreat, and having become separated from his unit, Dune was captured by Cossacks who belonged to the Green movement. The Greens, identified not by red or white ribbons but by leafy twigs stuck in their caps, opposed both Reds and Whites in favor of local autonomy. Dune was soon reunited with hundreds of captives from his unit, and all were handed over to the advancing White Army. Dune's party of prisoners was taken to a village adjacent to a railway station and put to work unloading freight.

In this place, the second scourge of the civil war—typhus— struck down Dune as it did to so many others. In fact, typhus claimed more victims during the war than did wounds from battle. Somehow, Dune found himself recovering in a hospital designated for White Army typhus victims and supplied by the British with clean linen and fresh medical supplies. At this point, in late 1919, it was the White Army's turn to retreat, and Dune was evacuated along with the hospital to the town of Novorossiisk, on the northeast coast of the Black Sea. Here in the prisoners' infirmary he made contact with a partisan organization inside the hospital, and he began to work in the group's "passport bureau," altering and forging documents (some acquired by trading cocaine stolen from the hospital medical stores) that would permit other prisoners to escape and rejoin the partisans fighting in the nearby mountains.

Dune remained in Novorossiisk, under treatment for a badly infected eye, and he witnessed from the hospital windows first White executions of captured partisans and then the chaotic evacuation of White soldiers and supporters from the port of Novorossiisk. With the arrival of the Red Army, he left the hospital and reported once more for duty. The Red Army had changed yet again from the army of conscripts he first joined a year and a half earlier. He was no longer an isolated Communist, and the political section of the division in which he served had become an empire unto itself, with dozens of organizers, agitators, and its own printing press. Dune was assigned to the Kuban, a rich agricultural region at the northern foot of the Caucasus Mountains, and charged with disarming the local population.

By the end of 1920, the military battle had been won. The Red Army, five million strong, had driven the last of the White Army out of the Crimea, and supporters of the White movement either melted back into Russian society or escaped to exile in Europe and America. But in the wake of victory, armed rebellions sprang up all around the periphery of the young soviet state. Dune's unit was sent "by fate" to the mountainous region of Dagestan, where an Islamic-led rebellion had erupted against soviet power in September 1920. Dune's account of his last battle in the civil war presages the Soviet Army's more recent experience in Afghanistan. The ill-prepared and war-weary Red Army had to face native dwellers high in the impassible mountains. Red losses were extensive, and only the Reds' superiority in supplies and numbers gave them the ultimate victory. Even in victory, Dune found himself perplexed by the special treatment given the "national Communists," confused that soviet authority allowed the Dagestan Communists liberties not permitted for Russians, puzzled why mollifying these Communists, who went from party meeting to evening prayer, should have higher priority than shipping local oil to the fuel-starved center. Here Dune uncovers but shows little understanding of the complicated relationship between national identity and socialist consciousness, a relationship that constitutes an enduring theme in Soviet history.

While Dune sat in his Dagestan fortresses aiding in the denouement of the war in the Caucasus, he caught distant echoes of the new politics of soviet Russia. His friend Sapronov was leading a movement of organized opposition to Communist rule. Factory workers in Petrograd and Moscow declared strikes to protest Communist policies. The once-loyal Kronstadt naval garrison rebelled and demanded a new government to replace the Communists in power. Shortly after this, in March 1921, the Communist party's Tenth Congress decided to relax its drastic and calamitous economic policies and to implement the New Economic Policy aimed at a partial restoration of markets and economic recovery. Barely conscious of these upheavals, Dune in 1921, at the memoir's end, appears still to be a committed Bolshevik, an internationalist, a believer in the necessity of a world revolution as the only means for the continuation of the Russian revolution.

Dune's subsequent biography, which included experiences even more harrowing than those recorded here, can be pieced together from scattered papers and writings found in his personal archive at the Hoover Institution. Dune remained in Dagestan with the occupation Red Army until mid-1921, when he fell ill with jaundice and then scurvy. After a long convalescence, he was demobilized, and because of his experience at Provodnik, assigned in late 1921 to one of the plants belonging to the new socialized rubber trust (Rezinotrest, for which the poet Maiakovskii wrote some famous advertising copy) as assistant director. This was a discouraging position for an idealist such as Dune still must have been. The plant possessed raw materials but no fuel, and consequently stood idle. Dune was the only Communist in the plant, the workers were discouraged, and they drank too much. From the latter part of the civil war, Dune seems to have worked as a member of the collegium of a military tribunal and then in the service of the political police, a matter about which he was rather quiet in his life as an exile. Perhaps through his connections with Sapronov, who had become an important official in the Central Executive Committee of Soviets and was still a leader of the Democratic Centralist opposition within the party, Dune managed sometime in 1923 to find a position in the Central Executive Committee bureaucracy. Here he met his future wife, Ginda Efimovna Zaretskaia, by origin Jewish and also a party member. They were married in 1923 and had a son, Volodia, in October 1924. (Many boys born in the year of Lenin's death were given the name Vladimir, or Volodia for short. Dune does not mention a namesake, and in fact, the name of Lenin rarely appears in his writings.)[5]

Dune's lifelong quest for knowledge led him to enroll in the fall of 1923 as a student in the biology-physics-mathematical faculty at Moscow State University, training for a specialization in biochemistry and physics. In an unpublished fragment about these years, he describes the split between apolitical students, who sought a university degree for the sake of a diploma, and the Communists, who came for the sake of knowledge itself. Dune's circle of political friends gravitated in this period toward the anti-Stalin opposition. Some of these friends saw Trotsky as the best alternative, but Dune did not, afraid that Trotsky would be as authoritarian in his own way as Stalin was in his. Scheduled to graduate in 1928, Dune was instead expelled from the Communist party in

December 1927 as a member of the "Group of Fifteen, " the Democratic Centralist opposition.[6] The Democratic Centralists, still led by Sapronov and Vladimir Smirnov, had been much more unwavering in their opposition to the Communist party than the United Opposition of Trotsky and Zinoviev during the political ferment of 1926–27. Even in defeat, the group issued to the Fifteenth Congress of the Communist party in December 1927 a stinging attack on the party. Their platform denounced the party's economic and internal policies and called the Red Army an "instrument for a Bonapartist coup."[7] The Congress responded to the challenges by expelling seventy-five members of the United Opposition and twenty-three from the "group of Sapronov" as "flagrantly counterrevolutionary." Dune was eleventh on the list of twenty-three.[8] Expulsion was followed by arrest. In January 1928 Dune was exiled for three years, first to Arkhangel province in the north and then, when he contracted tuberculosis, to Semipalatinsk in Kazakhstan. Dune continued to communicate with his fellow oppositionists even in exile, and in 1929 they issued a "platform" denouncing the "dictatorship of the petty bourgeoisie." He returned to his family from exile in 1929, after declaring that he had dropped all opposition to the regime, and he was restored to party membership in 1930. He found work as a scientific researcher at the new institute of rubber and synthetic rubber, but his political past continued to haunt him. After another wave of arrests of former oppositionists, Dune was reassigned to work as a biologist in a small town. There he worked until he was again expelled from the party in December 1935 in the growing assault on old party veterans, and in April 1936, Dune was arrested again, this time "for counterrevolutionary Trotskyist activities." He was sent to Vorkuta, a notorious penal colony beyond the Arctic Circle. He was assigned to work hauling coal, but his lungs were so badly damaged by the four-month journey to the camp that he could not fulfill his assigned norm, the basis for receiving food. With little to lose, Dune joined a hunger strike in protest against the camp regime. He survived even this, and when he recovered, a camp doctor placed him in charge of the infirmary's medical laboratory. Like another camp inmate, Eugenia Ginzburg, this inside job probably saved Dune's life.[9]

In 1941, he was released from Vorkuta, having served his five-year sentence. He was able to rejoin his wife and son, now seventeen (the same age Dune had been when he participated in the 1917 revolution) in the city of Vitebsk, in the western republic of Belorussia. His family had been exiled there as relatives of a political criminal, and even in "freedom," neither Dune nor his family could leave the city without permission from the political police. Released from Vorkuta in April, Dune arrived in Vitebsk at 6:00 A.M. on 22 June 1941. Three hours earlier the German army had invaded the USSR. Vitebsk was abandoned to the Nazis on 9 July and set afire. Dune and others were ordered to leave the city and organize guerrilla resistance; his wife and son fled the city for the security of the Russian interior. In August, her party was captured by the Germans. Dune was told, and he believed to the end of his life, that she and the boy, as Jews, had been shot. Dune was also captured, but as a civilian without documents (he had been ordered to deposit these with the city soviet before leaving the town), he was returned to Vitebsk and assigned to work for the Germans in the laboratory of the municipal hospital.[10] In 1943, the entire hospital was transferred to German-occupied France, in Evian-les-Bains on the shore of Lake Geneva. Soon after, Dune made contact, through German-speaking Alsatians, with the French resistance movement. Only later did he learn he had joined up with a section of the Francs-Tireurs (FTP), organized by Communists, rather than the French nationalist FFI, since at the time he knew neither French nor the difference between the two organizations. In September 1944, the FTP dismissed its Russian members and sent them via the Red Cross to Annecy, for repatriation to the USSR. To escape a return to certain imprisonment, Dune, with no money and little knowledge of French, walked to Marseilles and signed up with the French foreign legion. On arrival in Sidi-bel-Abes in Algeria, he was pronounced medically unfit for active service, but he remained in the legion until April 1946, when he returned to France to qualify for a French passport.[11]

In the final years of his life, Dune worked in a factory in Crémieu in the department of Isère until 1950 and then in a factory on the outskirts of Paris. He was active within the Russian emigration, among both old and new emigres. In 1948 he made contact with the Menshevik circle that published the newspaper *Sotsialisticheskii vestnik*, whose numbers included Rafael Abramovich, Boris Dvinov, Boris Nicolaevsky, and Solomon Shwarts. He became the Paris agent for the paper in 1950, wrote for it under the pseudonym of Ivan Ivanov, and dispatched it to subscribers throughout the world.

Dune was extremely ill and impoverished during these last years of his life. He corresponded extensively with Rafael Abramovich, the editor of *Sotsialisticheskii vestnik,* about emigration from hungry Paris to the United States or Canada, but the U.S. quota for Latvian emigrants was too small and Dune's communist past a problem. He also explored the possibility of finding refuge in New Zealand or Australia, far enough away to be safe even from Stalin or the atomic bomb, wrote one of his friends.[12] In late 1950, Dune was operated on for stomach cancer and given three months to live. He survived on remittances from New York for his work for *Sotsialisticheskii vestnik,* on payments for articles he wrote in the emigre press about his experiences and about politics in the USSR, and on charity. Sometime in 1951, Abramovich must have given Dune's name to the Russian Archive of Columbia University, which with the Ford Foundation and other funding was commissioning memoirs from participants in the Russian revolution.[13] Hoping to be placed on a regular salary for his work, Dune began to haunt the libraries of Paris to compile material to support his recollections and to write. But he was beset by doubts. He feared his manuscript would not appeal to the archive because of poor literary quality. "Who would read this, let alone pay for it?" he wrote Abramovich in February 1952. Carrying stones under the hot African sun was easier than literary work, he moaned. Dune sent his initial chapters to Columbia in May 1952, but for five months received no payment. And an honorarium for another article he had written was misdirected to the wrong person. "To put it bluntly, I was of a mind to throw myself into the Seine," he wrote a friend. Although payment eventually arrived, Dune's health continued to deteriorate. Still he kept writing. He had sold the 1917 portion of his autobiography to Columbia's Russian Archive; in July 1952 he mailed a second section on his experiences in the civil war to Boris Nicolaevsky in New York.[14] Dune planned to continue his recollections through the 1920s, with chapters on the Communist opposition, factory unrest, and the rise of Stalin. Of these, only a fragment on university life and some bits on politics can be found in his papers. Accounts of his experiences in Vorkuta, Vitebsk, and in France had been published earlier in *Sotsialisticheskii vestnik*. Late in 1952, Dune was cheered by the prospect of a German edition of his memoirs, but no evidence exists that the publication ever appeared. His spectacular luck ran out in early 1953; Dune died in a Paris hospital on 21 January at the age of fifty-three, the same age at which his friend and mentor T. V. Sapronov had died fourteen years before.[15] In 1956, in a supreme and poignant irony, Dune was rehabilitated and posthumously readmitted to the Communist party. The petitioner on his behalf was his wife, Zaretskaia. She had somehow survived the retreat from Vitebsk and believed thereafter that Dune had perished somewhere with the Red Army during the war. Neither one knew that the other had survived.

The ability of Dune to recreate the idealism of his youth despite the tragedies and suffering he endured in the intervening years gives the memoir its special quality of authenticity. Dune's uniqueness as an observer derives precisely from the distance he achieves as an outsider—as a Communist oppositionist reminiscing about years of communist enthusiasm, as a Latvian in a Russian city, as a night school student among factory workers, as an urban worker volunteer in a peasant conscript army. Dune is a sensitive observer of others and a man of broad sympathies, but he is not an unbiased witness. Dune perceives his environment— whether the factory, peasant settlements on the Don, or mountain villages in Dagestan—with the eyes of an urban, educated, skilled proletarian, and this colors his estimation of other types of workers, of peasants, of professional army officers, and of other socialists.

But through this filter, Dune's memoir offers the reader insight into the Russian revolution in several important ways: in his description of society and social structure, in his view of the political process, and very significantly, in the values he reflects. His detailed portrait of factory society includes a marvelous description of seasonal peasant workers, their love for rhyming ditties, and their disdain for indoor work at a machine. He carefully describes the hierarchical world of work, from the construction workers and haulers, seasonal laborers employed outside the plant, to imported laborers from Turkestan and China, to skilled workers, at whose apex stood the dozen or so engravers who came to work in clean clothes, starched collar, and tie. Yet all these laborers were considered quite distinct from clerical and administrative staff, even if pay levels were similar. A worker who dated a female clerical worker was considered very rare, almost scandalous: these classes did not mix.

Dune's vignettes about shop floor culture are equally valuable: the symbiosis as well as antagonisms between foremen and skilled workers figures as a significant feature of factory life. The foreman agrees to let Dune work an eight-hour day, knowing full well that Dune can arrange his work in order to produce the same amount as in ten or twelve hours and that if he forces Dune to stay at the plant for that long, his output will not be any higher. Foremen who displease workers, for unfair treatment or sexual harassment of women, find themselves covered in a filthy sack and carted out of the factory. Dune's account of this traditional practice is one of the best in the memoir literature.

Urban-rural relations constitute another important element in this story. The Provodnik factory was typical of a large number of Russian industrial enterprises located not in cities but in small rural settlements. Thus relations between workers and peasants were intimate and complex. Dune looks down on the seasonal workers, bumpkins with their shaggy haircuts and long beards, finding their conversations about land and the harvest tedious and oddly discordant with their factory surroundings. It makes no sense to him for these peasants to sink their hard-earned wages into ailing farms for the sake of a few cabbages in the summer. He sees their determination to salvage their farms as emanating solely from proprietorial instincts: he cannot see that the plot of land not only provides them with much-needed security in the event of sickness, injury, or old age but symbolizes independence and self-respect to the peasant. Whereas Dune's own family relies entirely on the company for its income and housing, the seasonal workers have a supplementary income from farming, are self-sufficient in food, and have their own homes in which they can live as they please. Dune found this inexplicable, until he returned to Moscow in the fall of 1918. Then the workers in the idle factory had to scrounge, beg, and even steal leftover potatoes from their peasant neighbors' harvests.

Dune's memoir also offers a glimpse of the revolutionary na-
scence of civil society, of an independent set of structures and organizations outside the control of the state. The flowering of this
society in 1917 was subsequently overshadowed by the reimposi-
tion of soviet state power in all areas of life. In fact, his compatri-
ots in Riga had already had substantial experience with independent urban organizations such as choral and temperance societies.
The formation of the medical fund at Provodnik—a joint effort
between workers and management—illustrates the extension of
this kind of activity, and the growth of the factory club as a location of autonomous civil activism at Provodnik also reflects a process occurring throughout urban Russia in 1917. Curiously, Dune
says little about trade unions in this account. His friend Sapronov
was an activist in both the Bolshevik party and the construction
workers' union, and the identity of the two was sometimes fused
in the minds of the working rank-and-file. A shortage of activists
meant the same individuals often held posts in soviet, party, and
trade union organizations, further diluting the claim trade unions
made on workers' loyalty. A union of rubber workers organized a
section at Provodnik and in Moscow grew to seven thousand
members by June. Dune was probably a member, but his failure to
acknowledge its work is symptomatic of the weak role played by
the union movement in revolutionary Russia. Independent factory organization, such as Provodnik's factory committee, played a
far more central role in the lives of most workers.

One of the valuable contributions of this memoir is the worm's
eye view it provides of the political process, however distorted
that view might have been. Whereas N. N. Sukhanov's compelling
account of the revolution in Petrograd conveys the immediacy of
the decisions made by the Petrograd Soviet and the Provisional
Government, Dune encounters the political history of the revolution only in snatches. The February revolution took Dune un-
awares; he just happened to spend the revolution's first day in
Moscow and was able to join the growing demonstration. Dune's
recollection of one of the key episodes in 1917, the Bolsheviks'
abortive July Days uprising, is badly confused, conflating several
different crises and decisions of the Moscow Soviet and Bolshevik
party. The confusion about political events in Dune's own memory, however, pales in comparison with the astonishing range of

understandings about Bolshevik politics that he encounters as a Red Army commissar. Dune's interactions with an old fisherman who thinks that Latvians are some race of one-eyed monsters, with the political commissar who regaled his rapt peasant audience with exotic, garbled, and obscene-sounding Chinese names, and with the Red Army veteran who believed that the Communists had taken control of the revolution away from the good Bolsheviks speak to the vast disparity between the political culture of the city and the provinces and indicate the enormous challenge that the Bolshevik government had to face in explaining and implementing its program.

The memoir is at its best in revealing the day-to-day political life of the revolution: the ways in which the Bolsheviks mobilized workers at Dune's Provodnik plant, the tactics of agitators when appealing to peasants or workers, and the endless rounds of meetings and discussions that characterized the vibrant revolutionary period between March and October 1917. At Provodnik, whole families would flock to the party club to hear speeches and to view new revolutionary entertainments. The plant began to serve as the agitational center of a large region north and west of Moscow, and speakers from Provodnik would fan out to factory and agricultural settlements to help organize new democratic institutions. Even the children of Provodnik workers had been caught up in this spirit. A newspaper report from 1917 describes how the children, who in 1914 had played at soldiers, now in 1917 organized formal meetings, elected committees and chairs, and marched in rallies carrying red banners that proclaimed, "Long live free children!"[16] The memoir also conveys the level of political discourse in urban Russia, which was carried out in the most simple terms: "For sociologists the question of the dictatorship of the proletariat was more complicated than it was for us," writes Dune, explaining the appeal of Bolshevik slogans in 1917.

Even this rudimentary level of political discussion fades from view in Dune's account of his Red Army experiences. The milestones by which standard histories of the revolution and civil war chart the Bolshevik consolidation of power are absent here. The struggle to create a soviet government with or without other socialist parties in November 1917, the Constituent Assembly and its dispersal in January 1918, the Red Terror of late 1918, the Kronstadt mutiny of early 1921—all these are far away from Dune's field of vision. Without newspapers and other forms of communication, none of the men in the field defending soviet power could know exactly what was becoming of that power they were sworn to defend. In this respect, Dune's ignorance of high politics is both typical and highly significant in understanding the development of the soviet style of government.

Aside from the February and October revolutions, one event does claim a long-term hold on Dune's consciousness: the peace of Brest-Litovsk. For military and diplomatic historians, the peace marked the withdrawal of Russia from the war with Germany and Austria. For Communists such as Dune, the peace was the culmination of weeks of bitter political and ideological debate about the nature of the revolution. The arguments about the peace exacerbated ideological splits that had already begun to divide the party. Lenin appealed to party pragmatists in signing an accord with Germany that stripped Russia of one-fourth of its population and arable land and much of its coal and oil deposits. Left Communists opposed this "obscene peace," preferring to die fighting for the world revolution rather than to make peace with such a capitalist enemy. Dune clearly sided with the Left Communists, with Sapronov and Bukharin, and against Lenin, Trotsky, and Stalin. The memory of this peace still rankled him thirty years later.

In addition to providing a rank-and-filer's view of the major events of the revolution and civil war, the memoir is especially valuable for the subjective values and attitudes that it conveys about the revolution and about revolutionary society. Dune's idealism, which permeates his recollections even after thirty years of struggle, repression, and personal tragedy, is particularly important for understanding the motivations of this entire generation of revolutionaries. The young people in Dune's revolutionary cohort believed they could create a braver and better world, they attributed setbacks to external forces such as foreign intervention and the failure of the revolution to spread to Western Europe. Socialism meant justice and equality, and its supporters believed it would transform the very nature of the human spirit. A picture of a strict revolutionary morality emerges at several points in the memoir, as committed revolutionaries like Dune attempted to bring about this spiritual transformation as they strove simultaneously to win the revolution. The Provodnik Red Guard unit rejected any applicants with a record of drunkenness, "hooliganism," or improper behavior toward women. Some of Dune's fellow Red Guards were tried in a comrades' court for pilfering pencils and rulers during the October 1917 assault on the telephone exchange. Dune took pride in the Bolsheviks' humane treatment of their prisoners, in stark contrast to White behavior; and he was therefore shocked when two captured White officers were summarily shot. Later, in the Kuban, he was embarrassed by the savagery of the Red occupying forces, who behaved no better than the Whites had done. And in his refusal to touch alcohol, Dune not only deprived himself of a chance to taste some well-aged wine kept by his Don Cossack host but he conveys a whiff of the revolutionary Puritanism that constituted an important cultural feature of the new society.

This revolutionary idealism had a specific class content, and attitudes attributable to Dune's working-class origin are likewise candidly revealed in the memoir. Dune's descriptions of factory and work culture illustrate what we might call the nobility of work. He exhibits a fierce pride in skilled manual labor and places a high value on education for its own sake. His attitude toward foremen and managers is ambivalent. In general, Dune recognizes the legitimacy of the managerial function, and he notes with pride that the Provodnik plant ran smoothly under "triple power" in 1917, when each partner in production understood its role and respected its colleagues. But foremen who transgressed acceptable limits of behavior were despised and punished.

Like many of his urban fellow workers and socialists, Dune displays little empathy for peasant Russia. Even during the period of revolutionary euphoria in 1917, peasants remain alien to him. Some agitators could successfully reach them, but his hero, Sapronov, himself a peasant by origin, had no success in village agitation. The minority of peasants who took jobs inside the factory were perceived to be a malign influence, since their individualism undermined the cohesion of the workers' collective. Their desire to earn as much as possible in the shortest time meant they had scant regard for the unofficial norms and practices of the workshop. Contrary to some stereotypes that portray peasant workers as recalcitrant to the discipline of the factory—unpunctual, restless, careless, etc.—Dune emphasizes their assiduity and compliance with authority. In the Red Army, Dune felt estranged, a "white crow," not only from the professional officers from the old tsarist army but also from the conscripted peasants in the rank-and-file.

Nor did Dune show much sympathy for Russia's hereditary intelligentsia. In describing how the soviet state took over former gentry estates after the revolution, he makes a point of the selfish and thoughtless behavior of the tenants of one estate loaned to the Union of Writers. Similarly, he recounts an anecdote from civil war Moscow about a famous ballerina stuffing herself on caviar, oblivious to the hungry party employees surrounding her. Worker-intellectuals like himself, he implies, showed far greater respect for the collective wealth of the country than the formerly privileged intellectuals; workers were the rightful new elite of socialist Russia. Remarking on the numbers of students he saw in the February demonstrations in 1917, Dune recalled, "I have no idea why this mass of narrow-minded, petty-bourgeois Muscovites should have needed a revolution." Such an attitude provides an explanation for the animosity workers and Bolsheviks felt toward specialists in industry and all formerly privileged members of society.

One attribute worth mentioning here is the role played by women in Dune's recollections. Dune says almost nothing about his personal or family life in the memoir, and his writing is distinctive for its nearly total lack of personal emotion or feeling. His mother, we learn, did not work outside the home, a point of honor for Dune's working-class father. He mentions a sister only once in passing, and not in his initial description of his family life in Riga. He says surprisingly little about women workers, and one would barely guess that women may have comprised a majority of the work force at Provodnik. This omission springs in part from a broader neglect of the semiskilled machine operators, with whom Dune had little daily contact, and in part from the fact that women, with the exception of his mother, appear to have played little part in his life at this stage. Other women figure as the apolitical chance companion in the February revolution, as the telephonists who seem to have been young women with education and "tone," and as the looters of shops in the Kitai-gorod. Dune's most positive and full descriptions of women are those who played a maternal role: his own mother, the farmers' wives in the Don who fed him and darned his socks, and the nurses at the typhus hospital. Other women are portrayed as defenseless and as victims, either of the foreman's capricious lust or of the Don Cossacks' gang rape. Perhaps Dune's aspirations to revolutionary asceticism caused him to minimize his own personal relations. We know he had a "sweetheart," because she appeared to him during his typhus-induced hallucinatory dream, and he reports that he, his pals, and some female secretaries in his army political unit enjoyed a lively camaraderie. On the other hand, his admiration for the "women of the Don" derived from his respect for their independence and capability rather than their maternalism. He criticizes workers (perhaps including his father) who insisted their wives be confined to the home, and he acknowledges the influence of Lily Braun, the socialist feminist whose writings stimulated Dune's own political radicalism. But overall, women are not treated here as equal players, intellectually or otherwise, in the revolutionary drama. Official socialist rhetoric to the contrary, the world of the Red Guards and the Bolsheviks was a man's world, and in this respect Dune's account is quite typical of the revolutionary record in general.

Finally, Dune's attitude about Russians and minorities is quite interesting. Although born in a Latvian family and brought up on tales of Latvian history as well as of internationalist class struggle, Dune appears to have had no trouble at all shedding his Latvian identity with his family's move to Moscow. Russian food was much tastier than his own, and he praised his mother's new Russian stove, with its high sleeping shelf and clay oven, "for there is no better food than that cooked in a Russian stove." Once at Provodnik, Dune seems to have had few linguistic or social difficulties in integrating with the Russian workers. He shared with his Russian fellows a sense of the Central Asian and Chinese workers as a race apart. Late in his life, when offered a chance to find refuge in the United States under the immigration quota for Latvians, Dune wrote scornfully that he had left Latvia in 1915 and had not used his native language since. He was no more a Latvian, he said, than his friend Abramovich, a Jew, was a Zionist. National origin did not for him predetermine national identity.[17] In times of heightened national consciousness, it is important to appreciate the lure that the Russian metropole offered to members of the empire's minorities. Not only Dune but many members of non-Russian ethnic groups, including Joseph Stalin, found a new identity as Russians and as Communists.

Dune's memoir ends with the Red Army's ambiguous victory in Dagestan, and he concludes with some sober reflections on the failure of the revolution to unfold according to the ideals of 1917. Dune's doubts about his cause had obviously surfaced already in the civil war years, and his experiences in Dagestan contributed to his confusion, but these reflections were also the product of the next thirty years of his life as a socialist.

Although Dune left no sustained exposition of his political ideas, it is possible to reconstruct them partly from the curriculum vitae that he wrote and partly from the articles that he penned for *Sotsialisticheskii vestnik*, the newspaper of the Menshevik emigration. To the end of his tragic life, he remained faithful to Marxism, with a particular fondness for Engels, whose works he knew intimately. In his obituary of Dune, Rafael Abramovich, former Bundist and guiding light behind *Sotsialisticheskii vestnik*, wrote that during his final years Dune had come over unequivocally to Menshevism. There is no doubt that Dune felt closer to the Mensheviks than to other left-wing currents of opposition to Stalinism. The distrust he felt in the 1920s toward the "Bonapartist" ambitions of Trotsky was carried over in the 1940s into a dislike of the authoritarianism and sectarianism of the Trotskyist Fourth International. Yet it is difficult to categorize Dune as a Menshevik in any straightforward sense.

For the Mensheviks, the October revolution had been a utopian experiment carried out by a ruthless minority party, which was doomed to fail because of the economic and cultural backwardness of Russia. Dune did not completely endorse this view. Even at the end of his life, he continued to believe that October was a popular revolution that had established an authentic "dictatorship of the proletariat" in Russia, however briefly. "The Bolsheviks sought to broaden the scope of the revolution, whereas everyone else sought to limit it." He believed that the revolution had begun to turn sour as the party lost touch with its working-class supporters during the civil war. Like the Mensheviks, Dune rejected the Stalinist state absolutely. He did not believe—contra the Trotskyists—that it still represented some kind of "workers' state," however degenerated. He saw in the planned economy a system of state capitalism dominated by a new class that owned and disposed of state property. Dune believed that capitalism world-wide was moving increasingly in the direction of state regulation and planning and that this process was accompanied by the growth of a technocracy that was the organizer of the state economy.[18]

Dune's analysis of how a popular revolution was transmogrified into a barbaric dictatorship is not especially original, although it has a couple of distinctive touches. Dune shared with the Trotskyists the conviction that Stalinism marked a violent break with Leninism, that, in Trotsky's words, a "whole river of blood" separated the two. At the same time, he did not entirely reject the Menshevik claim that the 1917 revolution had been inspired by utopianism. In an exchange with Rafael Abramovich in 1950 he wrote: "The utopian character of the socialist revolution in 1917 lay in the unrealized hope of achieving material abundance on the same archaic energy base on which capitalism had arisen."[19] For Dune, like Trotsky, the key to the evolution of a new ruling stratum in the Soviet Union lay in material scarcity—scarcity that had persisted in spite of the industrialization set in motion by the Five-Year Plans. But, unlike Trotsky, he seemed to believe that even had the revolution triumphed on a world scale it would not have been possible to achieve an authentic socialism because the requisite global "energy base" did not yet exist. This distinctive notion of an "energy base," rather than the more conventional Marxist concept of "productive forces," perhaps reflects Dune's training as a scientist. It was rooted in a type of economic determinism that was characteristic of Menshevik thinking, but for Dune a developed "energy base" was only a necessary and not a sufficient condition for a classless society. He saw nothing progressive in state ownership of the means of production; indeed he believed that it was actually contrary to true socialism. Instead, in a way that was calculated to provoke his Menshevik comrades, he counterposed to state ownership a quasi-syndicalist conception of social ownership, via cooperatives of workers, technicians, engineers, and white-collar staff, remarkably similar to the one popularized by the anarchists in 1917: "factories to the workers, the collective farms to the peasants." At the deepest level, therefore, in his view that the material base for socialist society did not yet exist, Dune was closest to the Mensheviks, but in his belief in social, rather than state, ownership and in his conception of democracy as the self-organization of producers, he remained true to the vision of socialism to which Sapronov had introduced him as a young teenager.

Eduard M. Dune, circa 1917, age 17. (Courtesy of the Boris Nicolaevsky Collection, Hoover Institution Archives, Stanford University)

Eduard M. Dune in 1946. (Courtesy of the Boris Nicolaevsky Collection, Hoover Institution Archives, Stanford University)

Enlistment of volunteers for the Red Army. (Al'bom Revoliutsionnoi Rossii/Album of Revolutionary Russia, circa 1920)

Review of the Red Army in Moscow, circa 1920. The banner reads "Defense of the Soviet Republic." (Al'bom Revoliutsionnoi Rossii/ Album of Revolutionary Russia, circa 1920)

"Long live revolutionary labor discipline." Red Army soldiers in formation, Moscow, 1920. (Al'bom Revoliutsionnoi Rossii/Album of Revolutionary Russia, circa 1920)

Note on
the Translation

The translation presented here is based on several typescripts found in the Boris Nicolaevsky Collection at the Hoover Institution Archive. Nicolaevsky was the self-appointed archivist and historian of the Menshevik movement, as well as being active in several emigre publications. Dune sent him copies of the memoir he had prepared for Columbia and the subsequent parts as well. After Dune's death, Nicolaevsky received all of Dune's personal papers, which remain in the collection. Our project to translate and publish this memoir originated in the editors' independent research into the role of the working class in Moscow and Petrograd in the 1917 revolutions. We had each encountered Dune's work while reading numerous similar but simpler accounts; Dune's candid descriptions of factory life, of the revolutionary process, and of the ambiguities of the revolutionary outcome rang very true to us, and we wanted to make the memoir available to a wider audience. Once we learned of each other's interest, this collaboration was the natural outcome.

A few words are in order about the text itself. "Notes of a Red Guard" exists in two different versions, and the translation is made from what appears to be the more finished version. In places, however, we have incorporated sections from the first version that are missing in the second and that are of historical interest. Even the second version is in no sense a final, polished piece. It is repetitious and ungainly in its organization, and we have cut out some of the repetitions and organized a few sections in a more logical fashion. We have tried, however, to avoid turning the text into a literary work by filling in its gaps and smoothing over its inconsistencies. We have only occasionally tried to modernize the style of the original, which is written in simple, colloquial Russian. Dune's prose is rather diagrammatic and disjointed, with none of the stylistic elegance, discursive detail, or richly metaphorical encapsulation of feeling that characterizes some of the published memoirs by Russian workers. But the very simplicity and unpretentiousness of the language lend a verisimilitude to the text, an honesty and accuracy to the observations that deserve to be preserved in translation. It is not always easy to do this: Dune, for example, frequently uses a form of free indirect speech that is not easily rendered into English except through correct reported speech. These recreated conversations are a rhetorical device commonly used in Soviet editions of other workers' memoirs, as well as in Dune's published writings about Vorkuta and the war years.

In transliterating we have relied primarily on the Library of Congress system, with occasional exceptions for well-known figures, such as Trotsky and Kerensky, and to render some place names more pronounceable (Khopyor River).

To place Dune's specific experiences in a somewhat broader context, we have prefaced each of his chapters with a brief survey of the relevant political and military events. Throughout the narrative we have provided additional information on individuals and events mentioned by Dune. Our policy has been to explain such references without overburdening the reader with too much detail. When Dune quotes a recognizable source, we have provided more precise documentation in the notes. We have appended a list of works about the revolution and civil war that we consulted in preparing this book for publication and a bibliography of Dune's published works. To aid the general reader, we have also included a brief list of suggested readings in English on the revolution and civil war.

PART ONE

The
Red
Guard

Chapter One

World War I began on 1 August 1914, pitting an alliance of Russia, France, and Great Britain (the Triple Entente) against Germany and Austria-Hungary. Opening offensives occurred on both the western and eastern borders of Germany. The Russian army tragically bungled their attack at Tannenberg in East Prussia, in which one hundred thousand soldiers died or were taken prisoner. But in the process, Germany had to rush eighty thousand troops from west to east to help push back the Russians. This weakened the western front enough to permit the French and British troops to stall the German march on Paris and set the stage for the four years of trench warfare and stalemate that followed.

In East Prussia, the German army began a massive offensive in the early months of 1915, provoking the "Great Retreat" by the Russian Imperial Army. From April until August, the Russians lost nearly a million dead and wounded and a million prisoners of war. The city of Riga was too valuable a center of war production to allow its capture by the advancing Germans, and tsarist authorities decided in the summer of 1915 to evacuate its major factories to safer locations inside Russia.

The retreat revealed Russia's gross unpreparedness for war. Shortages of munitions and weapons, along with a series of military defeats, led to a growing crisis of confidence in the government. Nicholas II sought to rally his forces by personally assuming the chief role at the headquarters near the front lines. This left the government in Petrograd (as St. Petersburg was renamed at the start of the war) in the hands of his wife, Empress Alexandra, and in the power of a collection of inept ministers chosen primarily for their loyalty to the imperial family. The war effort also produced growing shortages in the domestic economy, causing widespread unrest in cities, towns, and countryside.

In fact, not all suffered equally. Industrialists producing for the war effort could count on lucrative contracts from government ministries, and they expanded their operations. Many of these entrepreneurs and other public-minded organizations, such as the Union of Towns, sought to gain more control over the war-industrial effort in order to rationalize it and make it more effective. Skilled workers also benefited from the war. Their skills were so necessary to military production that such workers were exempt from military service (although the threat of the draft hung over them should they misbehave or participate in protests). The high wages of these skilled workers reflected their value to industry.

The combination of these conditions—dissatisfaction with the war effort and the exemption from military service of skilled workers—made it possible for socialist agitators to find an audience for their message of revolutionary change. Tsarist police tried assiduously to track, identify, and arrest these underground agitators, but popular discontent with the war and its conduct continued to grow. By the end of 1916, Russia was faced with growing dissent at the highest levels of society, among elected representatives to the State Duma, and even among the royal family. The mood of protest was also spreading in the streets of the cities and in the trenches at the fronts.

To Moscow

When the 1914 war broke out I was still at school in Riga, a youth of fourteen. My mother was delighted that her son had been born in the fifth year of her marriage and not in the first: otherwise he would have been called up for the war. My father, aged forty-seven, worked at the Provodnik works of the Franco-Russian Joint-Stock Rubber Company and he, too, was not called up. Our hope was that the war would not disrupt the monotonous working-class life to which we had become accustomed over the years and that we would be able to live through the war in the same old way. The newspapers said that the war would not last long and would be over in two or three months. But for a whole year we ran out each day for the newspaper to find out what was happening at the front. The front continued to approach ever closer.[1] There were now more soldiers in the city than civilians. One evening my father came home with the news that they were getting ready to evacuate his factory to Moscow and that they had proposed we go with it, promising him more pay, his moving expenses, etc. But how would we survive in such a faraway place—over six hundred kilometers distant—where there were such severe frosts, where everyone went around in fur coats and *valenki*,[2] when we had only coats with quilted linings? We would surely freeze . . . But we couldn't stay in Riga without work or money, since that would mean certain starvation.

The factory was receiving many orders from the War Department, and the work force had already grown to fifteen thousand.[3] Many of the workers had been employed there for years and had acquired skills and work habits and built up a resistance to the peculiar smells of india rubber and benzine, which had initially poisoned their bodies, causing them to faint, until they got used to them. It was proposed that all such experienced workers and, of course, foremen, should move together with the factory. In Riga the production departments and stores of the factory occupied a huge area. It would have been impossible to find so large a site in Moscow, so different shops were sent to different sites throughout the country. The section that made asbestos products, linoleum, etc., was transferred to the town of Pereiaslavl'-Zalesskii;[4] the section that made automobile tires to a site under construction in Moscow; and the section where my father worked was moved to the village of Tushino, about fifteen kilometers from Moscow.

In August 1915 our turn came to set off for this unknown and distant place, and I left my school and my studies. In later life I was to "evacuate" many times, but this first evacuation was not like being forced to flee or being forcibly resettled. Our small family was given a whole freight car, complete with a small stove, so that we could move all our possessions, furniture, and kitchenware. We traveled with the haste of refugees, and within a week were in our new home. Because we were refugees, either a hot dinner or supper or rolls or sandwiches awaited us at every station. We ate these, not because we were hungry but because the food seemed so tasty. In fact we had already heard in Riga that Russian soldiers' bread was better than our own. Most important, it was not as cold as we had expected—no colder than Riga.

In a village close to the Tushino station we were given a big room, complete with bedbugs. Our landlady said that we must have brought them, since bedbugs had never bothered her. For my mother there was immediately a further misfortune, worse than the bedbugs: a big Russian stove, to which she just could not get used. None of our pots and pans were suited to it. I praised it to the skies, however, for there is no better food than that cooked in a Russian stove. And it wasn't just the stove that made me happy. I could now spend whole days by the river fishing, whereas in Riga I had had very little time for it. Now from early morning for days on end, I strolled along the banks of the Moscow River and along the stream that flowed through our village.

It was an hour on foot to the factory, though it was less distance across country through the fields and woods. The village lads were puny in comparison with me, but they were already working at

Figure 1. European Russia in 1917.

the factory, whereas I was twiddling my thumbs. I decided to have a word with my father: couldn't he get me a job at the factory? He replied that I hadn't gone to school in order to work on the shop floor and that I should wait a while until the factory got going and they required office clerks. Somehow I befriended a local lad, however, and, through want of anything better to do, began to help him lug heavy machine parts to the factory. The gang leader suggested that if I wanted a job I should turn up the next day for work, at one and a half rubles a day. On the Saturday I brought home my first wage packet, my mother was proud and delighted that I could earn so much money for such easy work. Once in Riga my father had fallen ill for six months, poisoned by lead dust, and I had spent each day collecting iron and other scrap metal from factory dumps, which I had then sold for ten to fifteen kopecks. Now here I was earning one and a half rubles a day!

The work consisted of delivering machines from the station to the factory. Because these machines were too heavy for horses, or else too bulky to take by cart, they were slid onto round logs and rolled inch by inch along the road to the factory. Two or three dozen workers, harnessed by long ropes, dragged the load like Volga boatmen. They did not hurry or strain themselves, so they never got tired. Along the way there were frequent stops for a cigarette, and once the frost set in, bonfires were built by the roadside, and we would stop to rest by them. We worked happily, singing as we went along, and whenever we went up or down a hill we would sing the "Dubinushka."[5] Until then I had only read about the "Dubinushka," so now I was hearing the real thing for the first time. I'm no romantic: in fact, I'm decidedly dull and prosaic. Verses don't normally send me into raptures, but even now, in old age, I remember with warmth our "Dubinushka" and those who led the singing. These leaders were such masters of improvisation that never once, not even in one *chastushka*,[6] did they repeat themselves. The *chastushka* would be about something topical—a foreman or gang leader, a woman or young girl, a priest or deacon. Each leader had his own specialty. I recall a fat, heavy-faced youth, a complete illiterate who on payday would drink away his wages, who was a master of the sharp-witted *chastushka*—admittedly, of a rather obscene variety. For every passerby he would invent some clever and totally unexpected jingle. He would break into an improvisation as the figure drew near, and then subside as they drew away. The appearance of the next person—whether young or old, handsome or ugly, fat or thin—would spark some new association, which would spontaneously form itself into words and rhyme. The words were rough and crude, but the rhyme could become tenderly caressing if a woman happened to please him. It would then seem as though a completely different person was singing the *chastushka*. Sometimes we would ask him to sing again the one that he had made up that morning about the school ma'am who had passed by, but he could never repeat himself. During the six months that I worked as a loader, I got to know several other illiterate poets and storytellers who improvised around various incidents or adventures in their daily lives. One of these poets befriended me because of our common love of fishing. When we were out fishing he would be silent and taciturn, becoming the poet only when a small crowd gathered.

As the machines were assembled, the experienced workers were transferred to them—transferred to well-paid jobs in clean, warm workshops. The ribald young poet and I were put to work on a press, but the poet never managed to come to grips with the job. He would complain how boring it was, saying that such tedious work would never interest him even if it were paid at two or three rubles instead of one. He would often go to the lavatory for a smoke and stop to talk or chat with anyone who came in. Anything except tend that boring machine! We were paid by the piece, but he hardly managed to earn the day rate and would come to me on payday and say: "Count this for me. That foreman's been cheating me again!" Soon he left his fifty-ruble-a-month job for one that paid twenty or thirty rubles—a shoveling job of some kind. There he found a job where he could sing his songs and have an audience. None of the poets managed to hold down a machine job: they all slipped off elsewhere. They found machine work quite intolerable—as tedious as learning to read or write. While we literate workers crawled along the ground, the poets floated among the clouds, unable to get along on the boring old earth, eating too little, drinking too much, dying in some obscure corner. I met similar people in the prisons and concentration camps: there, too, accomplished storytellers and singers would stand out from the crowd, enjoying their popularity and success like artists on the stage.

Apart from the workers who had been evacuated from Riga, there were many locals who worked in excavation and construction. The factory had formerly been a textile mill, and now the premises were extended and two stories built onto them. Living accommodations for the work force were added, along with a sewage plant, drains, a steam pipeline, stores, stables, and garages. This all required a lot of labor, which was difficult to get outside the city. Even in Moscow there was little surplus labor and no unemployment. This labor shortage forced up wage rates, attracting workers from the nearby small textile mills who were still being paid at prewar rates. Many local workers continued to live in Moscow, traveling the fifteen kilometers each day to Tushino. For them the working day lasted from early morning until late at night, for in addition to the ten-hour day, overtime working was widespread, which meant that the working day lasted twelve to fourteen hours. If you add on to this time spent traveling to and from Moscow, then there were only a few hours left for sleep. A fair number of the unskilled workers later transferred to jobs inside the factory: from navvies and carpenters they were transformed into rubber workers, and their wages doubled as a result. In the soft rubber goods department, where they manufactured pharmaceutical and surgical goods, almost all the workers were women, either the wives and daughters of male workers or women from the surrounding villages. These women were particularly happy, for the war had increased their wages to one and a half or two rubles a day, which they compared not with the subsistence minimum but with the fifteen kopecks a day they had been earning in the small textile mills before the war. Now these mills stood empty and idle because of the labor shortage.

All the construction and ancillary work was done by seasonal workers, who had temporarily left their villages and domestic crafts. These workers sent their wages back to the villages to sink into farms that could no longer support them. They lived in semi-starvation, feeding on bread and a little herring or pickle. We, the evacuees, used to watch these Moscow peasants with incomprehension. They lived in the village, had a cow or horse and a piece of land on which they could grow only potatoes or oats if they were drivers with horses to feed. They justified working at the factory by saying that their land was barren, mere clay. Yet with the arrival of spring, they would all leave their jobs and go off to plow the piece of land that could not feed them. In the time they spent plowing the barren clay, they could have earned at the factory more than the total value of their land, but the little plot of earth drew them back, it gave them their very own cucumbers, cabbages, and potatoes, even though it would have been cheaper to buy them at the market.

The seasonal workers tended not to be drawn to the workshops, even though the wages there were much higher than in the factory yard. If seasonal workers did take a machinist's job, paid on piece rates, then the other workers would have to conduct a "trade union" battle with them. For seasonal workers would always try to earn as much as possible, not understanding that the total monthly wages bill was fixed by the administration and that raising the level of output merely resulted in a lowering of the general rate. The seasonal workers would arrive at the factory long before the whistle blew in order to start work as soon as the machines were set going. They would leave their benches only after the machines had stopped and the whistle for the end of the day had blown. If the older workers tried to persuade the newcomers not to work so fast, they would listen with incredulity. Sometimes novices would reply: "Well, if they stop paying me as much, I'll find myself another job." In such cases, it was in the interest of the collective to lower the seasonal workers' output to the average norm by sprinkling talc or graphite on the transmission belt of their machines, thus reducing the number of revolutions, or by giving them raw materials or semifinished products of poor quality to bring down their output to the average or even lower. One didn't, of course, have to explain to the experienced workers that their individual interests and the collective interest were one and the same.

Sarts,[7] conscripted from Turkestan, worked in the factory yard. They wore turbans and striped, quilted robes made of a smooth cotton fabric. As soon as it was time for prayers, they would quit work and perform their ablutions at the side of the road, heedless of passersby. There were also several hundred Chinese at the factory who, like the Sarts, could not understand a word of Russian and so had no contact with other workers. Observing them from a distance, it seemed to us that they were interested in nothing except their wages, but no doubt the onlookers from the administration thought the same about us workers. The Chinese lived in their own mud barracks under the command of their contractor,[8] a fat man who was always protected by a dozen men carrying long knives in their belts. In March 1917 when we were holding meetings and demonstrating with red flags, we learned that the Chinese, too, were having a revolution. They had sent the contractor and his retinue packing and chosen a new cook. They were left, however, without food and money, since all negotiations with the management had been conducted by the contractor, who managed to make off with all the wages advanced to the gang. Not long after, all the Sarts and the Chinese left the factory.

In each workshop a single foreman directed several hundred workers, without the assistance of any other supervisors. The foremen comprised the elite of the factory collective. Formally, they were "staff," not workers, but because they had begun as workers, and learned every detail of the production process and all the little tricks used to lessen the burden of work and increase pay, they willy-nilly pandered to the interests of the workers and were basically part of the collective. Both sides recognized the dual role of the foreman and behaved accordingly.

The highest category of workers proper—those engaged in physical work—were the dozen or so engravers. They came to work in clean clothes, with white collars and ties. And they were never in a great hurry to take off their blue working clothes, since these always seemed to be newly washed, the trousers neatly pressed. Whereas the average wage of an unskilled laborer was 30 to 40 rubles a month, they earned an average of 100 to 150 rubles on piece rates. These men were artists who loved their work, who carried cases in which they kept their fine chisels, their precise measuring instruments, and their magnifying glasses of different shapes and sizes. The secrets of their work were their own personal property. Behind them came the turners, the milling machine operators, and those who worked on the specialized machines for rubber production.

The most dirty and physically harmful work was done in the "black" department, where they prepared the primary mixes of india rubber and other ingredients. This work was not badly paid. Rival firms, such as the Treugol'nik and Bogatyr companies,[9] sought out the experienced workers from this department to persuade them to come to their companies for much better pay. It was in this department that all the secrets of production were to be found: the compounds of such-and-such a rubber, the composition of rubber-based lacquers, and so forth. To safeguard these secrets from the workers who prepared the compounds, the usual names of the ingredients were replaced by numbers or special names. Of course, any intelligent worker who worked there long enough came to learn the names for india rubber, sulfur, talc, lead oxide, and the rest, and in what proportions they went into each particular type of rubber. So that such a "chemist" should not leave the factory, the administration would assign him a high wage, according to his experience and length of service.

Such a worker was part of a labor aristocracy, both because of his material position and because of the quality of his work, which involved his brain, not brawn. Such a worker did not leave work totally exhausted. He had leisure in which to read and not just time in which to recover from exhaustion. His wages allowed him to raise a family and to give his children a school education, without his wife needing to go out to work. If it happened that because of illness or accident he was deprived of his normal wage and his family was forced to live on the fifteen to twenty rubles a month assistance from the medical fund, then he would still not allow his wife to work, out of false pride. His ten-year-old son would also consider it shameful for his mama to work at the factory.[10] In such a situation, it was usual for the son, and not the wife, to help the family by going out to work or by earning a bit on the side. After getting home, the labor aristocrat would spend time reading. He developed interests outside his job, and he might spend his spare cash on newspapers and books. It is no accident that it was precisely among this layer of highly paid workers that a worker-intelligentsia formed. It was also noticeable that the highly paid workers did not get drunk, whereas the less skilled workers, on leaving work, would head straight for the tavern.

Neither rates of pay nor total wages were laid down according to any scale. Nevertheless a certain gradation of wages was observed between skilled and unskilled workers. A highly skilled metal engraver or metal turner was paid more than a turner of vulcanite or a metal fitter. And in the different rubber workshops the pay of an unskilled worker had to be lower than that of the machine operators. The relation of the wages of different categories of workers was incomprehensible to the "seasonals," who assumed that wages depended entirely on the diligence, concentration, and ability of the worker. It took many months for them to grasp that the pay scale was unregulated by any law or set of rules and to learn to accept the same as their fellow workers, without stretching themselves to the limit.

As a general rule, piece rates were determined by voluntary agreement between the worker and the foreman: only the total wage bill was subject to the control of the factory administration. If a foreman would not accept the terms put forward by a worker, the worker would refuse to work on piece and would be transferred to day rates. The worker would earn only half the piece-rate wage, but the situation would last for only a few days. Because he would deliberately lag behind the rhythm of the machine, the worker would produce far less than normal. Even if the foreman timed the movements, he would usually end up accepting the worker's terms and restoring him to piece work. The advantages of piece work were not only that the worker earned two or three times more than the day rate but also that the foreman no longer watched his every move. The worker could work quietly, without straining, and go to the lavatory as often as he wished.

I never saw a case where the foreman failed to agree to the worker's terms, but I know from my father's stories that there were rare occasions at the Provodnik plant when a whole workshop of three hundred to five hundred workers would rise against the foreman. On coming to work, the foreman would discover a sack nailed to the door of his office as a warning. If the warning did not suffice, he would be thrust into the sack, carried into the yard, and dumped in a wheelbarrow and, amid general laughter, mirth, and joking, wheeled through puddles or to the dung heap in the stable yard. A foreman who had floundered in a sack amid the hoots and jeers of the crowd or wallowed in a puddle while trying to crawl out of the sack would not easily forget it and would bear the stigma for a long time. In order that the instigators should remain undetected, this would all happen without warning or in some other department, as the foreman was passing through a crowd of workers. Someone would come up from behind and throw the sack over his head. The guilty person was never discovered, and if he had been, the foreman would have been in an even more dangerous position. Such methods as the sack were also applied to strikebreakers and to stooges who refused to participate in the defense of the collective interest for the sake of personal gain. During the three years that I worked at Tushino, we had recourse to the sack only once—when we wheeled out engineer Krause to the dung heap. This young chemical engineer ran the department that produced sanitary goods, a well-lit workshop, where the work was clean and childishly simple. He would, however, hire only beautiful young women. Each of the women who worked there had her boyfriend, who jealously protected her from the pestering attentions of engineer Krause, and it was for his misconduct that he ended up in a sack.

The relationship of the administration to the work force was similar to that between state and society: one did not seek to swallow up the other, and each had its own written and unwritten rules. The individual was subordinate to the interests of the collective, but the collective was not antagonistic to the interests of the individual. We felt ourselves to be more like electrons than "free" atoms. Workers who leapt out of the common orbit were rare creatures. Each of us gave up a part of our freedom for the sake of the collective, but this transaction was not regulated in writing or by binding norms. Individuals who did not like the extent of their freedom could either try to increase it through the collective or rely on their own forces. I now feel that that was a world of ideal freedom, but as a youth I felt that freedom lay in breaking the unwritten rules. At the same time, we were prepared to forego freedom for our ideal, which was then much clearer, which shone from afar in the form of our own workers' state.

Am I idealizing the past, like all old men? Certainly, at the material level, we did not always live in clover, as I did when I first began work at the factory. There were times when we ate only black bread and crushed hemp seed instead of butter. There were times when fishing was a necessity and not just a pleasure, times when we could not afford a school outing for want of five or ten kopecks. And my freedom was regulated by the ruble. I had to refuse a ticket for a Shaliapin[11] concert, for instance, because it cost five rubles—the cost of a pair of shoes. But then to miss Shaliapin was no real sacrifice . . . And within the collective we had the freedom to fight against those who undermined the general will . . .

The majority of the three hundred to five hundred workers of the ebonite[12] section where I worked belonged to the highly paid category. We frequently received orders for articles we had not made before the war and about which the chief engineer and fore-man knew no more than the workers. These orders were assigned to the experienced, older workers, who had to begin by experi-menting since no one knew what quality of raw materials would be required nor the length of time that would be needed to make the articles. The best thing was that very high wages could be earned on such orders, for only workers who could read technical drawings were able to execute them and there were no more than a dozen of us in the section. This led to my being promoted, as a fifteen-to-sixteen-year-old youth, into the ranks of the skilled, highly paid workers.

I began to earn twice as much as my father. My mother said with a smile: "Now that you're earning more than your dad, we'll have to get you a cash box." It was agreed that I should contribute as much to the household expenses as my father and that the re-mainder should be mine. Because of my "cash box" I was able to smarten up my appearance, and every Sunday I would go into Moscow, quite the dandy.

In Riga, I had read a great deal, avidly reading anything that came to hand, anything in the school library that was at all inter-esting. The more entertaining books were passed from hand to hand. Among them I can recall *The Count of Monte Cristo*, Sher-lock Holmes, and Pinkerton,[13] which were published in thin pa-perback and were very popular. Because of my addiction to read-ing, there were often quarrels at home. My mother would demand that I put out the lamp when they went to bed, or she would tear me from my book to run an errand, just as I had reached the most interesting point. To avoid such disturbances, I would often spend hours in the municipal park on my way home from school, finish-ing the latest adventure.

Once when I was sitting on a park bench an older fellow came up to me. We started to chat and he advised me to read something more interesting. It turned out that he worked in a printshop and knew what he was talking about where books were concerned. He regarded what I was reading as children's stories, fairy tales, but the "more interesting" book he brought me was one I could make nothing of, and I returned it to him unread. Later he gave me Lily Braun's novel *Diary of a Socialist*.[14] This I found more interesting, more true-to-life. Instead of counts and detectives, this story concerned things close to my own life and that of my family. My new friend gave me other things to read. But soon he went away to work on the construction of the Murmansk railway[15] in order to avoid being drafted. Later in Moscow I remembered my friend, Jan Apin, with gratitude for directing my reading toward the field of social relations.

From my earliest years I knew about factory life because of the tales my father told. Each day his return home would be accompanied by stories of what had happened at the factory. And my mother would talk about the latest domestic happenings, about the details and calculations of everyday life, about how to survive until payday, what to buy and what to put off buying. After supper my mother would close the shutters and putter about the house, while my father lay on the bed reading the newspaper aloud. Occasionally he would read a revolutionary leaflet to my mother. Neither paid any attention to a child like me, and I would not have paid any attention to what was being read had it not been for the circumstances of secrecy. I could already understand my father's stories of strikes, of how they carted a certain foreman out of the factory. Tales of Cossacks,[16] of arrests and torture by the Riga Okhrana,[17] of people hanged, and others forced to flee to some unknown destination became more interesting than adventure stories. After reading *Diary of a Socialist*, these things all began to occupy a special place in my life. I began to look for more challenging reading. The little book I had read had raised new questions, and I searched for answers to them in other books.

I always returned from Moscow with a parcel of books bought from the second-hand booksellers at Sukharevka.[18] The books there were generally very cheap, and even old publications were usually in good condition, the pages often uncut. These books represented a kind of continuation of the *Diary*. At Sukharevka I obtained books such as *The Condition of the Working Class in Russia*—whose author, P. Berlin,[19] I would come to know thirty-five years later—*The Condition of the Working Class in England, British Trade Unions, History of the International*, and so forth.[20] Because of my greed for books and my fear that the books I wanted would have been sold next time, I used to buy far more than I could possibly read in a week.

On one occasion I returned to Tushino in the company of a worker from our factory named Ribel'. Seeing that I was carrying a stack of books, he asked me where I was studying. I replied that I could not study because I had to stick around the factory all day. I explained that my books were not textbooks, but simply books to read. He then told me how it was possible both to study and to work and that one could even earn a high school diploma as an evening student. This was the first I had heard of it, and my interest was aroused. He told me how every day after work he traveled to Moscow to the evening technical institute. He said that since I had already done seven years at school, they would accept me into the first course without having to take an exam. To get into the second course, however, I would have to take an exam in trigonometry, about which I knew nothing. Ribel' was already doing the second course, and I could see from his conversation that he knew more than I did, even though I had seven years' schooling behind me. It appeared that nothing interested him more than trigonometry, and he spent the whole journey telling me about it.

Ribel' was a man of about thirty-five, married but with no children. In Riga he had also worked at the Provodnik plant and gone to evening class. On the basis of the qualifications he had acquired there, they accepted him into the second course at the Moscow technical college. He urged me insistently to study, saying that I was still young, that it was silly to wait until the war was over since no one knew when that would be. "Get on with living. Take it from me, it will be a lot harder to study once you're married." I definitely wanted to study, but at the technical college one was required to study higher mathematics, which interested me about as much as last year's snow. After three years, however, I could take the high school equivalency exam without troubling my parents for the cost of my education. It was the latter consideration that gave me the energy to walk five kilometers to the station each day, take the train, and change trams twice in order to get to the technical college. Towards 11:00 P.M. I would do the whole journey in reverse. By that stage we were no longer living in the village but in a factory hostel, where we occupied two rooms and a kitchen. I lived in a permanent hurry, in constant fear of being late. There was never enough time for reading, leisure, or sleep. That intimate little thread that had bound me to the collective of other workers was broken. My whole working day was spent with one thought in mind: not to be late for the train, not to be late for the evening class.

Two other workers and I had been assigned a "responsible" job making magnetos for airplanes.[21] A magneto has many bronze screws of different diameters and one had to ensure that the distance between threads was absolutely accurate. If there was the slightest error, the job had to be scrapped. When our rates were first fixed, allowance was made for wastage, but I discovered that the screws became slightly distorted during vulcanization, because of the unevenness of the heat, thus causing an expansion of the diameter of some of the screws. If I made allowance for this, wastage was reduced to almost nil. The engineer and foreman did not know my "secret" and tried to make me work fifteen hours a day, as this was an urgent military order. I insisted on downing my tools as soon as I had completed my ten-hour stint, however, in order to rush off to the station. When the foreman learned the reason for my refusal to work overtime, he raised my "price." From then on, because I had no deductions for spoilage, I began to earn far more than the other two doing the same job. They didn't mind, since they were already earning close to the maximum allowed in the shop. Taking this into account, I asked the foreman to let me leave work as soon as I had finished my quota for the day. I could easily do this in five hours, but as too great an intensity of effort would have led to a lowering of rates, I stretched it out to eight hours. This meant that I could take my time in getting to the technical college and also have time for a good sleep.

Because I could earn five rubles a day with my eyes shut, I devoted all my energies to the technical college. I even stopped going to the Sukharevka to buy books for lack of time. Having money in my pocket, I rented a room in Moscow, which I shared with someone. I slept there, and in the mornings caught the works train, which stopped near Tushino-Pavshino, only one verst from the factory instead of five.[22] This allowed me to work and study, and with money in my pocket I no longer felt myself to be a fifteen-year-old youth but an autonomous independent adult.

A desire to study was not so exceptional. It is true that in Tushino, fifteen kilometers from the city, Ribel' and I were oddballs. Yet every morning on the works train it was rare for someone not to read a newspaper or book, rare if you lived only for your wage and your family. The postal carrier, who served many hamlets and villages in this district, came each morning to the factory, bringing newspapers and journals for the workers who lived there rather than letters. On holidays he would come to the factory for tips, saying: "I bring more things to you than to all the villages put together. Since you read so much, how do you have time for work?"

Uprooted by the war from the urban environment to which they were accustomed, the workers in Tushino felt themselves to be sojourners, temporary residents. In Riga there were all kinds of public organizations and voluntary associations, from choral societies and temperance societies to the Society of Friends of Learning, which ran evening classes, lectures, and so forth. Moreover, the printed word circulated widely: there were many newspapers, books, and pamphlets in our native language. The lessons of 1905 had left their mark, and although the circle of political activists had narrowed, circles continued to work illegally underground. None of these Latvian Social Democrats had ever heard of Mensheviks or Bolsheviks, nor of the disputes between them, for the Latvian Social Democratic organization was a unified one.[23] My father was not a member, but he would often bring home leaflets or proclamations to read.

With the outbreak of war, interest in "politics" slackened. Social discontent was overtaken by patriotism. I think that in the Baltic region the distinctive patriotism of the Letts and the Estonians was stronger than Russian patriotism. This Baltic patriotism had a particular social as well as a nationalist flavor, for in the Baltic, Germans made up the social elite, and these descendants of the Teutonic Knights still preserved their privileges. Until the formation of the Latvian republic,[24] the German barons owned the biggest estates and castles and comprised the capitalist and administrative elite in the town. The power of the Russian governor was merely formal. With the outbreak of the war, Germans within Russia were relieved of their duties and expelled.[25] In Latvia, however, this measure was not carried out, since Germans, ignorant of the Russian language and knowing even less Latvian, made up the whole of the ruling class. Their position was reflected in the external environment: street names, for example, were in three languages—German, Russian, and, lastly, Latvian. After the outbreak of war, all the street signs were changed: Russian now came first, followed by German, and then Latvian . . . Yet actual power remained in German hands. Among the Germans there were no proletarian wage laborers of any kind. There were certainly poor people—impoverished nobles who were employed somewhere for a pittance—but even they behaved haughtily and would not associate with the local people.

A German victory and a German occupation of the Baltic region[26] would intensify not only the national yoke but also social oppression. For Latvians, therefore, the war against Germany was also a war for freedom. Patriotism manifested itself in the volunteers who enlisted in the Lettish Battalions. Originally intended to be only battalions, these were soon transformed into three divisions. And this among only one and a half million Letts![27] Various public organizations rallied to serve these divisions long before the Union of Towns[28] took on a similar task in Russia. For Latvians, Russian monarchism was less dangerous than German. Hence the issue of defeatism, or the peace formula proposed by the Zimmerwaldians, was perceived differently by us. We wanted peace—but not at any price.[29]

Baltic patriotism began to wane as setbacks at the front increased and as Riga was threatened. The speeches of the Russian Duma opposition leaders once more became popular. Workers spoke openly of treachery at the front. Our soldiers were fighting courageously—more was written about the heroic battles of the Latvian Rifles than about the Siberians—and yet here they were being ordered to retreat by the generals.[30] Workers were working day and night, the supply points were full of shells, and yet there were none at the front . . . It was obvious treachery! What could Nikolai Nikolaevich[31] do when his orders were being countermanded by the German tsarina![32] And as for the tsar, well he was neither fish nor fowl. He was more interested in icons than in the war . . . He prayed to Rasputin,[33] not to God . . . Nicholas was not the tsar, but a holy fool in tsar's robes . . . Count Fredericks[34] knew more than the high command about when and where the Russians would attack next . . . Sukhomlinov[35] was Russian, of course, but he was a lackey of the tsarina . . . No good would come of all this . . .

Such conversations were carried on almost openly, and little restraint was felt in front of strangers. Mostly, it was the politically "grey" masses, not the "politicos," who spoke in this fashion. In any village teahouse people would talk louder and longer than did the workers in the factory. Once, for example, when I was having dinner in a Moscow tavern, I heard a loud conversation along these lines. A police officer, who had dropped in to warm up with a nip of vodka, soon got involved in the conversation. "There's no other word for it but treason," he pronounced as he sat there.

In 1916 there was so much vodka available that the peasants ceased to distill their own, since it was no longer profitable.[36] In every tavern vodka was dispensed from the teapot under the guise of tea, and people used it to drown all the misfortunes and mishaps at the front. There was more money around. Peasant girls, who before the war had earned fifteen kopecks a day in the textile mills, now earned a ruble, so they began to dress in the urban style—in the obligatory silk dress—and to shower themselves in perfume. The wages of the townsfolk increased just as much: workers no longer had to count every kopeck. Yet a smoldering discontent was rising, which was apparent even at our factory, where no one complained about the wages. This discontent erupted unexpectedly in a stormy incident. An inexperienced worker—a greaser—got his apron caught in a conveyor belt and was badly injured. Shortly afterwards, another worker got his hand crushed in a roller and lost several fingers. Although such incidents occurred all the time, these gave rise to a virtual general strike in support of demands for better safety levels and for the organization of a medical fund.[37]

The administration did not resist the demand for the organization of a medical fund, for it was anxious to make concessions and avoid exacerbating relations with the workers. Organizers of the fund were found among the former members of the medical fund in Riga and from among local workers. Each member of the medical fund was given a little book in which was recorded his or her contribution, together with the contribution of the same sum by management. If a worker lost the capacity to work, he or she would be paid a flat day rate (not their average wage on piece rates) for the period during which they were incapacitated. There were no conflicts with the administration over the organization of the medical fund, since it saw no danger of "politics" in this example of workers' self-activity. The administration agreed to the decisions of the general meeting of the deputies of the medical fund, without consulting the police. And the deputies did not attach any great significance to their work, since they were unaware that local Social Democrats saw in the organization a potential vehicle for conducting political work. Although some Latvian Social Democrats had come to our factory, they kept quiet until the end of 1916, and no one knew of their existence. Only when Russian Social Democrats arrived did illegal political work revive.

One day my mother told me that a painter, who was working in our hostel, had seen my books and asked if he might read some of them. I replied that she should let him take whatever he wanted. I had no time for books because I was too busy rushing to the technical college. This proved to be the beginning of a new friendship, which was greatly to determine the course of my future life.

The painter who arrived at our factory in November 1916, under the name of Aleksandr Shirokov, had recently escaped arrest in Moscow. Later I learned that he was not "Aleksandrov," as we called him at meetings, but T. V. Sapronov, a man in his thirties who had been born into a peasant family in 1883[38] in the village of Mostushka, in Sitovskaia *volost*, Efremovskii *uezd*, Tula province. He joined the Russian Social-Democratic Workers' party (RSDWP) in 1910,[39] and in September 1914 was elected secretary of the union of construction workers. As such he was a member of the Central Bureau of Trade Unions until it was raided by the police on 15 February 1915. Those who were not arrested, including Sapronov, continued their political and trade union work. Members of Social Democratic committees in Moscow were arrested on numerous occasions during the war.[40] A city district committee was created from among individual party members who had escaped arrest, and this committee took on the task of creating a new Moscow Committee of the RSDWP under the title "Workers' Bureau of the Moscow Committee." Its three members included Sapronov, but he was arrested on 22 April 1916 and charged with authorship of a leaflet. The evidence was inconclusive: during the interrogation the police chief joked that such an illiterate leaflet could only have been written by Sapronov. He was soon released from jail and exiled to his birthplace in Tula. Having spent three months in the countryside, however, he returned to Moscow again and with a false passport in the name of Shirokov, began work as a painter at the Provodnik plant.[41]

As soon as he started, a deputy of the medical fund, Filipp Kalmykov, proposed that he become a member. He thus immediately became acquainted with those workers from Riga who were deputies of the medical fund. All of them had been members of the RSDWP in Latvia or else participants in the 1905 revolution. With Sapronov's arrival, the medical fund began to operate successfully among the construction workers. He also organized a union among them, since their interests were in key respects different from those of workers in basic production. The administration hired construction workers through a contractor, who paid the workers himself and who was responsible for seeing that a particular job was carried out. The workers suffered from the tyranny, abuses, and downright lawlessness of the contractors, and by taking up the struggle against them, Sapronov managed to recruit workers to the union faster than to the medical fund.[42] By January 1917 there were already 250 building workers in the union and a month later this rose to 400.[43]

Word went round that some newspaper was making things hot for the factory administration. Everyone was interested, and we all began asking each other which newspaper had written about our factory. After all, nothing very interesting had happened recently, one day was very much like another. Then we heard that *Printworkers' Voice*[44] had published an article about working conditions in the rubber industry, saying that the administration cared so much about the shareholders' profits that it could not be bothered to install ventilation in shops where workers were being suffocated and poisoned by harmful fumes. From this article, many workers learned for the first time that everything was a consequence of the capitalists' pursuit of profits. Following the publication of the article, the spirit of protest increased: someone obviously cared enough to write about us. The piece was signed "Forgotten" and was written by Sapronov for the journal edited by Polidorov.[45] This article, along with the news from the front and from the Duma, influenced everybody's attitude. The factory director, engineer Konoshenko, without consulting the police, allowed a meeting to take place of all deputies and ordinary members of the medical fund. Some workers were alarmed at this prospect, others hoped that the hundreds of workers at the meeting would run riot. In the event, the meeting was poorly attended: who wanted to spend their Sunday discussing illness and hospitals . . . ? The organizers of the meeting behaved too conspiratorially, emphasizing the practical side of the meeting and playing down its political side, and so it passed off without incident.

Parallel with the organization of the medical fund and of the construction workers' union, some broader political activity developed. By January 1917, Sapronov had managed to create three cells of the RSDWP—each of five or six people. These were very inward-looking circles of personal friends or close acquaintances cut off by the need for secrecy from other workers and with few political links outside the factory. Sapronov himself never went to Moscow for fear of arrest, so Oskar Shmidel' or Filipp Kalmykov would go to see Polidorov. Any leaflets they brought back were for the internal use of members of the cells, not for the rest of the workers, who did not display any great inclination for public activity, still less for revolutionary action.

A week before the revolution, on Sunday 22 February, members of the underground organization at the factory held a party in Spasskoe village to discuss their future work and to sing and do some drinking. Sapronov, Shmidel', Eduard Mazul', Martikinus, Dits, Kalmykov, D'iakov, Zaliais, Vever, Shkuntik, and others— all future activists of October and the civil war—were there. They had all been connected with factory life from childhood and had participated in the 1905 revolution, but none of them had any inkling that they were on the threshold of revolution. Decisions were taken to prepare to celebrate May Day, and Sapronov was entrusted with the task of writing and printing a leaflet on a homemade hectograph about local hiring conditions and work at the factory. In the event, the leaflet never saw the light of day, for the revolution intervened.

Chapter Two

By the beginning of 1917 the capital city of Petrograd was awash in labor unrest and political intrigue. Various groups in well-to-do society sought to restructure the government in order to restore Russia's fighting capacity. One focus of opposition was the Fourth State Duma, elected in 1912, whose leaders now advocated the appointment of a "ministry of confidence," officials who could command the public trust. Another focus of opposition was the tsar's own cousins, who idly discussed the removal of the empress or even the abdication of Nicholas in favor of his uncle. In the streets and factories of the capital, food shortages and the pressure of war production provoked strikes and walkouts, and underground socialist activists busied themselves with efforts to mobilize and channel this discontent.

The February revolution began in the streets on 23 February 1917. (Russia at that time still used the Julian calendar, thirteen days behind the rest of Europe. In Paris, this day was 6 March.) Protests at empty bread shops turned into factory walkouts in the industrial neighborhoods of Petrograd. The next day, crowds began to converge on the Duma in the center of Petrograd. The city's garrison, reserve troops fearing to be sent to the front, received the order to shoot to break up the demonstrations. They refused, and several important military regiments mutinied and crossed over to the insurgents. The tsar and his officials were powerless.

At this point, leaders of the Duma convened a temporary committee to consider how to control and channel this protest. With support from most of the military commanders, they first recommended and then demanded that Nicholas abdicate as the only path to the restoration of order. When the tsar gave up the throne on 2 March, the Duma formed the Provisional Government whose task it would be to continue the war, to supervise the implementation of a new constitutional structure for Russia, and to enact basic social reforms to satisfy the populace. At the same time, however, representatives from factories and socialist organizations in Petrograd created their own council, or soviet, of workers' and soldiers' deputies. The soviet directly represented the aspirations of the disenfranchised members of society, and it saw as its task to defend the popular demands of the revolution from manipulation and betrayal by the Provisional Government. Thus began the period of delicate revolutionary balance known as "dual power." Neither the Provisional Government nor the soviet felt it could govern Russia exclusively by itself, but no constitutional mechanism had yet been developed to balance the competing interests represented by the two bodies.

Moscow too was abuzz with rumors and labor unrest in the first weeks of 1917, but not on the scale of Petrograd. When mass demonstrations began in Petrograd, tsarist officials first tried to prevent any news of this from reaching other cities. When news of the revolution did reach Moscow on 27 February, the city's population poured into the streets to add its voice to the protest against the tsarist order. The representatives of the old regime did not resist, and in just a few days, a new revolutionary government assumed power. As in Petrograd, power was shared. The Committee of Public Organizations, representing nongovernment citizens' groups, assumed the functions of the former city government. Workers and soldiers also elected soviets of deputies, and these two soviets acted as watchdogs over the committee's public actions.

The soviets represented a generally socialist point of view, and three major socialist parties emerged from the underground to exercise leadership roles. The Mensheviks and Bolsheviks represented two wings of Marxism, and they found their most solid support among workers in factory neighborhoods. The Socialist Revolutionaries had emerged from the Russian agrarian socialist movement and sought to represent the Russian peasantry. But the SRs, as they were known, also commanded substantial support from soldiers, the urban lower middle class, and workers too. Among the several nonsocialist parties represented in the Fourth State Duma, the Constitutional Democrats, or Kadets, emerged in 1917 as the party most closely tied to the interests of wealth and privilege, although the party's leaders themselves saw their role as defending the interests of the state rather than of any class.

The
February
Revolution

Moscow continued its normal existence. On this Saturday the technical college was packed as usual with mature students.[1] Tired after a day's work, they were not very talkative. Buried in their exercise books and textbooks, they did not pay much attention to their neighbors. Although it was Saturday, I decided to spend the night in Moscow, so that on the following day I could buy some things I needed. For once my roommate, a student from the Petrovskaia Academy,[2] was not asleep, but relaxing by the samovar. He told me that the students were going to hold a demonstration the following day in protest at the cost of living and in support of their colleagues in Piter.[3] I didn't attach much significance to what he was saying, but remembered about it on the way to Sukharevka. On Sunday afternoons there were normally a lot of people taking their leisure, but today there were more than usual, all making their way toward Sukharevka. Scurrying between the stalls or standing in groups were police officers armed with rifles. This, too, was unusual. Apparently, they had no idea why they had been summoned there and were languidly, almost reluctantly, holding back the curious with cries of: "Halt, it's not permitted to go any further."

The crowd stared but did not disperse. Then, following some order, the police went off in disorderly groups along Sretenka. The crowd followed, pursuing them with wisecracks, jokes, and laughter. We noticed that along Sadovaia another crowd was coming toward us. At its head fluttered a small red flag on a pole. In the crowd were many students who explained that a revolution had begun in St. Petersburg. I have no idea why this mass of narrow-minded, petty-bourgeois Muscovites should have needed a revolution, but the news swept through them like a breeze and created an extraordinary atmosphere. People began to embrace and kiss; strangers became close friends; some wept for joy. In five to ten minutes people seemed reborn. A pretty girl came up to me and took me by the hand, as though we had known each other for ages. Then hand-in-hand, in a warm embrace, and without asking each other's name, we proceeded toward the Krutitskie barracks.

As usual, sentries stood at the gates of the barracks. The yard was empty, but the windows from top to bottom were packed with the silent figures of soldiers. We called out to them: "Come out, there's a revolution!" We couldn't hear what they answered, but the sentries said that they were under orders not to come out.

The crowd grew bigger and bigger, and somewhere in the distance one could hear the well-known refrain of a revolutionary song. By this time it was so crowded that it was quite impossible to get to one side or the other. We continued to hold hands, as though we might get lost. Slowly, barely perceptibly, the human stream moved toward the Red Gates, where I knew there was another barracks. It was the same scene there, except that the soldiers were shouting loudly, waving and greeting us. We couldn't make out what they said. Near Pokrovka we ran into a group of police officers, but instead of greeting them with good-natured jokes, thousands of voices yelled fierce, threatening cries: "Pharaohs![4] Your time is up! Get away for your own good!" I don't remember whether they did go away or whether we just passed by. We moved slowly and could see neither the front nor the back of the crowd, for the street was blocked solid. For the first time in my life I sensed that atmosphere of joy, when everyone you meet seems close to you, your flesh and blood, when people look at one another with eyes full of love. To call it mass hypnosis is not quite right, but the mood of the crowd was transmitted from one to another like conduction, like a spontaneous burst of laughter, joy, or anger.

The majority of the crowd consisted of people who that morning had been praying for the good health of the imperial family.

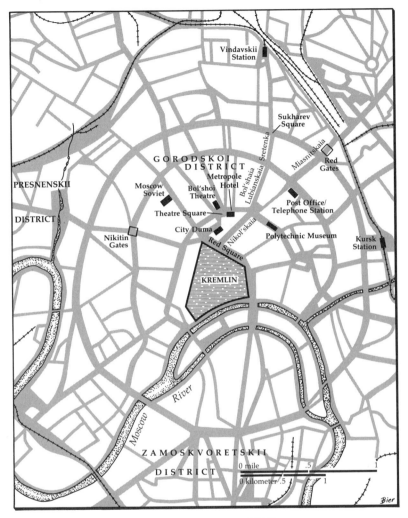

Figure 2. Moscow, 1917.

Now they were shouting, "Down with the Tsar!" and not disguis-
ing their joyful contempt. My companion was a good example. She
showered me with questions: Where are we going? Why are we
marching? Why is there a revolution? How will we manage without a tsar? It seemed like a mere holiday to her—Sunday's carnival procession, complete with mass participation. Tomorrow—
Monday—humdrum working life would begin again, just as usual.
Without asking a question, as though talking to herself, she sud-

denly said: "How good it would be if there was another revolution tomorrow!" What could I say? Tomorrow? Probably tomorrow the police would arrest us. But today there was a festival on the streets.

We were approaching the Iauza River when, over the muffled din of thousands of voices in the crowd, we heard a distant shot. "It's started," I thought. It wasn't possible to see what was happening ahead. The crowd bunched together more tightly, but still kept going. Word came that the police would not allow us to cross the river, yet when we got there, there were no longer any police in sight. Things became a little more relaxed as the crowd dispersed along each bank, watching something in the river. We also turned to look. There in the unfrozen water by the foot of the bridge bobbed the body of a police sergeant in a gray uniform. Eyewitnesses explained that in spite of the rifles of the police barring the way across the Iauza, the crowd had surged forward under pressure from those behind. The police sergeant had shouted and brandished his revolver, but had not been able to stop the crowd. He had then fired a single shot, wounding a young boy. In an instant everyone laid into him. The gray overcoat of the police sergeant was seen flying through the air above the heads of the crowd toward the railings and into the river. His peaked cap was flung after it, and it stuck on the ice a long way from the body.

This was the first time I had seen the body of someone who had been killed. I felt a certain unease inside. My companion seemed to feel the same. She kept looking at the corpse and talking about the boy who had been wounded, saying how sorry she felt for him. Then she turned toward the dead man and pronounced: "It serves him right." But judging by her tone, she hardly seemed convinced that there had been no alternative. Our exultation disappeared, and no one wanted to talk about what had happened. Earlier my companion had pushed ahead, but now she seemed to hold back.

After many hours spent walking halfway round the crowded city, we arrived back at Sadovaia. Close to the barracks a crowd of soldiers mingled with civilians. The yard of the barracks was overflowing with excited men, but they were unwilling to come out on the streets. Our mood was also joyful, for we were convinced that a new and better life had begun. They told us that their officers were in hiding, that the noncommissioned officers were afraid they would be punished for mutiny, and that they themselves didn't know what to do. People said that they should go and liberate other barracks and on to Khodynka.[5]

There were no police to be seen, nor trams, nor drivers. Everywhere red flags were glistening, and more red ribbons could be seen on the demonstrators' chests. By evening, traders had appeared selling an item hitherto unknown—red calico ribbons for five kopecks apiece. The supply disappeared in seconds—there were not enough to go round. Those who had bought ribbons tore them into pieces and shared these emblems of revolution among outstretched hands. Who could refuse to sport a red ribbon on his chest? It was amusing to watch the fervor and determination with which everyone tried to get a little bit of material and the pleasure of those who succeeded. Well-dressed people wore ribbons almost the size of table napkins, and people said to them: "Why are you being so stingy—share it out among us. We've got equality and fraternity now."

Students were held in high esteem. Everyone turned to them with questions and for advice. As street orators, they were listened to by us all. The groups around these orators were particularly dense. Speakers were held aloft above the crowd so that everyone could hear. Their speeches consisted of little more than a series of slogans—"Down with the autocracy!" "Long live the revolution!"—but the crowd was quite satisfied. As they lifted the orators there was a buzz or roar of approval. Even the traders of the Sukharevka market shouted: "They've drunk our blood for long enough."

I hadn't eaten since morning, nor had a drink, but I didn't notice. I wasn't hungry. I arrived home late as I always did after the technical college, too late to go back to the factory. My roommate wasn't there. My landlady, who was wearing a red ribbon on her blouse, proffered the samovar in a state of great agitation. Sitting down, she started to speculate: "What will happen tomorrow? It's a revolt against the tsar, and they'll drag me off to the police station—all because I rented a room to students. What kind of people are you, I really don't know . . ."

I don't know how I managed to sleep on that triumphant night. I woke up in the morning to find that I was lying on the sofa, fully dressed, with my shoes on. I hurried to get washed and rushed for the train to get to work. At the station there was a red flag and everyone was still in the same carnival mood as on the previous day. Everyone was talking about the day's events—what had happened in each district. There was laughter and joking. There were no police, but the trains were still running normally, although according to a timetable of their own choosing. Only the milkmaids had gone on strike because they were afraid to go into Moscow.

The previous day, as soon as news of the events in Moscow had reached the factory, those in the underground party organization had arranged a special meeting, at which they decided to disarm the factory guard. They set about this task with their bare hands, at some risk to themselves. But instead of attempting resistance, the guards handed over their revolvers and sabers and then vanished to avoid further trouble. The factory whistle was blown, as was done if there was a fire, but the great majority of workers were absent because it was Sunday. Two dozen men, with a few sabers and revolvers, took over from the guard, declaring themselves a revolutionary defense force.

Now on Monday it was decided not to sound the whistle for the start of work. Workers arriving for work filled the factory yard, all talking about the same thing, not knowing how to act or what to do next. The clerical employees sat at their desks and pretended to work as normal, although they were watching what was going on in the yard.

Surrounded by comrades, Sapronov was overjoyed and started to make a speech about the long-awaited revolution, about the exploitation of the workers by the capitalists, about the end of autocracy and the beginning of a new revolutionary life. He proposed that the general meeting call a strike to demand an eight-hour day, freedom to meet, and so on. The other orators said the same things, in almost the same words. Nearly everyone who spoke was elected to the strike committee, which, followed by a crowd, headed for the office to put demands to the factory administration. We waited to see what the director would say.

Another meeting followed, at which the delegates reported that the administration was willing to make concessions. It had agreed to an eight-hour day, on condition that part of the work force begin work immediately. It was in our interests to do so, since otherwise there would be no power, the furnaces would cool, and the water and steam pipes would begin to crack. It was agreed that the rest of us would not start work until the revolution had triumphed throughout the country. Those who had disarmed the guards of their sabers and revolvers on the previous day were unanimously declared to be the armed detachment of the factory, and the same people were elected to be the factory committee and the fire brigade. It was agreed that no one should enter or leave the factory without their permission. The office staff and engineers were forbidden to enter the factory workshops until the strike was over, but they seemed as pleased about the revolution as we were. The director went about beaming and talking to people. We also agreed that no finished goods should leave the factory without the knowledge and consent of the workers.

At the same general meeting of workers an announcement was made about enrolling in the local branch of the Russian Social-Democratic Workers' Party (Bolshevik). The chair of the branch was comrade Aleksandr (Sapronov), and the secretary was E. Mazul'. The accounts office donated a large account book and Mazul' began to enroll members to the first legal cell of the RSDWP at our factory. At the same time, the branch committee dispatched comrades Aleksandr, O. Shmidel', F. Kalmykov, and others to the Moscow Committee of the Bolshevik party, though they were uncertain whether or not it still existed or whether there were just individual comrades, such as Polidorov, K. V. Ostrovitianov, and N. L. Meshcheriakov, who had managed to avoid arrest.

Recruitment to the RSDWP, and to the trade unions of rubber workers and construction workers, got underway.[6] Many did not really understand what they were joining—whether it was the party or the trade union. The older workers who had taken part in the revolutionary movement in the Baltic provinces came along to help, by explaining and clarifying things. The seasonal workers sought not to get involved, saying they were poorly educated and that we could make the revolution without them.

Sapronov returned from Moscow with a proposal to elect delegates to the Moscow Soviet of Workers' Deputies.[7] This was another opportunity for a meeting and for explanations of what a soviet was, of how a revolutionary power should be created, of who would rule the country in place of the tsar, and of what a republic and socialism were. Not only did workers come to these meetings but their wives and children did too: nobody wanted to stay at home. Meetings went on for hours—people would leave, others would arrive, but the platform would never lack a speaker, speaking in Russian, Latvian, Polish, or Lithuanian. People would listen without understanding, and on many occasions we were obliged to interpret for the speaker. If it came to electing someone, then those who had spoken the most times would get the most votes, even though there was no shortage of candidates to vote for. The result was that the same people were elected to everything. Because we were on strike, we were able to spend our time at these meetings, but our elected representatives were constantly giving speeches, traveling to Moscow, conferring with the administration, or conducting technical matters in the factory committee, trade union, or party branch. Consequently, they had time neither to sleep nor eat, and their wives brought their meals to them wherever they were working.

The director accepted all the demands of the factory committee, not refusing a single request. The factory committee, and not the administration, had responsibility for organizing the protection of the factory, for hiring and firing workers, and for setting guards at the factory gate. Even the dispatch of finished goods could not take place without the committee's stamp. In this way, workers' control was born quite painlessly. The strike came to an end on instructions from the Moscow Soviet, and working life returned to normal, its rhythm regulated by the factory whistle. Henceforward all meetings and conferences took place in the evenings. Nevertheless the members of the factory committee spent more time at their public duties than at their jobs, and so earned much less than the rest. And delegates to the Moscow Soviet went there almost daily. The management agreed without any fuss not only to pay us an average wage for the days we had been on strike but to pay the same to members of the factory committee, the armed detachment, and the soviet.

The administration also paid for the repair of a large wooden hut where we organized the Third International Workers' Club. Again came the questions. What was a club? What was an International? Why was it the Third and not the First International? The workers listened to a long speech from Sapronov about these issues, and those from Riga described how temperance societies and libraries had been organized.[8] Newspapers and pamphlets were snatched from one's hands, as people tried to comprehend things that were not clear from the speeches of the orators. In the past, for instance, no party or Sunday had been complete without vodka, but now in the new club vodka, and even beer, were to be forbidden. And if you had a tipple in a teahouse and then came to work, people would start to talk about you, embarrassing you at general meetings, saying you were lacking in class consciousness. In pamphlets such matters as temperance and the struggle against drunkenness were explained in detail. A library was set up that provided an outlet for all the books I had bought at Sukharevka that were still lying unread. Among them was one entitled *History of the International,* but I couldn't find anything in it about the First, Second, or Third Internationals.

Sapronov was able to explain how Marx organized the labor movement, how the First International was set up, how the Second International collapsed after the German Social Democrats voted for war credits, thereby giving support to their government and to a war that was still bringing suffering to the world. He explained that our task was to create a Third International under the leadership of the one party that was opposed to the fratricidal war, which had raised the slogan "Proletarians of All Countries Unite" as a way of liquidating the war, and which stood for revolution not only in Russia but throughout the world. Sapronov could answer any question and had command of both the spoken word and the mood of his audience. Speaking in plain, unbookish language, he reached his listeners with every word. He seldom used revolutionary jargon, and if he did, he would immediately explain what he meant by *socialism, democracy,* or whatever. During these speeches, his audience identified completely with the thought and life of Aleksandr, or Aleksandrov, as they respectfully called him, regarding him with warmth and affection.

The workers knew from the newspapers that there were other parties besides the Bolsheviks, but it was not until April that the RSDWP (Menshevik) organized a branch of about a dozen people, at a time when the Bolsheviks had already recruited over five hundred members. Menshevik and Socialist-Revolutionary newspapers and leaflets were available, however, as well as those of the Bolsheviks. Still, much remained unclear. Sapronov took me along to see his friend, Ostrovitianov, later a pillar of Stalinism. He was about thirty, with a worn face, probably the result of lack of sleep, and wore a student's double-breasted jacket. The Moscow Bolshevik Committee was a scene of confusion, with piles of newly printed newspapers and pamphlets everywhere. To the right lay *Spiders and Flies*, to the left *Down with the Materialists*, a short exposition of the theory of historical materialism. We were not yet up to philosophy, we were looking for answers to topical questions relating to the programs of the Bolsheviks, Mensheviks, SRs, and Kadets.[9]

The club organized various amateur evenings. It had its own orchestra; it held readings of Chekhov's stories, recitals of the poetry of Nekrasov and Nadson,[10] evenings of songs and *chastushki*, followed by dancing. Sapronov found time for all of this. Before the revolution it had seemed that most workers were interested only in their wages, that other issues were alien or of no interest to them. Now the club became a center for those whose education had been inadequate, for those who sought to supplement their knowledge and to broaden their social outlook and activities. Apart from the library and reading room, a dramatic society was formed at the club. T. Bankovich, the wife of Ribel', discovered that she had a talent as director and makeup expert. She teamed up with some young workers who were as drawn to the theater as she was. Among the painters at the factory was a man who had learned his trade as an apprentice maker of stage sets. Now, remembering what he had learned in his youth, he began to paint sets for us that were as good as those in any provincial theater. It was a real eye-opener for many, who were seeing theater for the first time and were captivated by our simple entertainments. They even learned to laugh at Chekhov's hairdresser-dentist and to wipe away a quiet tear over the disappointed love of poor Lisa.[11]

There was an entrance charge to all our social events, with the proceeds going either to victims of the old regime or to the library and other club facilities. It was always difficult to accommodate everyone who wished to visit the club. Artistic hand-drawn posters were put up in railway stations, workshops, villages, and hamlets a long way from the factory, and a lot of people turned up to the social evenings from factories and villages with which we had previously had no contact. Friendships were forged at these social evenings, which were to be significant for the work of the party and the activities of the club. The club orchestra and dramatic society were invited to hold concerts at factories up to twenty or thirty kilometers away, and the party branch began to organize activities beyond the walls of the factory. For two years we had lived there without having contact with the countryside, yet two months of revolution were enough to bring young peasants flocking to us. Young workers and peasants became friends. The white-collar staff at the factory, who had formerly kept their distance from the workers, also came along to the theater, so the barrier between them and us began to break down spontaneously.

Chapter Three

When the Provisional Government created its cabinet in March 1917, leaders of the soviet agreed that the socialist parties should remain outside the formal government. To explain this decision they relied on the Marxist argument that this was a bourgeois revolution and that socialists should not participate in a bourgeois government. At the same time, the soviet remained watchful lest the Provisional Government enact policies that harmed the interests of the workers, soldiers, and peasants. In such a system, conflicts were inevitable, and the first serious one arose in April, when the Provisional Government was pressured by Russia's allies to clarify its war aims. Publicly, to satisfy the soviet, the government declared it had no territorial ambitions. Privately, the government's foreign minister, Pavel Miliukov, assured the allies that Russia continued to fight for the territorial gains agreed upon in secret treaties. When the contents of this private note leaked to the public, the result was a mass protest demonstration in Petrograd. Key government ministers were forced to resign, and the remaining officials appealed to the soviet to abandon its hands-off policy and to join in a coalition government. Bolsheviks in the soviet rejected this suggestion outright, but Mensheviks and Socialist Revolutionaries reluctantly agreed. The coalition now faced the tasks of negotiating an end to the war, implement-

ing reform, and calling a constituent assembly to construct Russia's new order.

Meanwhile, economic conditions continued to deteriorate, and growing inflation led to a spiral of strikes and mutual recriminations between workers and industrialists. On Russia's borderlands, nationalist groups took advantage of the center's weakness and pressed claims for more autonomy. Much to the distaste of the statist Kadet party, the Ukrainian national parliament, or Rada, declared its sovereignty on 3 July, provoking a government crisis and the resignation of the Kadet ministers. At the same time, radical Bolsheviks in the party's army organization decided to put an end to the coalitionist nonsense and to seize power for the soviets by force. Petrograd was gripped by street fighting for two days, 3 and 4 July, until the Petrograd Soviet prevailed on the insurgents to abandon their assault. (They were helped by the publication of documents alleging that the Bolshevik party was in the pay of the enemy, Germany.) A new coalition, led by the moderate socialist Alexander Kerensky, was formed to try to repair the damaged central government. Bolshevik leaders were arrested and imprisoned for their alleged role in the uprising. Vladimir Lenin escaped to a hiding place in Finland, to return secretly to Petrograd only at the end of September.

The new coalition also found the problems of the war, economy, political power, and national sovereignty to be insoluble. Furthermore, the-liberal-socialist coalition within the government belied a growing polarization at all levels of Russian society. Workers and soldiers increasingly demanded a definitive socialist and pacifist solution to the crisis of power and war, while conservative and liberal elements looked more and more to a strong military leader to restore law and order domestically and Russian military prestige abroad. In late August, General Lavr Kornilov, a hero of the war, led his "Savage Division" against Petrograd in

an attempt to suppress what he reported to be a Bolshevik insurrection. There was no insurrection, and workers and soldiers rallied around the soviet to defend the city and the revolution.
Meanwhile, the Bolsheviks had recovered from the period of repression that followed the July Days fiasco. Bolsheviks won ma-
jorities in the Moscow and Petrograd soviets and in the two city
councils in September. In response to increased demands for a
government that would end the war, implement land reform, and
solve the nation's economic crisis, the soviet leaders agreed to call
a national congress of soviet deputies in late October. The Provisional Government also convened two consultative assemblies in
September and October to attempt to shore up its waning authority. Lenin and other Bolshevik leaders saw in this crisis the opportunity to move the revolution beyond the bourgeois stage and to
seize power for the proletariat. Only a true proletarian government, they argued, would properly defend the working class's revolutionary goals of peace, bread, and democracy. Only a proletarian government would convene the oft-postponed constituent
assembly and resolve the questions of land reform and power.

The Bolshevik Central Committee conspiratorially organized
the seizure of power to coincide with the assembling Congress of
Soviets. Kerensky attempted to suppress the radicals, and this
permitted the Bolsheviks to couch their action as a defensive one,
to save the soviet. On 25 October, within a matter of twenty-four
hours, Bolshevik military units had seized control of strategic
points in Petrograd, such as the telegraph office, and they arrested the members of the Provisional Government early in the morning on 26 October. Power was now in the hands of the soviet congress.

Moscow's October was not so decisive. Once news arrived of
the transfer of power in Petrograd, defenders of the Provisional
Government mobilized some seven thousand troops, mainly mil-

itary cadets, to defend government institutions and points of communications. An equal number of Red Guards attempted to take over these points. After ten days of sporadic street fighting, the defenders of the Provisional Government surrendered, and power in Moscow passed also to the soviet.

Workers'
Power

Three months had passed since the revolution. The factory continued to work normally and to manufacture the same quantity as before, in spite of the fact that the working day had been reduced to eight hours and that all overtime working had been abolished. Overtime work was allowed in exceptional circumstances, but only by permission of the factory committee. The basic rates remained the same as before the revolution, but wages had not fallen since we now kept busy for the whole of the working day without shirking, no longer afraid of lowering the rate.

The workers' control commission, which was made up of representatives of all the factories owned by the Provodnik joint-stock company in Moscow, was a help rather than a hindrance to the administration. All daily production passed through its hands right up to the point when goods left the factory gates. There were no misunderstandings—even where financial matters were concerned, these also being handled by the workers' control commission.

Supplies of raw materials were guaranteed for many years and continued to come in, filling up the stores. But fuel supplies were a different matter. Even before the revolution holdups in coal supplies had occurred. By using its existing reserves, the factory had managed to avoid stoppages, even for a single day, but now these reserves were coming to an end and the factory was facing closure. The administration was powerless and turned to the factory committee for help in getting hold of coal. A new function was thus vested in the workers' control commission, which extended beyond the factory itself. The administration was now persuaded of the competence of the Soviet of Workers' Deputies, since what it could not obtain through the Ministry of War or through the War Industries Committee[1] it got via the soviet, with the help of its staff.

Somewhere in Piter was the Provisional Government, and in Moscow there were the city duma[2] and other new organs of government. Yet the power of these bodies was only formal. To get anything done, you had to go through the soviet. Formally, there appeared to be dual power, but it did not seem like that to us. Within the factory there was dual and even triple power—the directorate, the factory committee, and the two party committees of Bolsheviks and Mensheviks. Disagreements between them were passed on to the factory committee for resolution, since it comprised representatives of all the organizations.

Elections to public organizations were decided not on a political basis but according to practical competence. The core of Mensheviks consisted of older, thoughtful, and widely read comrades. They were also the most skilled workers in the factory. Their revolutionary ardor had cooled during their lifetimes, but their knowledge and experience were considerable. Many of them worked in the commissions of workers' and financial control, on the board of the workers' cooperative, and in other technical bodies. We had more faith than knowledge and had no desire to use arithmetic to solve tasks of the revolution. They, on the other hand, could not manage without it. Perhaps because of this the Menshevik branch played second fiddle on all issues and did not attract significant numbers of workers. Either the workers did things for themselves or else they gathered around Bolshevik enthusiasts, leaving the Mensheviks on the sidelines.

In May we discussed Lenin's letter,[3] which we decided to draw to the attention of a general meeting of the work force. Sapronov first explained who Lenin was and why he had not been allowed back into Russia before now and then went on to talk about the future course of the revolution. He didn't deliver a treatise on revolutionary perspectives or on the bourgeois and socialist revolutions, he spoke in words all those attending could understand. Did we need a government composed of representatives of the bourgeoisie and former tsarist officials or should we transfer power into the hands of the representatives of the revolution, the representatives of the working class, the Soviet of Workers' Deputies? The Bolsheviks said that the transfer of power to the soviets meant creating what we already had at the factory—a dictatorship of the proletariat. We no longer had guards and police, we worked an eight-hour day at the old rates, yet we earned as much as under the old twelve-hour working day. We lacked the tsar and the police, yet order was better than before the revolution. There was no robbery or stealing, no drunkenness or accompanying hooliganism. If we could organize a revolutionary government in one factory, then why could we not create a similar order across the whole of Russia? Let the bourgeoisie continue to trade and build its mills and factories, but power must rest with the workers, not with the factory owners, traders, and their servants.

How was this power to be organized? No one had a clear idea. Everyone was more or less like us. The soviets were doing some thinking, but even Lenin had not written anything about this matter in his Theses. Many wished to speak at the meeting. They did not speak in well-turned, prepared speeches, but gave voice to what people were thinking. Representatives of our workers' aristocracy, the Mensheviks, also spoke. They were against the idea; before workers could come to power they had to learn a great deal: not only how to run a factory but how to run the whole country, a country where workers were fewer in number than peasant-soldiers. On the question of the dictatorship of the proletariat, they quoted from memory what Bebel,[4] Lassalle,[5] and Marx had written. A socialist revolution could occur only when the country was mature economically and culturally, and then the transition from bourgeois-democratic revolution to socialism would be as natural as our revolution had been in February.

The meeting listened carefully to all the speakers, but with less attention to arguments about the socialist and bourgeois-democratic revolutions, supported by citations from the works of Bebel and Marx. How could one know whether the bourgeois revolution was finished or whether Russia was ripe for socialist revolution? The Bolsheviks spoke in a way that was more comprehensible. We must preserve and strengthen the power we had won during the revolution, not give any of it away to the bourgeoisie. We must not liquidate the soviets as organs of power, but transfer power to them instead, so that there would no longer be dual power, but a single revolutionary government.

More people spoke at this meeting than ever before, and those who spoke most were those who had said very little until then. As well as workers from the factory, migrant workers from the countryside and invalid soldiers who had been demobilized also spoke. Some talked of workers' power, others said that the new government must give the landlords' estates to the peasants and bring an end to the futile bloodletting of the war. The meeting continued a long time, but the atmosphere of intense discussion preserved us from exhaustion. We had a break, so that we could take a snack or have supper, and then resumed our debate. The meeting dragged on, but at midnight the club was still packed to the rafters. Although the windows were wide open, beads of sweat glistened on the brows of the speakers. For sociologists the question of the dictatorship of the proletariat was more complicated than it was for us. We wanted only one thing: the establishment of a revolutionary government that could be trusted and the strengthening of those practices that had been tried and tested by the experience of revolution. We were for land to the peasants, for an end to the bloody war, for everything that workers in other countries wanted. There was no revolution anywhere else as yet, but there would be. Foreign soldiers trusted their officers as little as we trusted ours and would soon follow our example. All those who spoke against power to the soviets were enemies of the revolution, hiding the fact that at a suitable moment they would act against the gains that it had brought about.

After this momentous meeting we began to pay more attention to the newspapers and literature that were hostile to the soviets and became convinced that the Bolsheviks were right, since the whole of the bourgeois press spoke against them.

The influence of the Bolsheviks grew by the day. The factory committee had long been deserted in favor of our party branch meeting, which was packed with people well into the middle of the night.[6] There new members of the party were recruited. There we could buy newspapers, and there we gleaned each day's news before we read about it in the press. Deputies would arrive back on the last train from Moscow and were expected to stop by with the latest information. The most lively gatherings took place in the party branch, attended by hundreds of people. In terms of numbers, these were the assemblies most competent to solve problems of all kinds. At the suggestion of the factory committee, the issue of the factory guard, or, more precisely, the organization of guards, was put to this assembly. It was decided that the guards should be paid by the administration. We also thought it necessary to establish a separate volunteer workers' militia along the lines of the voluntary fire brigade, which consisted of workers living on the factory premises and which had been in existence since before the revolution.

Recruitment to the workers' militia was as strict as to any other organization. The candidacy of each prospective member was discussed at a session of the factory committee, and applicants were often turned down on the grounds that they were regularly drunk or engaged in hooliganism or had behaved coarsely with women. The volunteers numbered 150 and were all drawn from among the young workers, with the exception of some three dozen older men. Twice a week we lined up and were taught military drill, tactics, camouflage, and the rifle manual. We had no weapons, so we learned the rifle manual using wooden staves. We also marched with these. Ensign Lygzdyn', son of a worker at the factory, was elected commander of the militia.

On one occasion, Sapronov had to go to a session of the Moscow party committee. Since the Bolsheviks would have lost his vote in the soviet and since there was an important matter of organizing the Red Guard of workers' militias on the agenda, he offered me his deputy's pass to the Moscow Soviet. The session of the soviet took place at the Polytechnic Museum with Nogin presiding.[7] He proposed a resolution on behalf of the Bolsheviks to protest the sacking of the editorial office of *Pravda* in Petrograd,[8] the reactionary offensive against the Bolshevik party and the persecution of its leaders. The majority of those who spoke supported the Bolsheviks. The hall was filled with constant noise from people condemning the first counterrevolutionary steps of the Provisional Government and from those attacking Bolshevik proposals to organize a protest demonstration and to set up a workers' guard in the mills and factories of Russia in order to defend liberty and the revolution.

In the vote on the secondary question of a peaceful demonstration the Bolsheviks had already won a majority. The opponents of the demonstration protested, accusing the Bolsheviks of having miscounted the vote. Another vote was taken, which produced the same result, whereupon the minority quit the hall in protest. In all the subsequent votes, the Bolsheviks obtained an overwhelming majority. After the resolution to organize the Red Guard had been passed, the session of the soviet was suspended so that everyone could take part in the demonstration that was being organized. Outside the deputies lined up four abreast and moved off in silence toward the soviet headquarters in Skobelev Square. The district soviets, mills, and factories were notified of the impending demonstration by telephone but, of course, did not have time to reach it. The column of soviet deputies was not particularly impressive, and few people joined us along the way.[9] I recall the pensive look of Smidovich,[10] who was inspecting the faces of the deputies inquiringly. Nogin no longer had a cheerful, confident expression, and he was possibly tired from constant meetings and conversations.

Skobelev Square was empty. People gradually arrived, but they were mostly onlookers and passersby. When the first contingent of workers from Presnia arrived, a rally began. Unarmed soldiers from Khodynka arrived, without their rifles, but continued marching in order to leave the small square free for contingents that were due to arrive but who were obviously in no hurry to get there. The demonstration turned out to be most unimpressive.

Afterwards propagandists remained on the square, surrounded by groups of glaring, inquisitive onlookers, obviously inclined to be hostile. Similar knots of unfriendly citizens had gathered around the numerous orators along Tverskaia Boulevard and were heckling them fiercely: "German agent," "Where's your German money?" "Adventurers," "Did you happen to come to Moscow via Germany?"[11] Toward the back of the crowd that surrounded me was a slightly rotund young beauty, beside herself with rage, who tried to stab me with her umbrella. I felt that any minute she and I would exchange punches. At that moment cries rang out—"Stop him! Catch him!"—amid coarse whistles and whoops of laughter. I saw a man running along the middle of the street. Everyone was watching him, though no one tried to stop him. I took advantage of this diversion to make my escape from the umbrella pointing at my eye. I listened to the conversations around me. "Who was that running by?" "Why didn't they stop him?" "Just you try to stop someone like that." "He'd throw another bomb." "Didn't you see the revolver sticking out of his pocket?" On the tram, too, there were many conversations hostile to the Bolsheviks. "They should crush those spies! Why does the government just stand there?"

No less lively was the discussion of events on the train, but here the tone of the conversation was set by the milkmaids from the outskirts of the city, who were unaware of any Bolshevik "uprising" and who were cursing the workers instead. "What are they short of? Why are they rioting? They should be given a taste of the Cossacks' whip, then they'd quiet down. I've been stuck in Moscow since this morning, selling milk, and you can't buy sugar anywhere. Yet look at these workers . . . They've got a cooperative where they can have as much sugar as they like. And there's not diddly for us."

At the factory the mood was vigilant. It was agreed that all members of the militia should sleep in their clothes and that if the whistle blew, they should go at once to the factory committee. The newspapers told of the arrest of Bolsheviks; of Lenin, Trotsky, and Kamenev making their escape; of *Pravda* being shut down.[12] The ensuing days testified to the pogromlike mood in Moscow. Yet in the mills and factories volunteers were being recruited to the workers' guard, just as they were at our place. We insisted that the factory committee get hold of guns instead of wooden staves, but this remained talk, and we continued to march with our old weapons. We each searched for a weapon for ourselves, but you couldn't buy rifles anywhere. At the Truba,[13] apparently, if you knew the right person you could buy a rusty old Parabellum[14] cheap or a "bulldog"[15] and cartridges. There was no other source of weapons, and we reckoned that one was sorely needed.

People of all walks of life cursed the Bolsheviks, yet at the same time there was growing interest in us. What did we want? What were we proposing? Delegates from small factories, dozens of kilometers away, visited us at the factory. We established contact with the workers at the Dedovskaia mill at Golytsino station and set up a Bolshevik cell there.[16] Not far away was the Pavlov settlement, where the 195th Reserve Infantry Regiment was stationed, with whom only now, in the wake of the July Days, did we establish contact. We arranged a meeting for the soldiers similar to the ones we had at the factory. We didn't bother with the soldiers of Khodynka, although they were near at hand, since agitators from Moscow came out to visit them. The Muscovites, however, were generally unwilling to go out into the sticks. To get there and back, they had to walk from the station along country tracks and through mud. For the sake of half an hour's speech, they had to waste a whole day, and so it fell to us to serve the factories, barracks, and country districts far from the railway line. The laborers of the Zvenigorod and Voskresenie districts knew the "Provodnik boys" better than the Muscovites.

Although there were several hundred Bolsheviks, few were natural orators. They could talk well enough among their friends, but if they set off for a strange factory, they never knew what to say. During the first months of the revolution we began to specialize. Sapronov was in his element only at big meetings of thousands of workers and spoke reluctantly, and to no great effect, at peasant gatherings. Such meetings passed off in a businesslike fashion, without much spark. The villagers listened willingly enough to speeches against the war and for peace but they didn't show much interest in the partition of the landlords' estates, which was what our orators mainly spoke about. Peasants in the Moscow suburbs were more interested in their nonfarm earnings. Artamanov, a worker at the factory released from jail during the revolution, specialized in speaking at peasant meetings. Either because he had an impressive bass voice or because he spoke the dialect of the Moscow suburbs or possibly for some other reason, he was a great hit with peasant audiences, who applauded him much more than Sapronov. In the villages we were unable to create party cells, but no other party had any organization. The SR, Vorob'ev, tried to knock together an SR group, but he remained a lone voice, if you exclude those who sympathized with the party in the peasant credit union.

Another of our speakers, F. Kalmykov, willingly toured the small workshops of the district—renamed Spaso-Tushino and covering a large area. He was a most gentle man who approached everybody with great warmth and affection. He was always surrounded by children, whom he sent to hand out pamphlets inviting people to meetings. He talked to them tenderly, as though he were their father. He was always in a hurry and never had time to spare, yet he would stop to exchange a few words with anyone he bumped into. He had a large family, a clutch of small children, and didn't earn much money. He went about dressed any-old-how, in down-at-heel shoes, never wearing a hat, since it would not fit over his thick, African-like hair. His beard, by contrast, was wispy and straggly. All in all, he looked rather like a tramp or a drunkard. The speeches he gave at meetings differed little from any ordinary heart-to-heart conversation. Perhaps for this reason he was warmly received at other people's meetings, to which he was ready to trudge many kilometers. Some of the folk from Riga would also speak, but as their Russian was not fully fluent, and as they had a marked accent, they didn't have the same rapport with the audience.

This was the time when the Bolsheviks were being persecuted, so there was heightened interest in our speakers from all quarters. Political differentiation became noticeable even at our factory. The Mensheviks sweated over purely practical work and agitated against the organization of a Red Guard, which none of them joined. The newspapers spoke of the Bolsheviks losing their influence on the masses, but in fact we noticed that it was growing, at least to judge by the number of those wishing to join the Red Guard detachment. Attached to it was now a nursing corps, formed by young women at the factory.

For more than a month we were dubbed "German spies," but in August came the counterrevolutionary rebellion of Kornilov.[17] At that point, the tactics of the Bolsheviks, as defenders of the revolution, became comprehensible to all. Naturally, we had greater prestige than at any time during the preceding months, and for the next two months our organization grew so rapidly that we even began to think of slowing down the growth. By October we had fifteen hundred members, and these were not just paper members, but people regularly paying dues and participating in social and political work. The Mensheviks still had the same one hundred members they had had in earlier months. This did not mean that one-third of the five thousand workers at the factory had joined the Bolshevik party: there were about one thousand members in our factory, i.e. one-fifth of the total work force. The rest consisted of family members—wives, older children, and teenagers—and peasants from the surrounding villages. In the countryside we didn't have our own party organizations, for we hadn't yet hit upon the idea of organizing small cells there. People gravitated to our factory organization, which became a kind of territorial branch. This was because we were close to Moscow, we had representatives on the Moscow Soviet and the Moscow committee of the party, we always had a batch of propaganda literature, and we had committed and experienced speakers. So not only small factories but also the Dedovskaia mill, twenty kilometers away, and the very weak district organizations of Voskresenie and Zvenigorod came into our sphere.[18]

After General Kornilov's coup, Lenin's April Theses on the dictatorship of the proletariat appeared in a new light—no longer something contentious or merely theoretical but something indispensable. We certainly did not understand the dictatorship of the proletariat as a dictatorship of the Bolshevik party. Quite the contrary. We were looking for allies, for other parties willing to go with us along the path of building soviet power. At the same time, we believed that Plekhanov had been right when he wrote: "The success of the revolution is the highest law. If this success demands a temporary limitation on the operation of one or other democratic principle, then it would be criminal to desist from this . . . We can imagine a situation in which we, Social Democrats, would speak out against universal suffrage. If elections to a parliament were unsuccessful, then it would be necessary for us to disperse it not in two years but, if possible, within two weeks." In 1917 Plekhanov no longer wished to remember these words, which he considered to be the "sins of youth."[19] But in fact the left wing of the Menshevik party was not very distant from us. According to Martov,[20] the choice posed by life was either the counterrevolutionary liquidation of the revolution or its continuation and development via a dictatorship of the forces of organized democracy and the realization of the tasks of revolutionary creativity. *Novaia Zhizn'*, the newspaper of the Menshevik-Internationalists,[21] enjoyed even greater success at our factory than *Pravda*. So we were by no means pure sectarians, for whom party truth was higher than the truth of reality.

Yet we were beginning to tire of words. Lenin's statement that "there can be no other way out, objectively speaking, apart from either a dictatorship of the Kornilovites or a dictatorship of the proletariat" spoke to us more than high-flown phrases. The workers thought that the conditions for a proletarian dictatorship had matured, that there was no time to wait, that danger loomed. The counterrevolutionary forces were ready, but the Provisional Government was doing nothing, confining itself to Kerensky's idle chatter. The cartoonists drew him in the pose of Napoleon, complete with cocked hat, not on a field of battle but on a stage set. He seemed to us quite a ridiculous figure, for in the wake of the Kornilov rebellion, the revolution required a commander-in-chief, not a persuader-in-chief. In our minds this actor was associated with the introduction of the death penalty in the army and with orders to disarm the Red Guard. We believed that he was unwilling or afraid to bring the general to trial who had acted against the revolution. Kerensky was not the man to implement the "dictatorship of democracy" about which Martov spoke.

Everywhere they were writing about the growth of our influence. At the same time in the soviets bitter debates about soviet power were taking place. A group of soldiers from Khodynka told us at the club that their long-absent officers had reappeared and that they were beginning to drill and exercise once more, supposedly to defend the revolution. They were told that the soviets were chattering while the Germans were preparing to occupy the capital and that the officers were not against the revolution, only against the idle talk of Kerensky, the soviets, and the Bolsheviks. The anti-Bolshevik newspapers wrote more about the weakness of the Provisional Government than we did. Conversations went on quite openly on the trains and trams about the uprising that the officers were preparing. Others said that the Bolsheviks were preparing an uprising in order to make the German victory easier. At the same time, they would mock the Kerensky government, saying that it was no more able to satisfy the country than a pacifier can feed a baby. There were also unsettling rumors that in Piter things were even worse and that the counterrevolutionary forces were concentrating there, that the Kornilovites were preparing another rebellion.

Toward the end of October, late at night, Sapronov returned and gave a detailed report on what was happening. He said that Lenin had sent a letter to the Moscow Bolsheviks proposing that they discuss whether Moscow should take the initiative in establishing soviet power.[22] In Piter, apparently, a great many counterrevolutionary forces had concentrated, against which the workers' militias could not possibly hold out and which would be destroyed before help came from other towns. There was no unanimity on the Central Committee on this issue, and so it was agreed that the party should act in accordance with the views of the majority of the membership, the workers of the mills and factories.

Our resolution expressed our readiness to act on behalf of soviet power and also the urgent necessity of arming the Red Guards, who were still marching with their wooden rifles. Our resolution was sent to the soldiers in Pavlov settlement. The delegation returned with the news that the soldiers had supported the resolution at a meeting but refused to hand over any rifles without permission from Moscow.

By this time we saw Sapronov only rarely, for he spent days and nights in Moscow. Several party organizations operated in the city—the Moscow city, oblast', and okrug committees.[23] Sapronov was our branch representative on the okrug committee. After the disturbing letter from Lenin about the situation in Piter, the Muscovites decided to create a single party center, on which Sapronov was once more a representative.[24] It was necessary to bind together all branches in the Moscow oblast', particularly those that were close to the city and that could offer it genuine help. But everywhere the situation was the same: a Red Guard existed but it had no weapons!

On Saturday, 26 October, news came that shooting had started in Moscow and that the officer cadets had attacked the soviet.[25] It was said that in Piter the situation was the same, and that the Moscow-Petrograd railway was not operating. Toward evening Sapronov returned to inform us that no rifles were to be had in Moscow. Because of disorderly shooting around the city, he had managed to get to the railway station only with difficulty. Armed cadets were marching through the center, the trams were not working, the workers' militias were ready but were staying at their workplaces for the simple reason that they had no weapons. We must, therefore, try again to negotiate with the reserve regiment of soldiers at the Pavlov settlement. We spoke on the phone with Demidov, the secretary of the party branch at Dedovskaia mill, who confirmed that the soldiers were in good spirits and that they would possibly give us rifles if Sapronov came along, since they all knew and trusted him. Demidov was waiting for us at the barracks when we arrived, and the meeting began right away, with Sapronov reporting on what was going on in the city.

Sapronov outlined what he had seen on the streets of Moscow and reported that cadets and officers were laying siege to the Moscow Soviet in the mansion of the governor-general and the party committee in the Dresden Hotel. The district was still holding out, thanks to the selfless efforts of several dozen Red Guards, armed with revolvers, but they had neither rifles nor cartridges. He explained that similar street fighting was going on in Petrograd and asked for the soldiers' help in overcoming the counterrevolutionary forces. The soldiers listened and several spoke in support of his appeal, but we didn't sense the same enthusiasm to join battle as there was among the workers. A representative from the soldiers' committee stepped forward and spoke for a long time about the blood flowing at the front, ignoring the blood that was now flowing on the streets of Moscow, but he finished his speech by saying they would hand over rifles as soon as the official order came. Otherwise, he said, they would be court-martialed. Sapronov, animated and indignant, replied that the officers who were shooting at unarmed workers were not stopping to ask whether their action was lawful. "We, too, stand for the law—but for the law that protects workers and peasants, not for that law that allows officers to shoot down the innocent. If you stand for the law that defends the gains of the revolution, I order you in the name of the Military-Revolutionary Committee[26] to arm all those who volunteer to fight for the revolution. If you need a piece of paper, I'll sign it!" A buzz of approval was heard among the soldiers. A definite shift in their mood had taken place. Speakers began to censure the speaker from the soldiers' committee and called on the soldiers to go to Moscow with the workers. One could tell in advance from the mood that the vote would be in our favor.

As they began to load rifles onto the carts, we realized that the regiment had only a few Russian rifles for guard duty. They gave us just 150 rifles of the Vetterli type. But a Vetterli was a Vetterli. All that mattered to us was that they were rifles.[27] At this stage, we couldn't tell one rifle from another. The boxes of rifles and cartridges were loaded quickly. It was fifteen to twenty kilometers back to the factory, and when we got back, everything needed to be ready and waiting for us. We telephoned to tell them not to go to bed and that we were bringing rifles.

At the factory they tired of waiting for us and many went off to bed. But as soon as the rattle of the cart was heard, lights appeared and lamps began to flicker. Everything sprang into life as though it were daytime. In the factory committee no one lounged about. The three hundred Red Guards had assembled, along with as many who were not. Seeing that we meant business, that it was no longer a matter of marching about, that battles lay in store, many demanded to enlist in the militia, ignoring the fact that we had only 150 rifles. The factory committee decided not to enlist any new recruits and to give the available rifles to young fighters who had no family.[28] Those who protested were calmed by the knowledge that in the event of battle there would be no widows or orphans. No one who received a rifle slept that night.

We young people had never held a weapon in our hands before, and here we were, face-to-face with a real "cannon." The long thick rifle was so heavy that we could barely hold it in a horizontal position on our shoulders. It was made still longer by the broad bayonet-saber. In addition, the several dozen thick cartridges with lead bullets were heavy enough to tear our pockets. As soon as dawn arrived, we resolved to study our weapons and use one cartridge on a test fire.

I felt proud as I arrived home to drink my morning coffee. My mother, seeing me with a rifle, turned away at once, softly wiping away a tear. If only she had scolded me . . . But it was not her way. Whenever she was displeased with me she simply fell silent and didn't speak. This affected me much more than any curses, and I immediately grew despondent. There was no shortage of words from my father, however, whose indignation knew no bounds. He bawled: "Be off with you! I know that sooner or later they'll start to hang you all, just as they did in 1905." My father was a "Menshevik." But what did he know? This was not 1905, but a real revolution. How could I be caught and hung when I had a rifle in my hands? They had hung revolutionaries then because they didn't have any weapons and had not been able to carry the people with them. Now the people were with us.

Only my little sister sympathized with me, as she got in my way: "Is this your gun?" she asked happily. "I want to have a look at it, how do you fire it?" I felt gloomy and angry at my father for clouding my keenness to fight with his talk of the gallows, and I didn't show my face again at home.

In the detachment we had lessons on cleaning and stripping our rifles. Once again we marched, but this time with a heavy rifle that slipped off our shoulders. We took careful aim for the first shot, but our rifles went wide of the target. The recoil from the shot hurt our shoulders, and our barrels leapt up into the air. We spent the whole day in this fashion until evening, when two railway carriages were ordered for us.

We traipsed the five kilometers to the station across woods and fields, under orders to walk in single file without talking or smoking. Everything was quiet around us, just like any other Sunday evening. There was a light, cold drizzle, but we felt warm. Our heads stirred with thoughts of what we would do when we got to Moscow. Would we march about, camouflage ourselves behind tussocks, and hide in ditches as we had been doing here? Somehow this didn't seem likely in the smooth city streets. There were few passengers in the poorly lit Vindavskii station.[29] The inspector checked the tickets and held one of us back for traveling without one. We were carrying rifles, but still got no respect. He asked to see each person's ticket, even though the fare for the whole detachment had been paid in a lump sum.

Meshchanskaia Street was unlit, and there was no traffic. Only our footsteps broke the silence. We continued to march in single file, with rifles in our hands, but there was something that was not quite soldierly about us. Somewhere in the distance we could hear solitary shots, which rebounded off the stone walls with a loud echo. As we grew accustomed to the darkness, we tried to make out what was ahead, but apart from the night watchmen, hunkering down motionless, we met no one. Sukharev Square was also in darkness, but flares were coming from somewhere, and in their light we could see little empty trenches.[30] When we reached the Romanov tavern, light was streaming through the window, and we could see movement inside.[31] Here we were met by our friends, who had been waiting ages for the "Tushintsy" to arrive.[32] This name stuck with us during the following days.

We learned that fighting was going on along Miasnitskaia Street near the post office. Others said that the post office had already been captured and was in our hands. The shooting we had heard was taking place at the telephone exchange, close to Sretenka. Because each shot was followed by an echo, we seemed to be surrounded by constant fire. Apart from the telephone exchange, shooting was taking place along Sretenka itself, where officer cadets were holed up in several buildings. They were firing on passing militia members. Our first unit immediately set off for the Kursk station to reconnoiter. By day there was no way through to the station; some cadets were ensconced at the Red Gates. Other units set off in different directions.

We walked in single file once again, but this time across the width of the street. Along Sadovaia there was not a night watchman to be seen. It was as though we were lost in a forest. It was pitch dark, but suddenly from the top floor of one building lights flickered and shots rang out. Against the rules, and without waiting for a command, we broke formation, took up positions on the sidewalk on the opposite side, and fired answering shots. We couldn't see whether we made any hits and heard only the clink of glass falling onto the street, possibly not even from our bullets. We were under orders to investigate the road to the station and come straight back, so were ordered not to linger or continue fire exchange. As soon as we moved off, the shooting stopped. The rest of the journey passed without any incidents. All the stations were lit, but only the railway staff was present. There were no passengers to be seen. On the way back no one fired from the dangerous building, but we let off several warning shots that remained unanswered.

We got back, hoping that we could dry our clothes and take a rest, for this was our second night without sleep. We were becoming used to our new life as fighters. As things became clearer, we felt calmer. In the tavern there was constant motion: people arriving and departing, people sitting on the floor with rifles in their hands. Some were lying across three chairs resting, using birch logs or cabbages from the kitchen for pillows. Most of the men from Tushino had not yet returned. Those we met no longer had Vetterlis in their hands, but light comfortable rifles of Russian make. The exchange of our "cannons" for these rifles, which had just arrived from Khodynka, was taking place in the staff headquarters at the tavern. Time passed quickly in conversation and questions, but I was ready for sleep.

It seemed as though I had just begun to doze when a cry rang out: "Tushintsy, prepare to leave." Sleep was snatched from me. My damp coat offered little warmth, and the cold before dawn was worse than frost. My new rifle was light, but seemed as heavy as the old one. Outside there was a damp silence, and out of 150 men from Tushino, only a score were on hand. We were led off to take the place of the night guard. Going along Sretenka, we observed the upper stories from which we had been shot at not long before. At each crossing we left two or three men to check on any firing from surrounding buildings and to stop enemies getting into Sretenka.

I was stationed not far from Lubianka Square. Across from me at an angle, on the other side, in the building where the headquarters of the Ministry of Foreign Affairs is housed today,[33] people were firing in all directions. The enemy was sitting tight in the tall building of the telephone exchange on Miliutinskii Lane, so we lay low. From there they controlled the length of the street with their fire and from the top commanded a number of adjacent streets and the Lubianka Square itself. Our shooting was to no avail—we merely hit the stone walls and revealed our positions. It was not too difficult in the dark to run the few dozen yards to the building, but the approach was protected by barricades made of neatly stacked wood, furniture, and rubbish. Because of the barricade, we risked being showered by a hail of bullets. Several attempts to run to the barricades ended in useless sacrifice, so we kept sheltered behind the corner of the street, waiting for we knew not what. If we so much as poked a gun barrel around the corner, the shooting resumed at once. We stuck up a white flag with a red cross. This time they didn't shoot, which meant that we could collect the wounded and possibly the dead. The wounded were lying motionless for fear of being shot at. Only one man was crying loudly, but as soon as the nurse got to him he got up. It turned out that his shoulder blade was shattered.

We were ordered not to fire in vain, to surround the building to prevent any reinforcements arriving from Lubianka Square and Miasnitskaia Street, and to be on our guard against any sorties from the surrounded building. Judging by the shooting, there were a lot of officer cadets in there. Besides, they had at least two machine guns, whereas we had only rifles. Everything became visible as day dawned. No one on our side was shooting, but odd shots rang out almost constantly. The enemy commanded a wide panorama and long distance, so they opened fire on any moving figure. We were out of the line of fire, but the corner opposite the building was riddled with bullet holes, and from time to time we were showered with bits of brick and plaster. Opposite us was a stone wall behind which a church tower was visible.[34] At a moment of intense exchange of fire, when the wall opposite was smoking with brick dust, I saw on Sretenka, against the light background of the wall, a black figure in a cassock. He was watching us with interest as we hid from the bullets. We could see the priest clearly, wiping the dust from his eyes. It was as though he were magically immune from the bullets. I waved at him to indicate that it was dangerous and that he should go away, but he didn't turn a hair. Then I pointed to my rifle. I don't know how he understood my gesture—perhaps as a threat—but he turned through the gate, leaving it not quite shut; from there he continued to watch this unprecedented spectacle through the crack. Of course, no one intended to shoot a priest, but bullets are crazy: some of our men were wounded as a bullet ricocheted.

The walls of the Kitai-gorod[35] that came out onto Lubianka Square were in enemy hands, and between them and the start of Sretenka shooting was going on everywhere. Yet it was uneven and inconstant. Sometimes it was possible to get up to the square without provoking a single shot, at other times a machine gun would bang away from the Nikol'skie Gates. Later on, as I was passing through these gates, I saw a pile of cartridge cases and asked myself how many deadly bullets had been discharged from there. Although machine-gun fire was only sporadic around me, we were actually threatened with greater danger from that quarter than from the telephone station.

Like Lubianka Square, the thoroughfare across Theater Square, where the cadets were sitting tight in the Metropole Hotel, was a kind of no-man's-land, subject only to our constant patrols. We managed to force our way across the square to Malaia Lubianka, from where we could more easily fire on the telephone exchange, but during one of our crossings, when we were not expecting any danger, shooting started up from behind us, from the upper stories and attics of what later became the Ministry of Foreign Affairs Building. We ran to the other side, under shelter of the building itself, but couldn't get inside, as this section of the street was under fire from the opposite direction. We had no alternative but to return fire. It was now daylight and we were clearly visible. The only cover we had were the iron posts of the street lamps, so we returned fire from behind them. At my side, behind the next lamppost, was Voitsekhovskii, who was slowly taking aim. He crouched lower—I supposed because the post was broader at its base and provided better cover. I did the same, kneeling on the ground. Soon, seeing the futility of our shooting, I cried to him: "Come on, let's get away." It was only then that I noticed he was stretched motionless on the sidewalk, with his rifle lying across his body. While I ran for the nurse, I thought how easy and quietly a man can die, without words or groans. Perhaps he had had a premonition of something painful, for he had been humming a sad and melancholy tune as we were coming on the train, and he had walked along, weary and silent. Later there were a lot of wrangles provoked by his death, for he was his mother's sole supporter and should never have been given a rifle. He was one of the few whose body we were able to send back to the factory before the fighting ended.

From that time on, many irregular Red Guards, who had not been part of the detachment earlier, appeared among us. The factory committee had refused to recommend Evel' for membership in the Red Guard on the grounds of his "hooliganism." He was a young, handsome plumber of athletic build, who enjoyed great success with women, regularly leaving one for another. At the time of the revolution, however, he had a constant companion, an office worker. They were much talked about because it was rare for a worker to marry an office employee. I noticed with some satisfaction that Evel' had managed to join up with us and was armed with a rifle. It emerged that he had come to Moscow by himself, turned up at the headquarters of the Gorodskoi district, and been given a rifle. I sympathized with him, for I liked his handsome, manly figure and didn't quite understand why he had been turned down for the militia on the grounds of "hooliganism." I assumed this meant that he had ditched some girl or other. It turned out, however, that our elders had been good psychologists in their fight to maintain standards within the detachment.

We were under strict orders not to leave our posts without informing the guard commander, but it was not always easy to remain standing in one spot when a few buildings away there was shooting going on. After a stretch on duty we would go back to the tavern to relax, have something to eat, and be sent wherever we were needed. We frequently used our free time to go off toward the sound of shooting. Occasionally, the Red Guards of the Gorodskoi district got as far as Krasnaia Presnia, and men from there would come over to us. As a rule, however, we maintained discipline. Evel' had no such discipline and was not tied to the militia nor even counted as a member of a unit of ten. He would act like a "hooligan," going wherever he pleased. He would tell us about battles at Nikitsky Gates or Arbat Square when we were supposed to be bound by the limits of our district. One day Evel' appeared with a rifle on his shoulder and a peaked cap in his hands. "You won't believe how crazy it is! What the hell! Another centimeter and I'd have been done for." He stretched out the cap: the peak shot through by a bullet. He could talk about nothing else, admiring the little hole all the while. And then he just disappeared—back to the factory.

Such lack of discipline was also characteristic of soldiers. They never showed up at the tavern headquarters, were never at their posts, and came and went as they pleased. Yet as soon as fire was exchanged, whether it was night or day, early or late, they would appear on the spot. During the seven days' battle many irregulars turned up, and we returned with more men than we had set out with, in spite of losses.

In our factory bakery there worked a middle-aged man who suffered from the occupational disease of all bakers—he loved to drink. He didn't take part in public affairs and had not joined the militia, but now he turned up. Shortly afterward, he was wounded in the leg and returned to the factory. At the end of the week, however, he reappeared, saying that his wound had stopped hurting after it was bandaged up and that he couldn't bear just to sit at the factory. Everything was gloomy there, people could only talk about the death of Voitsekhovskii—it was worse than being here.

Among the irregulars was also E. Mazul', father of two children. He was our deputy in the soviet, the secretary of the Bolshevik cell, and, of course, a member of the fighting detachment. I don't know how he got hold of a rifle, but he was a most disciplined and, at the same time, a most enterprising member of the militia. At the factory we had been more than zealous in studying marching, and now we heeded the advice of the general staff and the soldiers. None of their advice, however, was suited to the conditions of street fighting. In the narrow alleys it was impossible to know from which direction bullets were coming, soldiers were lost and pressed close as we did to the salients of the buildings, rather than lie on the ground in accordance with rules of field battle. No end to the siege of the telephone exchange was in sight. It was impossible to get close to it, and there was no place from which we could keep it under constant fire. Mazul' noticed that the telephone exchange was on a street on which there was a two-story building, whose facade was peppered with bullets from top to bottom. All its glass was smashed and curtains flapped in the empty windows. It was unlikely that there was anyone in the house, since it was exactly opposite the barricades.

One dark night, as the shooting quieted down, we broke into this house. We climbed to the second floor and realized that Mazul' was right—the inhabitants were nowhere to be seen or heard. As dawn broke, we could see both the telephone exchange and the barricade, and there was no sign of life. Settling by the window, we opened fire, but immediately shots were returned, forcing us to take cover behind the piers of the windows. We could hear odd shots coming from our side and machine-gun salvos from their side. The rooms were filled with acrid plaster dust that would not settle, and in spite of the drafts, it was difficult to breathe. If it became easier to breathe in one room, it became more difficult in the next. There was no point, therefore, in firing aimlessly into the air without a clear target. We couldn't see what was going on outside, though we knew from the shooting that our comrades were trying to help us. If the officer cadets took it into their heads to make a sortie, they could not get to our building since the length of the street was exposed to fire from our side. But we were cut off. We gradually blocked up the windows with tables and overturned cupboards, piling mattresses and pillows on top of them. Thanks to this less than perfect cover it was not too difficult to poke our rifles through and take aim.

Evening came and we had to think either of getting back or of getting help. There were about twenty to thirty windows in the building, but only a dozen of us fighters. This time the shooting didn't die down with the onset of night. It seemed to intensify. Faced by such fire, there could be no question either of a return sortie or of waiting for certain death. Ten rifles could do little against machine guns, and we didn't know why the cadets fired so bitterly and incessantly. We decided anyway to barricade the front door and leave someone downstairs to watch the approach to the building. We all wanted to stick together, however, and no one was eager to stand guard downstairs. We proposed a rotation for guard duty—as soon as one person came upstairs, another would go down—but it was hard to find people willing to crawl up and down the stairs in the dark through plaster dust and under uninterrupted fire. We passed the night in great anxiety. By morning the plaster was behaving more decently, and the machine gun was silent, though bullets continued to hit the outside wall, making a dull smack on impact.

We cheered up as dawn broke and stopped being afraid that the enemy might dislodge us from below. We paid no attention to the incomprehensible sounds from outside, for although they were no longer firing from the telephone exchange, our side was firing without respite. Who were they firing at? Were they attacking them from the rear, from Lubianka Square? Through the cracks we could see some motion behind the barricades, but firing was not coming from there. At that moment our building shook from the force of an explosion and the windows were darkened by clouds of smoke or fog. We perceived that an armored car had turned into our street from the direction of Miasnitskaia and fired on our building or, possibly, lobbed a grenade at us. We could see that the armored car had stopped at the barricade and that they were taking something away. Then it came back, and the front door of the car was let down. The corner of our building had been demolished by the preceding explosion, and we now prepared to meet our end under the ruins of the building or in a conflagration. They were watching us keenly from the telephone exchange. After the explosion a hail of bullets had rained on us. But the armored car did not linger and set off in the direction from which it had come.

After this shock, all we wanted to do was eat and, above all, drink. Two soldiers among us brought up a jar of jam from the cellar and we fed ourselves on it. After we had eaten, we decided that we must get away as soon as darkness fell and return only during the final storming of the telephone exchange.

We stole out through the back entrance over several fences until we came to Sretenka. We arrived at the tavern as though we were coming home, and everybody fell on us with questions about what was happening. The rumble of artillery from the Nikitsky Gates had intensified and the glow of a blazing fire was visible. The headquarters was as poorly informed as we were, and had no idea what was going on in the other districts. All we knew was that the outlying areas were in our hands, including the railway stations. By now the place was crawling with rumors that the Cossacks and a regiment of guards were heading toward Moscow. The Dvintsy[36] were downcast and played on each other's depression: we won't get the better of the Cossacks. There were also soldiers from Khodynka among us who, like the men from Dvinsk, had arrived in dribs and drabs, rather than as an organized unit. They were not subject to the headquarters and acted as they pleased. Our unit of ten was sent to patrol the stations, and these soldiers joined us, so we set off almost as a platoon. The soldiers wanted to go to the station to hear news of what was happening in Piter, but at both the Nikolaevskii and Riazan'-Ural'skii stations there were no passengers, and the railway staff were not talkative. It was difficult to talk with people who didn't ask us anything and who didn't appear to be interested in what was going on in Moscow. They acted as though things were always like that and as though they were quite used to seeing unshaven men with rifles in their hands.

Our district was cut off from the Military-Revolutionary Committee and from the Moscow Soviet and we received no instructions from them. We were fired on from upper stories when we least expected it, just as before, but now we had some experience and didn't expose ourselves to the bullets. When firing started we would run across to the doorways of the buildings, force an entry, and start to negotiate. Usually the concierge or "guard" would come and we would demand that he either let us into the building or stop the shooting within "two minutes," threatening that if he did not, we would set fire to the house or blow it up with grenades that, of course, we didn't have. Usually we would get the reply that they weren't firing from that building and that we should wait while he checked the attic. After "checking," he would open the door to us and we would go up and find that there was nobody shooting there. As we descended we would be accompanied not only by the guard but by terrified women who would ask when the shooting was going to stop and whether the bakeries would soon be open. But though we were masters of the street, we had no bread ourselves. Some bread was brought to headquarters from the military barracks, but so little that it was quickly snatched up. The soldiers ate by themselves, the Dvintsy eating in the kitchen of some infirmary. They, too, said that they had only a small amount of bread, though as much flour as they wished for.

The telephone exchange continued to pester us. We figured that there were three hundred officer cadets ensconced there. Without this threat from the rear, we could have begun the battle for the Kitai-gorod, which also gave us no peace. The battles at Nikitsky Gates had quieted, however, and help came from that quarter, probably from the soldiers. A mortar was dragged from Khodynka, which we decided to use to renew the attack on the telephone exchange.

Under cover of darkness the mortar was placed on top of an unfinished building, and we resolved to rush the barricade as soon as it was fired. The first explosion of the mortar shell was as much of a shock to us as it was to the defenders of the exchange. It seemed as though the walls of the buildings were about to roll right over us. After the second—and last—shell, we rushed at the exchange without firing. Initially, the besieged occupants didn't fire at us, so shaken and confused were they by the swaying and shaking of the building. I can't explain the accuracy of the mortar, but both shells hit the roof of the building, and the top stories were half-destroyed. The machine guns fell silent.

Running up to the barricades in tight ranks, we got in each other's way and were unable to dismantle the wood from which the barricade had been assembled. After several minutes firing began again, but by this stage we had crossed the barricade and, protected by the walls of the building, returned their fire, shouting: "Give yourselves up!" With the butts of our rifles we battered down the door, the noise being so great that we couldn't hear who was speaking with the beleaguered occupants or what they were saying. From the third floor a white flag appeared, though spasmodically, after long periods of silence, shooting would erupt again.

We demanded that they hand over their weapons and surrender. They agreed on condition that they were allowed to disperse to their homes.[37] We replied that only the headquarters could decide that. As they came out, they piled up their weapons at the exit. Including those without rifles, there turned out to be no more than us, not quite two hundred. We had assumed they were all officer cadets, but we discovered that there were many civilians among them, including some in student caps. They were very confused and frightened, and their transfer into captivity was a noisy affair. The soldiers greeted them with cries and threats and made as if to hit them, reminding them of the bloody reprisals that had been meted out on soldiers guarding the Kremlin by officer cadets.[38] We, the militia members, outnumbered the soldiers and stood up for the crowd of prisoners, who had now been rendered harmless. As they trooped out, time dragged tediously, and we engaged in not entirely amicable conversation with the soldiers. The downcast figures of the terrified prisoners evoked our pity, and we felt no malice toward them. But the soldiers told how they had been turned out of the Kremlin by deception and how they had been fired on by machine guns as they walked away. Now they peered into the faces of the prisoners to see if they could recognize any of the officers. They were angry at the deception and insisted that we should use the same methods with these prisoners as they themselves had used. "So what that they are children," the soldiers complained. "When all is said and done, they still wish to be addressed as 'Your Honor.'" Our arguing with them perhaps would not have helped, but at that moment there appeared some nursing sisters with the wounded. Behind them, in a disorderly crowd, laughing for no apparent reason, came the "young ladies," the telephonists. They had been inside for seven days, having failed to escape before the fighting started. The appearance of these "young ladies" calmed the bellicose soldiers. Instead of shouts, curses, and vulgar abuse, they answered smile with smile, and some even twirled their moustaches.

The women dispersed and the prisoners were led to the staff headquarters. The next day in the tavern there was an excited protest meeting after it transpired that the staff had released all the prisoners. Staff representatives pointed out that no accommodation could be found for the prisoners and asked whether any of us was willing to guard them. We didn't have enough people for guard duty in addition to patrols. Nevertheless those same militia members who had protected the prisoners against violence from the soldiers made a formal protest censuring the staff.

When the occupied building had been cleared of all the prisoners, we were told to go around the rooms in search of any people still hiding and to collect weapons and cartridges that had not been handed over. We couldn't get to the top floor, as the staircase had collapsed after the explosion of the shell. The other floors were intact, but the windows of all the rooms were either smashed or peppered with bullet holes. Under a layer of dust, plaster, and broken glass, the parquet floors no longer shone. Tables and cupboards had been moved from their original places. Apparently, people had been sleeping on some of them, for pillows and stacks of paper were piled on them. Everything else—inkwells, pens, pencils, rulers, a lot of clean paper—was strewn on the floor. The thrifty ones among us cursed because so much of the people's money had been wasted. The soldiers said: "There is more order and cleanliness in our barracks than there is among these nobles." We went from room to room, collecting cartridges, taking them downstairs, and then returning upstairs. The nurses asked us to look out for bandages, cotton wool, and medicine. Bandages were found, but they were covered in blood, having been thrown on the floor once the dressing was done.

We went away happy that the telephone exchange had been taken. Its fall seemed to presage the end of battle, though Moscow still echoed with spasmodic gunfire. Morning came, a bright day, and explosions could be heard in the distance. These were not as powerful as those made by the mortar, but more frequent. We had not heard such sounds before, and our anxiety increased in the face of the unknown. Perhaps the Cossacks had arrived and were firing heavy artillery. The sound of distant battle cut short our work in clearing the telephone exchange of cartridges. We headed for staff headquarters to find out what was happening and to receive instructions as to what to do. The mood at headquarters was one of joy: it was our side that was firing cannons from Khodynka onto the Kremlin. A member of the Military-Revolutionary Committee, V. M. Smirnov, had made his way there, persuaded and organized the artillery soldiers, and liberated the Moscow Soviet from blockade. We also learned what was happening in other districts. Our forces were closing in on the center; the Aleksandr Military School[39] was under artillery fire; and Colonel Riabtsev[40] had begun negotiations to end the battle.

Units of Colonel Riabtsev occupied the Kremlin, the Kitai-gorod, the district of the Aleksandr Military School, the Arbat, and Ostozhenka. Forces were thinning out on the outskirts and concentrating in the city center. Meanwhile our forces were growing, as contacts were established with other districts and as reinforcements arrived. We met the militia members from the Dedovskaia mill, who told us that the soldiers of Pavlov settlement had decided to go to Moscow and had organized two companies of volunteers, headed by an ensign and noncommissioned officers. They had set off for the Nakhibino station, accompanied by the whole regiment and its band. But while waiting for the train, they had dispersed. When the train arrived, the commanders had vanished and the volunteers, like a flock of sheep, had decided not to go to Moscow. Nevertheless more and more soldiers were joining us, now that the artillery had gone into action.

We were faced with storming the high walls of the Kitai-gorod from narrow medieval lanes. The difficulties facing us were no less than those that had faced us at the telephone exchange. We hoped that the cannons would breach the walls or break down the gates and, with experienced soldier-fighters now at our side, we determined to do this. After a breakdown in the negotiations, we set about our task. It turned out that the defendants had moved on to the Kremlin, so the Kitai-gorod fell to us with little bloodshed. We went along Nikol'skaia to Red Square, where the enemy fired on us from the Kremlin, which stood as unassailable as ever. We had heard that it was partially ruined and that it would not be too difficult to get inside. The Cathedral of St. Basil was intact, though there had been a rumor to the effect that our artillery had fired on it with the aim of destroying this sacred Russian shrine and historical and artistic monument.

Chapter Four

Power did not pass seamlessly to the Congress of Soviets after the October revolution. Mensheviks and SRs in the congress denounced the seizure of power as unlawful and demonstratively walked out, refusing to share in the administration of that power. Some SRs remained, cementing a split in that party and leading to the consolidation of the Left SR party that continued to cooperate with the Bolsheviks. Many Russians who were unrepresented by the system of soviets—nobles, estate owners, merchants, industrialists, bureaucrats, professionals, lower middle-class shop owners, and white-collar employees—remained alienated from the new political structure. State officials declared a protest strike against the new regime, and employees of the State Bank refused to issue money to the new government.

The congress, notwithstanding substantial opposition, plunged ahead, creating a new executive body, the Council of People's Commissars, and enacting several key decrees. A decree on peace proposed an immediate peace without annexations and indemnities and called on workers in other warring countries to help implement the peace from below. Another decree abolished land-lords' rights to own land and transferred privately owned and church lands to land committees and peasant soviets. Land was to belong only to those who toiled on it, and hired labor was forbidden. In fact, the decree on land was purposely vague, but for the time being, it signaled to the peasants that their traditional dreams of control over their land would be fulfilled.

Implementation of a socialist economic program came more slowly. Outright nationalization of industrial enterprises was not on the agenda at first. One of the first economic measures of the new regime was a decree on workers' control, giving workers in industry the right to supervise all aspects of production and to have access to all spheres of administration, including the financial side. Private ownership of large houses was abolished in early December 1917, and such houses and apartment buildings were transferred to ownership of local soviets. The Supreme Economic Council was created in mid-December 1917 and assigned the general administration of the country's economic affairs. This body would eventually supervise enterprises that were nationalized, first individually, and then in a more sweeping blanket nationalization in mid-1918. Later in December banks were nationalized and banking declared a state monopoly.

Noneconomic measures also signaled the regime's determination to transform the old society. A declaration on the rights of nationalities officially recognized the right of self-determination for national groups. Women were given full legal equality with men; marriage and divorce were simplified and removed from the jurisdiction of the church; children born out of wedlock received full legal rights. The complete separation of church and state was decreed in early 1918. Religious teaching was prohibited in schools, and religious organizations could not own property. Even the Cyrillic alphabet was reformed to eliminate superfluous characters. And on 1 February 1918, the government decreed that henceforth Russia would follow the Western calendar and immediately advanced the date to 14 February.

Rob the Robbers

Earlier we had walked the streets with caution, expecting shooting to break out from any of the large buildings. Now such incidents were rare, so we walked boldly, not bothering to take cover. People reappeared on the streets, mostly women with bags on their arms. During the week of fighting they had used up all their supplies and had sat indoors half-starved. Now they ventured forth, searching for something to eat from their friends, the shops still being shut. From time to time, somewhere in the far distance a shot would ring out. We had got so used to the crackle of gunfire that we took no notice, not even listening to the shot unless we could also hear the whistle of the flying bullet. The local inhabitants who came onto the streets behaved differently. They passed by quickly, almost at a run. Hearing several shots, they would throw themselves to the ground. After a minute they would get up, only to lie down again, not realizing that the shooting was far away. It was rather funny to watch these antics: hardened by experience, we knew that lying flat on the ground made you a much easier target than if you were standing against the wall.

In the niches of the inner wall of the Kitai-gorod there were wooden provisions shops. Some of their shutters had been torn off, and hungry folk now descended on them, dragging sausage, lard, and smoked meat through the holes in the frontages. Some were more interested in the general stores than in the food shops. Along Nikol'skii there were some leather shops whose shutters had been wrenched open and windows broken, perhaps long before our arrival. At all the gates to the Kitai-gorod guards were set up to con-

fiscate stolen goods from people going out. But the sentries wanted to know how they were supposed to guess whether something
was stolen or not. We told them that anything that was edible
should not be considered stolen property. After dinner I took over
guard duty at the Il'inskii Gates. In the gateway was a handwrit-
ten notice that said something along the lines: "Comrades, safeguard the people's property! We declare war on looters. We will
detain all robbers and hand them over to revolutionary courts."

On the ground beneath this notice lay a heap of goods confiscated from passersby: a horse's harness with metal flashes for expensive turnouts; cardboard boxes full of knives, forks, and
spoons; pocket watches and watch chains. On top of the boxes
were clocks without their wrappings, broaches made of gold or
silver, or maybe just brass. Who could tell? The old guard went off,
and we were told to put any goods confiscated on this pile. They
promised to send a cart, though we never saw it. Meanwhile the
pile continued to grow.

It was mainly women who passed through, silently opening
their bags. Others, feeling guilty about the goods they had "acquired," apologized that their children were sitting at home starving. But we didn't bother about food. Men also passed through—
some well-dressed, others poorly dressed. Some went through
empty-handed, so we didn't pay attention to them. Later, however, after a typical "police officer's" experience, we began to watch
these men more carefully. In the distance we noticed a rather ridiculous figure clad from head to toe in a Siberian fur coat. It was
not yet winter, yet he was wrapped up to his nose. He had an old
cap on his head, dirty boots on his feet, and this expensive fur coat.
As he approached, he greeted us with an ingratiating smile. We
said to him: "Why are you going about in a fur coat when it's not
cold?" "My dears, I'm not the only one. It's a pity to leave such
good things. The shop is open, people are taking anything that is
the least bit expensive, so I thought this coat would prove useful."
Under the fur coat he was wearing an old sheepskin jacket. Afraid
that we would arrest him, he began to tell us that he was a poor
coach driver, not a robber. He had nothing in his pockets, so we
ordered him to leave the coat on the pile of confiscated goods and
let him off with a warning. The little old man was delighted, but
began to scold us, saying that it was useless our standing there
when a short distance away thieves were pilfering the wealth of

the country. Having thrown off the fur coat, he had become a defender of other people's property. He said that his neighbors were thieves—they knew a shop where the owner was absent and the goods that lay inside it. After this incident we began to pay less attention to the women's bags and more to the men. In one man's bulging pockets we discovered a large number of watches. The pockets of another were empty, but he had dozens of rings on his fingers.

I was furious at the sight of these narrow-minded people hunting for any booty that was not protected, trying to grab anything that was not under lock and key. We had been without sleep for a week, fighting for a better and brighter future. We were not under orders to detain the guilty, only to confiscate what they had stolen, so we confined ourselves to scolding them and shaming them for looting the people's wealth.

We finished our round of duty. The next day the Kremlin surrendered without a fight.[1] Sunday passed almost without any shooting. We walked around Moscow, looking at where the shells had hit the Kremlin. Already there was not a great deal for us to do. On the following day, Monday,[2] we prepared to go home. The stint of being a police officer already seemed a rather insignificant experience.

We traveled home tired, indifferent to everything that was happening around us. We had no sense of having been participants in "seven days that shook the world."[3] We had not been fulfilling a sacred duty, merely carrying out our responsibility. We had been excited when we arrived in Moscow, for we faced the unknown, possibly the gallows. Now all we wanted to do was to sleep, and we dozed as we trudged toward the station and slept with our eyes open as we waited for the train. We only came to when we heard a triumphant victory march being played by a brass band. We had arrived in Tushino. Off the train!

We had left in silence on a rainy evening, with no words of farewell for our relatives, friends, and loved ones. We returned on a sunny afternoon to be greeted by an enormous, noisy crowd of workers from the factory, a large number of women, old folk, and children, accompanied by music. Oblivious to others, some embraced and kissed, others wept. Not all the tears were joyful since not everybody had returned.

My drowsiness passed and I felt warm inside as I heard the

emotional speeches and the ceremonial music at the rally. As we listened to the speeches of greeting, we became aware that we had made a piece of history. Each of us had done his bit—in a simple, ordinary fashion, just as when we had marched with only our wooden rifles. The band accompanied us the whole way to the factory, solemn marches alternating with revolutionary songs. Everyone from the smallest to the largest sang in time to the music, loudly and enthusiastically. The peasants no longer stood aloof, and our procession grew into a vast sea of people. But the first moments of joy and good cheer gave way to exhaustion. After seven sleepless nights, I only wanted to sleep. I don't remember what happened at the factory during the first days after our return. I only recall that we were required to make another journey to Moscow in order to attend the burial of those who had fallen in battle.

This time Moscow looked different: there were speeches about those who had fallen, recollections of those who had watched our battles, and the role of the "Tushintsy" was duly noted. To the actual participants, everything had seemed rather mundane. We did not even know how many had perished. We assumed that there had been no more than a few dozen victims, but were now given different figures. From the Gorodskoi district alone seventy of our men (out of a total of five hundred) had been buried in a mass grave at the Kremlin Wall on Red Square.[4]

During the days of the fighting the factory had stopped work. Now it resumed with nothing much changed except that the Red Guards no longer marched with their wooden rifles on Sundays. At a general meeting of the work force Sapronov made a routine report on the situation in other towns, saying that soviet power was growing stronger and spreading wider and that the time had come for constructive work and for strengthening the popular government. The bourgeois newspapers wrote each day in a quite different spirit, saying that power had been usurped, that disaster would soon overtake those who had seized power, and that robbery was endemic.[5] Much later, when political passions had subsided, our opponents wrote rather differently about these matters. "In late summer 1917 the civil militia became so bankrupt that ordinary folk had to take their own measures, in the form of night watches and guards, to defend themselves against robbery and raids on private houses. The measures taken by the new government were so effective that soon after the establishment of soviet power, there was no longer any need to resort to private defense. If only in this respect, it became easier to breathe."[6] Yet after the new power was established the entire press began to clamor about robberies by the Red Guards, and peasants and workers at the factory did likewise.

We discussed this at any number of factory meetings. One speaker declared that several militia members had behaved dishonorably in Moscow, that they had besmirched the revolution with their unclean hands. Sapronov replied that it was inadmissible to make vague accusations and to repeat the lies of the bourgeois press, which was only concerned to compromise the new workers' government, not to uncover crime. Whoever knew of unworthy conduct by Red Guards should say so specifically, naming those who were guilty. We were vitally concerned to see that the guilty were brought to justice and the honor of the Red Guard restored. The above-mentioned baker, the one who had been wounded, made a speech in which he told the meeting what he had seen on the streets of Moscow. He said that during the battles the shops had been closed and that no one had got into them. Only during the last couple of days, after the shooting had quieted down, did inhabitants appear on the streets in search of food. From then on, rumors began to circulate about shops that had had their windows smashed and been looted. But we had not had the forces to protect broken windows at that stage, since we had been preparing to retake the Kremlin. He also described the scene inside the telephone exchange, where all kinds of valuables lay scattered on the floor untouched. Dipping his hand into his pocket, he pulled out a pencil with a metal point protector, and said: "I picked this up from the floor of the telephone exchange, it is all that I looted." The mood of the meeting lightened, but the baker was pestered with various spiteful questions: "Do you plan to make bread with a pencil?" "What do you need a pencil for?" Although it was nothing serious, people criticized him from all sides, forgetting that he had been wounded, that he had gone to Moscow to fight not steal, and that the value of the pencil was no more than a kopeck.

He was followed by the technical secretary of the factory committee. She had been one of the nursing auxiliaries and had risked her life under fire on several occasions. She had been with us on the night that we seized the telephone exchange and was also one of the most active women workers at the factory. Now she confessed that amid the destruction in the telephone exchange she had picked up a nickel-plated metal ruler, which was now in the possession of the factory committee.

Sapronov asked those at the meeting to decide who had compromised themselves by dishonorable actions and uncover those who had not had the courage to come clean. But no one knew anything very concrete, all quoting gossip and rumors. The upshot was that Mazul', Shmidel', and Sapronov, the most respectable in terms of age and authority, began to reproach and inveigh against the secretary because of the nickel-plated ruler and the baker on account of the pencil. They said that although this was not technically theft, such trifles compromised the fighters and gave ammunition to the enemies of the revolution. They said that it was not enough merely to censure the guilty. They must be punished. There then arose an animated discussion as to how this should be done. Should their names be published in the press? Should they be fined a large sum, which would go to assist the widows and orphans of the Red Guards who had died? Someone proposed a more original form of punishment. The guilty parties should go around for a certain number of days wearing a sign on their chest and back, saying "I stole a pencil" and "I stole a ruler."

The guilty parties kept quiet. The secretary began to cry, and the baker left the meeting. It was only when I saw how the secretary of the factory committee went about for three days wearing a placard at home and at work that I realized that a great injustice been done, and we workers were responsible. The humiliating punishment had been ordered by the general meeting of workers, which had the force of law. We had acted stupidly merely to shut up idle gossips and to justify ourselves before the enemies of the revolution. We so idealized the new government that we believed we could jump straight from the "realm of necessity" into the "realm of freedom."[7]

What is theft? My mother taught me as a child that a thief who stole a piece of bread to satisfy hunger was not a criminal, but a poor person too ashamed to beg. We should pity that thief as we would a poor, hungry beggar. Later in Riga at the Commercial School of the Society of Friends of Enlightenment, our religious instructor had argued that a thief who stole because of hunger was more honorable than a trader who grew rich by selling goods at a higher price than they had cost to buy. To what category of thief did the comrade belong who had picked up a ruler that was lying around, not even for her own use but for that of the collective? We were trying to create a morality appropriate to an impending paradise on earth, trying to turn the factory collective into an order of sinless monks. Later, when the Red Guard was at the front, we continued to apply this same "monastic morality." We regarded "heroics"—actions going beyond the call of duty that went undistinguished by decorations or gold epaulets—as a self-evident obligation. In order to discuss our morality more generally, however, I will not cite examples from our heroic actions during the war but examine how we allegedly "robbed the robbers."

The peasants of the Moscow region did not greet the new government's Decree on Land with the same enthusiasm as we workers. It was an abstract empty slogan, since land hung like a heavy weight on the peasants of our region, chaining them to their miserable allotments and houses in the countryside. For these peasants, partitioning the landlords' suburban estates, most of which were small in area, supplemented their plots by inches rather than yards. Moreover, the government had no apparatus in the localities to implement the decree. Such an apparatus was created only with difficulty and with "squeaking wheels." The village and volost' soviets did not yet exist, so they were not able to carry out the confiscation of the landlords' estates: instead it fell to the workers' organizations. In the factory committee we typed or wrote out orders that said that on the basis of the decree of the Council of People's Commissars, such-and-such an estate was confiscated as people's property and that any deliberate misappropriation of the property of the estate would be punished by revolutionary law. There was not even a police force to protect the confiscated properties. These orders were then delivered to properties lying within a radius of several score kilometers of our factory and handed over to the estate manager or stuck on the gate at the entrance. Later, after the organization of uezd and volost' soviets, this work fell to them, but I am speaking about the first months of the revolution.

In this fashion the estate of Prince Golitsyn, Arkhangelskoe, was nationalized.[8] In the autumn of 1918 I happened to drop by there. Our authorization was still pinned to the gate and the property remained in the same state as before the revolution. Yet there was plenty to steal. The parquet floor, covered by large carpets, shone as though it had just been polished the day before. The bookcases along the wall were full of books. There were writing desks, display cases filled with expensive ornaments, statues carved from ivory. On the walls were pictures and tapestries. In the office was a huge safe. I asked who had the key. "I don't know, they didn't leave it with me. It has been shut since the princess left."

"Are there any valuables in there?"

"Probably, but I have never seen the inside of the safe, so I don't know what's kept there." In other words, neither the uezd soviet nor thieves had got in. To placate the peasants it was enough for the manager to refer to our order. Evidently, this estate remained intact during the succeeding years, for in 1923 Trotsky stayed there.

Another estate, the palace of Prince Shakhovskoi at Pokrovskoe-Streshnevo station, was subject to a similar order.[9] But in contrast to Arkhangelskoe, everything inside was covered with dust. The small windows and thick portieres let in little light. There were few ornaments, but the walls were covered with pictures and heavy canvases, as in a museum, and the shelves were laden with books. This estate, situated about twelve kilometers from Moscow with convenient access, was soon transferred to the People's Commissariat of Enlightenment. Lunacharskii, staunch advocate of the preservation of historical and artistic treasures, set up a vacation home there for artists of the state theaters.[10] The Russian intelligentsia, "the salt of the Russian earth," who looked down on us workers, came here for their holidays. Once we asked them to put on a concert at our club, and they agreed, but only on condition that we pay them so many sacks of flour, so many pounds of sugar and butter. We didn't turn to them again: by the autumn of 1918 we had already gone on starvation rations, the Red Army ration having become an unattainable dream. Yet still they tried to trade in sacks and pounds!

Five years later, I visited this estate and chatted with the manager. We recalled 1918 and he took me to look round the holiday home to which the artists came during the summer. I asked him why the bookcases were half-empty and the shelves completely bare. Had the books been taken to the central library in Moscow? "No," he replied, "they've been borrowed and not returned. They take them off to Moscow, without asking, and then forget to bring them back." He led me around the rooms, silently pointing to the frames without canvases and to the empty places where pictures had formerly hung. Some windows had no curtains or blinds. With a bitter smile of reproach, he explained that they, too, had been borrowed and not returned.

I do not wish at all to suggest that there are more thieves among the intelligentsia than among the workers. But we considered the things we had won as ours collectively, as the "people's property." Books, pictures, and statues said little to the workers, yet to things they did not understand they had an attitude of sacred awe. An incomprehensible book was as mysterious as an icon, not something to be read as a way of passing time. Such things had become "ours." Who would think of stealing them? For the artists who lived here, however, this property was not theirs, it was someone else's, some philistine's.

I witnessed this devastation and passionately wanted to tell Lunacharskii just how the intelligentsia were preserving historical and artistic treasures. I remembered how he had collapsed in hysterics during the first days of October, when rumors reached him that we had destroyed the Kremlin and the Cathedral of St. Basil with our bombardments. They say he wept with indignation, yet his eyes didn't even water when five hundred Red Guards were buried. They had died for the sake of the Great Illusion—in the hope that a kingdom on earth might be built on the foundation of our hope and faith.

Two years after seeing this, I was walking home with my wife after seeing *The Red Poppy*, performed by Gel'tser.[11] I was in raptures, captivated by the graceful figure of the dancer, who looked as though she were a young girl. My wife remarked: "You may well be in raptures. She is over sixty, but she has just married a twenty-seven-year-old violinist in the orchestra." She then added, "I admired her, too, until I saw her treating herself to caviar." That was in 1920, the year when hunger was at its worst. At that time Avel' Enukidze arranged regular receptions for artists as a way of paying court to the intelligentsia.[12] At these soirees they were given the very best, the most refined things that old man Kalnyn' could obtain.[13] At one of these evenings they were served caviar canapes, my wife related. We, as employees of the All-Russian Central Executive Committee of the Soviets, waited upon them. In addition to waitering, we hung around, hoping there might be something left for us so that we wouldn't go home hungry. These artists were not to know that junior staff in the Kremlin went as hungry as they and that in the Kremlin canteen, where the elite ate, even horsemeat cutlets were seldom served. Around the city, however, many talked of orgies in the Kremlin, of this as the only place in Russia where people did not starve. The Russian intelligentsia, knowing that the treasures of generations of Russian tsars were preserved there, assumed the Bolsheviks must be stuffing their faces, while the people went hungry. Consequently, they came to these receptions not so much to show their faces, as to get their hands on some of the good things of life and to have themselves a real treat. When the caviar arrived, Gel'tser had already finished eating. Sitting at a table in an uninhibited pose, she languidly engaged in conversation. In between phrases, she licked the caviar off the canapes with the tip of her tongue, not even with a knife, and piled the canapes she had licked clean in neat little piles on her plate. She cannot have known the indignation her behavior caused among us. In any other company she would not have dared to take such liberties, but among us . . . "Imagine! Such boorish people! What do they know about good manners? Robbing the robbers!"

It is worth citing one other example of "robbing the robbers." At our factory, production had stopped because of lack of fuel. In 1921, after a long break, I returned there on leave. Instead of the several thousands who had worked there, now there were just a couple of dozen old workers, guarding and repairing the factory buildings. Three years had passed, yet it seemed as though the factory had been shut only days. The machines were oiled to prevent rusting, the windows were in good order and unbroken, and the roof was not leaking. The workers were hungry, living only on potatoes, which they grew on the factory grounds. Nevertheless in the storerooms there were all kinds of goods in short supply, including white canvas for rubberized materials and transmission belts, nails of all sizes, screws, tools such as files, axes, hammers. But as NEP began, the Rubber Trust laid its paws on the factory, demanding that it hand over all its supplies so that they could be used by factories that had already recommenced operations. The workers who had stayed on howled in protest, and their complaints reached Sovnarkom. They refused to hand over all this wealth, demanding that their own factory start production. For one box of nails, for one axe or file, these workers could have bought over one hundred pounds of flour, yet they chose to eat potatoes and to swell up from hunger, in the expectation that their factory would eventually resume production and that the supplies they had preserved would be required.

After thirty years, reading the unintelligible arguments of sociologists seeking to explain the success of the Bolsheviks and their subsequent defeat, I learned that this was a revolution carried out under the slogan "Rob the Robbers!" Possibly somewhere, at some time, someone did express themselves in this fashion, but we, the participants in this action, were certainly not guided by this slogan when we were seventeen years old, and I repudiate the charge even now. Such a "materialist" slogan could never have attracted the millions, only that scum that always forms when the sea is rough. No, our slogan was rather "Peace to the Hovels, War to the Palaces." Similarly, theoreticians who believe in the primacy of economics over politics are mistaken when they ascribe to Stalinism the primacy of politics and see in this an abnegation of the materialist principle. In actuality the two are inseparable; they interact with one another, as the example of the Crusades clearly shows.

Chapter Five

The consolidation of soviet power in the waning months of 1917 did not proceed smoothly. In the south, two areas stood out in resistance to Bolshevik rule. One was Kiev, the capital of Ukraine, where the nationalist Ukrainian Rada seized control back from the Bolsheviks in early December. On 3 December the Rada proclaimed Ukraine a people's (not soviet) republic, and declared itself the sole authority in Ukraine. (Eastern Ukraine, with more industry and a larger Russian population, refused to follow Kiev's lead, and a rival soviet government was organized in Kharkov.)

Another center of resistance was Rostov-on-Don, capital of the Don Cossack territory. Under the Cossack ataman General Kaledin, the Don territory declared its independence from Russia in mid-November 1917. Rostov became a refuge for conservative political leaders, merchants and industrialists escaping from the northern cities, and officers from the tsarist army (including General Kornilov of the attack on Petrograd). These military leaders made their way to Rostov to begin to build the nucleus of a volunteer army that would win Russia back from the Bolsheviks. The ataman's declaration of independence met with substantial internal resistance, since the conservative ataman was opposed by many landless inhabitants of the Don region, militant miners and workers in the Donbass coal and industrial district, and the remnants of the tsarist army who refused to submit to Cossack authority.

By December the soviet government decided it must crush these main centers of opposition, and Lenin appointed Vladimir Antonov-Ovseenko, one of the architects of the seizure of power in Petrograd, to take command of operations against Kaledin and the Rada. Antonov raised a small, loosely organized force of some six thousand troops, recruited mainly from among Baltic fleet sailors and volunteers from among Petrograd and Moscow Red Guards. The troops were divided into several partisan detachments, given some machine guns and artillery pieces, put aboard trains in Kharkov, and sent south. Driving the Ukrainian Rada from Kiev in early February 1918, Antonov's forces turned to the Don region. They joined the "railway war" of the winter of 1917–18.

The independent Don government had at its disposal the growing might of the Volunteer Army plus partisan detachments of Don Cossacks. But Cossack ranks were divided, and in early 1918 a Cossack conference had elected a rival military revolutionary committee to oppose Kaledin. Red forces sought to capitalize on these divisions with a two-pronged assault on the Don from the south, along the Sea of Azov, and from the west. Although the Reds had superior forces, their troops were ill-trained and generally fought with little enthusiasm. On 31 January the Cossack leader Chernetsov inflicted serious damage on Red troops at Likhaia, but this was the height of his success. Several days later Chernetsov was captured by insurgent Cossacks and executed. Ten days after that Ataman Kaledin realized the hopelessness of his situation and shot himself through the heart. On 23 February a Red Guard unit under General Rudolf Sivers entered Rostov. The remnants of the Volunteer Army, meanwhile, had fled south to the borderland between the Don, Kuban, and Stavropol prov-

inces, north of the Caucasus mountains, in what would become known as the heroic Ice March of the Volunteer Army.

A far more serious threat to the survival of the soviet regime loomed in the shape of the German army. After declaring its intention to make peace with the Germans immediately after the October revolution, the Bolshevik government carried on cautious negotiations with high officials from the Central Powers at the border town of Brest-Litovsk. Leon Trotsky, Russia's chief negotiator, played for time, hoping that revolutions in Austria and Germany would sweep these diplomats and generals from power. The Central Powers negotiators went along with these tactics at first, but in mid-January the German high command issued an ultimatum. Peace could be had if Russia agreed to a new border running north from Brest-Litovsk, removing Poland, Lithuania, and western Latvia from Russian sovereignty. Separate talks were carried on with the Ukrainian Rada, which had not yet been ousted by Antonov's troops.

The German ultimatum sharply divided the Bolshevik government. Lenin favored accepting the Germans' terms; left-wing communists led by Nikolai Bukharin demanded rejection and, if necessary, revolutionary war against Germany. Trotsky successfully advocated a compromise position, "neither war nor peace," and the Russian army ostentatiously threw down its arms. The Germans immediately launched an offensive, advancing unimpeded along their entire front. Within four days they felt strong enough to dictate new terms: all the Baltic provinces plus Finland were to be evacuated by Russian troops, and Ukraine would be independent. There was bitter opposition to these terms within the soviet government, but Lenin vowed he would resign if the peace were not ratified. The fifteen-member Bolshevik Central Committee voted seven to four, with four abstentions, to accept the German ultimatum, labeled an "obscene peace" by many embittered party members. Shortly after the peace treaty was signed at Brest-Litovsk, German forces entered Ukraine, where they would remain until the final German surrender to the western powers in November 1918.

The
Russian
Vendée

The country required a centralized power able to end the war or to bring it to a victorious conclusion. This task was beyond the capacity of the impotent government of Kerensky, which had pretensions to be a "democratic dictatorship" and which was aware that the major danger facing the revolution came from a military dictatorship. As early as April 1917 it knew that the Congress of Don Cossacks had decided to go back to "hoary antiquity" and reestablish the Cossack assembly and an elected ataman[1] independent of the central government of Russia.[2] Only after the rising of General Kornilov, however, was General Kaledin,[3] the ataman of the Don community elected in July, summoned to Petrograd. But the community assembly (krug) told the government that "there is no extradition from the Don." This provided Kerensky with a suitable excuse for a speech, and he declared General Kaledin a "traitor to the motherland." No concrete measures were taken to liquidate this nest of counterrevolution. On 18 October 1917 the Kuban Cossack assembly decided to form a government of southeastern Russia, including the Don, Kuban, Terek, and Astrakhan Cossacks and the proud people of the Northern Caucasus.

General Alekseev replaced Kornilov at the general staff, but continued his policy.[4] On his instructions 10,000 rifles from Petrograd and 12,800 from Moscow were sent by the Chief Artillery Board to the Novocherkassk Artillery Depot in the Don. Artillery stocks and cartridges were also sent there under the guise of reserve stocks for the Army of the Caucasus.

In the Don, freed from the government of Kerensky, officers and generals of the tsarist army began to congregate. The far-sighted generals prepared a bridgehead to commence the civil war against the government. From there General Alekseev wrote to Diterikhs,[5] the quartermaster general of the Supreme High Command: "Units returning from the front, especially Don Cossacks, have become no less infected than those of the 'comrades.' Time is now needed for the older, more solid Cossack element in the locality to knock the nonsense out of the heads of the younger Cossacks . . . I am now addressing the task of gathering together forces for a future attack, preceded more broadly and actively by political measures. It is first necessary to send here everything possible from the front under a plausible pretext: to transfer the Czechoslovak regiments[6] from the Don, in order to lay a firm foundation for the establishment of an effective force; to authorize the formation in Stavropol of a supposed reserve regiment whose core should be the Georgievskii regiment in Kiev, since its officers and a small number of soldiers are already here; to liberate the region of all the reserve regiments that have gone Bolshevik since they are not only no longer useful but harmful and dangerous; to disband or disarm the latter and send them to the front against the Germans and withdraw battle-worthy units from the front and send them to the Don. The Kiev Artillery Academy has already arrived in the Don 'on its own initiative,' but its equipment remains in Kiev."

In the Don weapons and equipment were needed for the units that were being formed, along with material such as hand grenades, transport, field kitchens, and entrenching tools. The formation of "six to ten regiments of Kalmyks" and of new units of soldier-volunteers also began there.[7] Alekseev proposed to study the question of Polish troops, "although I reckon that they will decline to participate in this campaign."[8]

Unable to rely on Russian soldiers in the rear, the Russian general proposed to send them unarmed to the front against the Germans and to remove from the front "battle-worthy" units to fight against the revolution. Unable to rely on his own men, he proposed to use Czechs, Poles, and Kalmyks. He had even less confidence in the Russian fleet: "We must reduce the size of the fleet and get rid of the most unfit and dangerous elements. We must rid

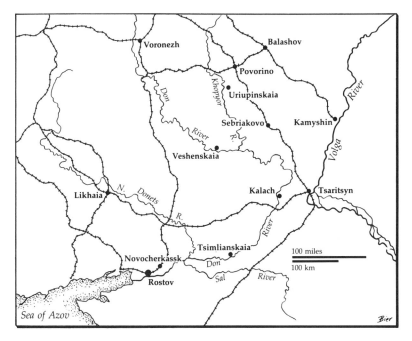

Figure 3. South Russia, 1918.

Sevastopol of its harmful garrison, occupy the fortress, and secure the Kerch Strait. The most important thing is to save the fleet, even if we have to buy people . . . Open struggle is not yet within our means, but it is possible and useful to search for ways of discrediting the enemy. We need to establish an intelligence section with a view to discrediting individuals."

Such was the morality and philosophy of the most talented enemy of the revolution. It is no surprise that the revolution could buy generals, but the generals could not buy men. The philosophy of this outstanding strategist of the tsarist army was that of the petty trader: "If you don't deceive, you won't sell" and "If you don't sin, you won't repent." Not without reason did Denikin complain in his memoirs that although there were huge supplies in the military stores of the Don region, we "could not get anything from there except by theft and bribery . . . and we did not have enough money to satisfy the Cossack committees, which were selling off everything on the side, including their consciences."[9]

Such was the legacy of Kerensky that the new government inherited: in addition to the external front, a civil war front was emerging in the south of Russia.

The new power had the assistance of the Council of People's Commissars (Sovnarkom) and the people's support, but it did not have an apparatus of government or an army. In the mining region of the Donets Basin (Donbass), a soviet republic was declared that opposed the Cossack government of Kaledin. The 272d infantry regiment rose against Kaledin's government, but it was disarmed by officer units.[10] On 9 December soviet power was declared in Rostov, but on the next day it was routed.[11] The boundaries of the "Don Republic" were maintained by Cossack and officer units, who began to disarm non-Cossack units. Grain, coal, and Turkestan cotton ceased to reach Russia, since railway traffic was controlled by troops of the new counterrevolutionary government. Moscow industry survived on existing supplies. Fuel supplies at our factory became exhausted and production came to a standstill.

Only one month after the battles of October, then, our detachment was called to fight on the Don steppes. About three hundred of us assembled for dispatch to the Don against the expanding counterrevolution. We faced a struggle against the Cossacks, and we workers had scores to settle that were still outstanding from the punitive expeditions of 1906–7. The composition of the detachment was no longer the same as it had been on the streets of Moscow. We had renounced the principle of accepting only young unmarried men, so Mazul' came along, as did many other older people. There were even whole families, such as the two Putnyn' brothers and one of their sons and a father and his fifteen-year-old son. Because the boy's mother had died, the latter asked that he be allowed to take his son to the front. We didn't give him a rifle, as he was too young, but his father said that he would prove useful in carrying cartridges during battle. His father's proposal came to nothing, for we buried the boy before we even got to Kharkov. Because of careless handling, a stray bullet from a neighbor's rifle killed him in the carriage of the train.

In Moscow we were billeted in a barracks and changed into soldiers' uniforms, so we ceased to look like a workers' detachment. The Tushintsy made up most of the detachment, though there were separate units of ten from other factories and mills. These warriors were about as experienced as we were, in as much as they knew how to handle a rifle, but had never clapped eyes on a machine gun. In our barracks we watched as the machine-gun crew stripped, cleaned, and oiled their guns. Our machine gunners were not Russian but Hungarian. They were also a musical group, and all had their own instruments.

Muralov,[12] the military commissar of Moscow, gave us a short speech and introduced us to the commissar of the detachment, a red-haired, gloomy old man. He also introduced us to our future commander.[13] As soon as we saw him we were on our guard, for he was obviously an officer. Well-dressed, well-scrubbed, with boots polished until they shone, he was a thick-set, rosy-cheeked, handsome, lively interloper who stood out sharply from the rest of us. He behaved in a familiar but not friendly fashion toward us. This lieutenant of the tsar's army was Vladimir Schreier. He was no Bolshevik, but said that when he was on the Romanian front he had spoken out for peace and against an offensive. His German name sealed his fate, for he had been arrested as a German agent and Bolshevik and sent to the Kiev jail. After the creation of soviet power he was released and sent to Moscow, to the War Commissariat. He was not in the least bit interested in social and political news, he never read newspapers, and could not understand the differences between political parties and did not wish to. "I am a military man, and my business is to fight."

While we were still in Moscow he "fought" with the girls, who often accompanied him back to the barracks. This handsome man, ablaze with health and vitality, invariably enjoyed success with women. We had the impression that the tsarist officers, in adapting to the demands of the new situation, generally tried to dress down, but our new commander was quite the opposite. Outwardly, he was as polished an officer as he had been before the revolution, except that he no longer wore epaulets. He thus stood out among us colorless characters, and even in an urban crowd stood out like a white crow.

On arrival at Kharkov, he and his aide-de-camp went off to the headquarters of Antonov-Ovseenko, and then disappeared for a long time until evening.[14] There was a huge commotion in our detachment after someone saw him walking around the city in his officer's epaulets. This turned out to be true for he came back wearing them. We held a meeting at once in the staff railway carriage. Why were the practices of the old order being upheld in a Red Guard detachment? Who had given him permission to wear his epaulets? Schreier gave his explanation. If it was what we wanted, he said, he would not wear his epaulets. He was no longer an officer of the tsarist army but of the army of the revolution, of the Red Guard. But how would people be able to distinguish him from other officers and the ranks? When he wore his straps, people acted differently toward him. The young ladies looked at his shoulders and could see that he wasn't an ensign but a lieutenant . . .

We then realized that it was the young ladies of Kharkov who were to blame and began to treat our commander with a certain condescension. We gave him an elementary lesson in political education about the abolition of privilege, explaining that we regarded epaulets as something more than a neutral means of distinguishing ranks. We advised him to hide his epaulets in future, since it would be safer to walk around the city without them in case some drunken soldier, who didn't know him, tried to attack or insult him. It is unclear whether it was our lecture or something else that had the desired effect, but he did not appear in the epaulets again. Later our commander showed his best side in battle and acquired authority among us even without his epaulets.

At Kharkov it emerged that we would not be disembarking and that all our fighting would be done from the train. We were living in the freight cars, and disembarking from them was a rather slow business, so it was decided that we should transfer to the passenger carriages. Our detachment was absorbed into the First Army of Red Guards under the command of a former officer and Left SR, Sablin.[15] The army had only just been formed and had no clear plan of campaign. It was in no position to attack regular Cossack and officer units. Instead the army, consisting of several detachments of Red Guards, was to be used to blockade and then gradually squeeze the borders of the territory occupied by General Kaledin.

It fell to us to disarm the special trains of Cossacks returning from the front to the Don. They came back in an organized fashion, as a military unit with all their officers and regimental property—money coffers, kit, food supplies, horses, and, not least, machine guns and rifles. They knew that they would be disarmed en route, and at each stop they brought out their machine guns in order to protect the train. We had no intention of impaling ourselves on their bayonets, for the weight of advantage was on their side. At the same time we were obliged to prevent any reinforcement to reach the insurgents. As a rule, we sent a delegation to negotiate with their committee. We argued that we could not allow arms through to the counterrevolutionary generals, and they objected that they themselves intended to make short work of the generals as soon as they got back. They said that their weapons and horses did not belong to the state, but had been acquired at their own expense and were therefore their personal property. It was true that a Cossack soldier was fitted out at his own expense, but what of the machine guns and rifles? When we explained that we had no designs on their horses, saddles, money-coffers, and other property, this usually lessened their initial hostility. We told them that it was not in our interests to shed fraternal blood and that we had the means to compel them to disarm without a battle. The engine drivers and stokers were on our side and could prevent the Cossacks from making any further advances. If they tried to seize the train by force, we would telephone the point men and further along the line their train would fly off the rails with inevitable casualties.

After cries, abuse, and threats, they would ask for time to discuss the situation among themselves. Usually, they would come back agreeing to hand over machine guns and some of their rifles. After this we would not carry out a search and would not try to determine how many they had hidden on the pretext of defense or guard duty. Later, before they reached the border of the Don, there would be another stop, and this time they would be disarmed completely. We ourselves had to deal with partially disarmed Cossack units, and generally they conducted themselves less aggressively.

There were very occasional incidents of armed clashes, when a temporary "front" would be created at a railway station. This happened when Cossacks arrived firing guns and machine guns as a deterrent and sent out a line of fighters to seize the station. In response we would deploy our forces and only then offer to negotiate. In such instances the railway crew would run off, out of the way of stray bullets, so the Cossacks would willy-nilly have to make peace with them by disarming or else sit in the station without any hope of getting locomotives to continue their journey.

During the campaign against the returning units of General Kaledin there was never any interruption to passenger traffic going from the center to the south or back. Trains coming from the south were checked somewhere in the Don region, and trains going into our opponents' territory were checked by us. At big stations, when the train stopped for several minutes, we would pass through the carriages demanding that people hand over their weapons. We didn't have the impudence or the experience actually to search anyone, we just relied on their consciences. I remember only two instances when we actually found arms in this way. An old man, who had not shaved for a long time, told us that he had a saber he had received for bravery, but no weapons. He unpacked his bag and took out the ill-fated saber. If he had not said anything, we would not have known about it, but now we had no time to go into the niceties of what constituted a weapon. As we took away the saber, he waxed indignant at the illegality of our actions, but the whistle of the train interrupted the altercation.

Another time, an officer in a second-class compartment, without epaulets, of course, but with a holster at his belt, said: "I don't have a revolver, only my holster. I heard earlier that you were confiscating revolvers and threw mine out of the window to avoid any misunderstanding." We had not at this stage developed a spirit of "vigilance," or even a desire to check the reliability of what he said by simply asking his fellow passengers. It's quite possible that as soon as we left, he and the passengers would begin to laugh at us simpletons. But the truth was that we simpletons had neither the inclination nor the conscience to fumble through the bags and suitcases of strangers. Anyone who had the will to flee south from soviet power, therefore, could do so without any hindrance aboard these passenger trains.

Our detachments represented no effective police cordon, thus, the government assigned this task to us in view of the lack of an administrative apparatus. And we did more than carry out police duties. We talked with the peasants, held meetings, and agitated for the dispatch of food and coal to the central industrial regions. Delegations of workers from the Donbass came to ask our advice as to how they should behave and what they should do.

This was the time when the white partisans of Esaul Chernetsov[16] were going about the Donbass, disbanding and disarming workers' committees and units of soldiers. Chernetsov's detachment and another under the Cossack lieutenant-general, Semiletov, comprised the most active force resisting our advance to the frontier of the Don republic.[17] In the Don republic the army of General Ponomarev, consisting of one reserve regiment and the Sixth Cossack Division, awaited us, along with several regiments and batteries under General Nazarov.[18] There would have been no question of our attacking their forces had it not been for the fact that much of their strength existed solely on paper. In practice, their soldiers and the Cossacks held meetings at which they declared the Red Guards to be representatives of the central all-Russian power and their own commanders to be counterrevolutionary insurrectionists. Even the Cossacks of the "independent Don" were alarmed by the flower of the Russian generals and of the Russian counterrevolution.

By this time, Generals Alekseev, Kornilov, Denikin, Lukomskii, Markov, and many other Kornilovite refugees had settled in Rostov. Having come to organize the army of the counterrevolution in the name of all Russia, they came up against not only Don separatism but more general hostility from the Cossacks. It was not for nothing that General Kaledin, in the name of the Don government, recommended that they "temporarily" leave the Don region and not engage in active operations, since their names were linked in the minds of the mass of Cossacks with the counterrevolution. The all-Don conference of *inogorodnye* (non-Cossack peasants) on 11 January 1918 (among whose 150 delegates were 40 Bolsheviks) passed a resolution calling for the disarming and dispersal of the Volunteer Army, because it was fighting against the advancing troops of revolutionary democracy.[19]

In the Don a Cossack revolutionary committee had been set up to support soviet power, headed by Cavalry Sergeant-Major Podtelkov, who also organized an armed detachment of Cossack volunteers.[20] The most effective unit of the 271st Cossack regiment, under the command of Lieutenant-General Golubov, was also under our influence.[21] We arrived, therefore, not simply as conquerors but as liberators from counterrevolution, and we were able to neutralize or demoralize the large force that had managed to gather there under the command of various generals. We clashed not with regular military units but with the same kind of volunteer partisan detachments as ourselves. At first we were disposed to act with great caution, because of the superiority of our opponents in terms of numbers, organization, and battle worthiness. But after several skirmishes, and after contact with Cossacks and negotiations with various delegations, we realized that words could be more effective than weapons.

Our army under Sablin had the task of cutting off the Don from the north and of taking Novocherkassk. The Second Army under Sivers was to advance from the southwest with the aim of seizing Rostov.[22] The staff of our army was accommodated in railway carriages at the Debal'tsevo station, from where detachments in special trains fanned out in all directions. This, too, was the base from which we were supplied with grain, canned goods, and cartridges. Cossack delegations and miners came to the staff headquarters on foot and by transport, and we arranged meetings for them. We thereby gained recruits from among miners and railway workers. The peasants sympathized with us rather than with the Cossacks, but they did not join our detachment. Seeing that we were living off canned food, they brought gifts of fresh meat and vegetables on their own initiative, in the name of their communities. They invited us to their villages for meetings to give reports on what was happening in Russia. They didn't hide their sympathy, but were critical of the figures we cut, telling us that they did not believe we could win: "They are all officers from the old regime. They have discipline. And the Cossacks do not want to share out the land."

At that time only 44 percent of the Don population were Cossacks, the rest were inogorodnye, with inadequate land holdings. Now, following the Decree on Land, they aspired to a share of the Cossack lands. At the conference in January the land question was fundamental for both inogorodnye and Cossacks. Among the latter, social differentiation by property had developed, so that poor Cossacks also wished for a slice of the lands of the big landlords and of the community (voisko). At the conference it was decided to transfer to the inogorodnye three million desiatinas of Cossack land.[23] For this reason, misunderstandings between the inogorodnye and the poor landless Cossacks grew, for the latter believed that the inogorodnye would be in a privileged position. All this made the situation difficult and complicated our political tactics in negotiations with the Cossacks and inogorodnye. We had no choice but to avoid giving straight answers, proposing that they decide for themselves what was the best and most just way to divide up the land. We could see clearly that it was too early to discuss the matter, when the generals had organized forces to preserve the old order in the countryside. We simply said: we will help you organize a popular regime and then you can decide the land question for yourselves.[24]

Because the officers ranged against us lacked mass support, they were forced to fight as we did—by special train. It was a strange war—unlike anything that had occurred during the war against Germany, and unlike anything we had seen in Moscow.

Crossing the border of the Don region, we ran into our Cossack opponents, who said they would not attack us if we did not invade Cossack land. Discussions began, followed by formal meetings and negotiations, which ended in their promising not to allow passage to the officer detachments of the counterrevolution and to drive them away. This was the position of the huge majority of the Don regular units, but they would not act against their commanders. Under the banner of "neutrality," one regiment of Don Cossacks occupied the Likhaia station, through which the Chernetsov detachment and officer battalions were launching a raid against us. The Chernetsov detachment, however, comprising only a few hundred rifles, had only to show itself, and the "neutral" regiment, consisting of several thousand rifles, ran off as the first shots were fired.

The railway operated normally, as did the telephone and telegraph lines, and staff informed us in advance which trains were going where. The trains traveled under their ordinary numbers, but if the staff attached a "B" to the number of the train they told us was coming, then we knew that we had to be ready and on our guard, for it was a military train. Our opponents probably knew about our movements the same way. We would advance until we ran into the enemy, then we would disembark from the train and begin to exchange fire. It sometimes happened that we occupied a station without a battle, in which case we stayed in our carriages until the enemy appeared and we could assess their strength. Battles lasted hours rather than days, enough to determine which side had the advantage. If the advantage was on our side then our opponents would retreat to their train, leap into the carriages, and set off back to where they had come from. We did exactly the same when the advantage was on the other side. Such skirmishes happened all the time. We would move forward one hundred kilometers, but if we did not feel confident that we could hold the advance we had just made we would then fall back the same distance.

This is what happened at the Zverevo station, after the Likhaia station had been occupied by Don Cossacks on behalf of soviet troops. Here the railways from Voronezh and from Tsaritsyn crossed, and there was no way to take Novocherkassk without seizing this railway junction. After the Cossack regiment scattered or was dispersed, we ourselves had to get to grips with the task. When we arrived it did not seem that the station was under anyone's control, so we prepared to stay there. Since we were not expecting the enemy immediately, our three detachments alighted. The steppe lay before us, smooth, with no knolls or hillocks. We had a wide field of vision, but there was not a blade of grass to hide behind, and we couldn't dig trenches in the frozen earth with our bare hands. Our trains stayed in the station, and we slowly formed a long line between one and three kilometers from the station. Some of our machine guns strengthened our position from above, on the railway bridge, some remained on the flanks of our lines.

After an hour, perhaps less, we saw in the distance the smoke of an oncoming train, which soon came to a halt. For this reason alone, we guessed that the enemy had arrived.[25] On the horizon we could just make out small figures in an extended line, but no shots broke the silence. Our machine guns on the bridge began to rattle away, but provoked no answering fire. Then, on a command, we began slow fire. Again the enemy did not respond, though we could see that the line was moving closer to us. My neighbor said: "They're officers, you can see their epaulets glistening." But I couldn't tell whether they were epaulets or their service caps. Nevertheless I, too, was certain that they were officers: who else except officers would attack standing up and without firing prematurely?

We were on the left flank, closer to the station, and the enemy was closer to our right flank. There the shooting was intensifying and we could see that both sides were now exchanging fire. The enemy machine guns began to fire away, but ours were fading, possibly jammed, firing two or three rounds, then falling silent. Our attackers were now so close that I could see that their glistening "epaulets" were, in fact, above their heads. I guessed that they were waving sabers. One of them shouted and, still without lying down, they shouldered their rifles ready for a volley.

Our commander cried, "Continuous fire!" but there was only disorderly shooting from our side. The commander flew into a rage, ranting and raving: "Stay down! Don't get up!" He leaped up to his full height, then crouched down and began to fire on his knees. From a distance it looked as though the enemy had got up to our right flank. They were now not far from us, but still they did not lie down.

It was the first time I had seen the enemy close, and my nerves were so tense that I didn't notice what was going on around me. I looked straight ahead and shivered at the unpleasant whistle of bullets flying past. At that moment a sharp whistle from the train pierced the air. Once, twice, three times—the signal to entrain. The other two engines also began to whistle. We didn't understand why. How could we board the train in these circumstances, when the enemy was in front of us and our commander was shouting frenziedly not about embarking but about shooting? We watched as the empty carriages of the special trains began quietly to pull out of the station. Then order broke down. We rose to our feet, still firing, turned around and ran after the departing carriages. Shouting and cursing, our legs carried us to the station. Behind us we could hear cries of "Hurrah!" as the shots became less frequent. Some managed to get on the train, others didn't. The rear train was loaded to breaking point, and the detachments were all mixed up. We sped back to the previous stop, where we gathered together to find out who had escaped, who had been left behind, and how many of us there were. Why had the signal to embark been given in the heat of battle when no one was in retreat and when no order to retreat had been given? Why had we run? Simply because everybody else had run . . . The engine crew explained that bullets had begun to fall on the rolling stock and that they had intended merely to pull it further back, out of the range of fire.

Hitherto we had always retreated under orders. Now we had

fled, gripped by panic, not out of fear of the enemy but out of fear of missing the departing train. At the first stop we counted our numbers and only then realized that one-third of our number were absent. The enemy was not in pursuit, so we decided to wait for those who had not managed to catch the train. It was impossible that one-third lay on the battlefield after so insignificant a skirmish. Our machine gunners were all there, but the machine guns had been left on the bridge, for there had been no time to remove them. Only that night did those left behind begin to reappear. Our right flank had been two or three kilometers from the station, so the majority of them had had no hope of catching the train and had rushed into a gully, along which they had headed away from the station, now occupied by the enemy. Some appeared dressed in oily miners' clothes, for they had hidden in a mining village.

Only several days later did young Putnyn' appear, after we had already mourned him. His father had caught the train and was convinced his son was not far behind, whole and unscathed. But his son explained that on reaching the station buildings, he had stumbled upon an officer, who, appearing as though from nowhere, had knocked him over and thrust a bayonet at his throat. While the disorderly shooting was still going on, the son had crawled to a house, where a sympathetic person gave him some civilian clothes and bandaged his wound, which was not very deep. He had stayed there until he had a chance to find the detachment. Some individuals turned up much later, after we had occupied the Zverevo-Likhaia region for a second time. How many died we do not know. Up to then, however, when calculating supplies, we had been reckoned a "complete account," whereas now they began to supply us according to a list of names.

Our damnable failure at the station of the same name[26] disheartened us for a long time. That over a thousand men should have been put to flight not by the enemy and his military superiority, but by the innocent whistle of a steam engine!

Our first serious defeat taught us that we should not be too defensive and should go on to the attack, since the enemy was operating similarly to us, in uncoordinated sections, throwing its forces from one place to another. It was these active partisan units, not the regular Don regiments, we feared most. Judging by the fact that Chernetsov was made a colonel on account of his success at

Likhaia and that he loudly celebrated our defeat, we inferred that the advantage had been on our side.

The Cossacks obviously sympathized with us but did not come over actively to our side, probably because of military discipline. If officers came over to us, however, then the units were willing to fight the partisan detachments of General Kaledin, and especially the officer units of the Volunteer Army.

This was illustrated by the 27th Cossack Regiment under the command of Golubov. After the success at the Likhaia station, Chernetsov's detachment, fortified by officer battalions, occupied Kamenskaia, a revolutionary Cossack town where the Don Military Revolutionary Committee had its seat. From there Chernetsov attacked Glubokaia, but there he and his detachment were taken prisoner by Golubov's Red Cossacks in the first days of February.[27] Almost simultaneously we began to advance in coordination with the Second Army of Sivers, operating in the direction of Taganrog-Rostov. We advanced to Shakhtnaia station, thirty kilometers from Novocherkassk, and waited for an order to continue. Large forces were assembled against us. At the Kamenolomni station were many trainfuls of partisans from Chernetsov's detachment, from Semiletov's detachment, from the cavalry detachment of officer cadets, and the Seventh Don Regiment under the overall command of General Abramov.[28] The presence of heavy artillery, erected on flatcars, and of machine guns, set up in coal cars and protected by sacks of sand, made us anxious. Because of the continuing traffic of goods and passenger trains, it was not difficult to find out this information, and our general staff knew that the impending battle would be more serious than any hitherto. It was perhaps for this reason that the attack was delayed. And for some reason, our opponents were as inactive as we. Only later, after the battle was over, did we learn of the suicide of General Kaledin. After a peaceful halt that lasted a week, gunfire warned us to be ready. This time, after our previous experience, the special trains were taken out of the station beforehand. We did not form lines to lie in wait for the enemy, but went on the attack with the aim of encircling them and penetrating their rear. Shooting was as intense and disorderly as before, but the enemy withdrew their special trains, and the soldiers pressed close to the departing stock. In this way we not only held Shakhtnaia but forced the enemy to retreat, notwithstanding their heavy artillery and machine guns. I didn't take part in this battle, as I had been elected by our detachment to the committee that was being organized at Sablin's headquarters, and I do not know the details of the battle.

From the staff carriage the overall situation appeared clearer, but the mood was not as confident as in the ranks. Dispatches from Ovseenko's headquarters calculated the strength of the enemy in rifles, sabers, regiments, and divisions, but in practice we never ran into such large units. Dispatches from Podtelkov's Don Revolutionary Committee, with which we were in daily contact, did not paint an optimistic picture: we were banking on the Red Cossacks, and they were banking on us.

According to these dispatches, after Kaledin's suicide, the forces of the enemy grew instead of diminishing. After their defeat at Shakhtnaia they became particularly active in organizing and recruiting volunteers. They invited many thousands of Cossacks to be recruited into Semiletov's detachment, handed out rifles at huge meetings, and formed them into detachments, which the building of the Cadet Corps at Novocherkassk could barely accommodate. The enemy was thus preparing no less actively than we for the coming battle for their capital. Decisive days of more cruel fighting had arrived, and we anxiously prepared for them.

Toward the end of February we reached the Persianovka station. Ahead of us lay the attack on Novocherkassk. We said farewell to our special trains, unloaded even our field kitchens, in order to go into battle on foot. We moved in a column several kilometers long across the snow-covered plain. We couldn't see the enemy anywhere, but it might appear at any minute from behind a hillock. Here and there in the distance Cossack villages were visible, from which men and women stared intently at our lines. It seemed a peaceful picture and no enemy activities were in evidence.

Away to our left we could see the gold dome of the cathedral of Novocherkassk and the town itself, situated on a hill. All about was calm and there was no sound of shooting. We were convinced that something unexpected lay ahead and were doubly on our guard. A reconnaissance party reached the outskirts of the town and waved to tell us to advance. Only when we had climbed the hill on which the buildings of the Cadet Corps were situated did we realize that the enemy had left that morning for the Don, having decided not to engage in battle. Golubov's Cossack forces were already in the town, having arrived before us.[29] Did this mean the end of the war? Why had experienced warriors, Cossack volunteers, cadets from the military academies, and officer detachments retreated in the face of poorly armed units without military experience?

In three months I had not once seen an officer cadet, even in captivity. Only on the day we occupied Novocherkassk, as we were carefully touring the town, did a sleigh rush toward our lines. Before it had got within half a verst, it halted and two figures jumped out and looked with incomprehension at our lines. We, too, stopped and displayed our rifles: we could see the glint of epaulets on the greatcoats of the passengers. Who were these people and where had they come from? In the sleigh a nursing sister remained seated, weeping. The officers, like the sister, were very young. With their revolvers in their hands, stunned by the unexpected encounter, they answered our questions, voluntarily, even volubly. They had gone to a Cossack village as someone's guests. Now they were returning to the town, having no idea what was going on and ignorant of our advance. They offered us their revolvers, since they were no longer needed, and set off in the same sleigh for staff headquarters at Persianovka. During this unexpected meeting no antagonism or coarseness was displayed as we talked and asked them questions. They had been taken prisoner, but prisoners were not enemies in our eyes since they were no longer dangerous.

I wondered if they would have behaved the same way toward me if I had fallen into their hands. I remembered the battle at Likhaia and what had become of the wounded who had been captured. We learned about this from local inhabitants when we retook the locality. They pointed to a little hillock in the distance, saying that it was the mass grave of our men. None of the wounded had been taken prisoner; there were only dead men. Officers do not take prisoners. Somehow I couldn't believe a man could kill an unarmed prisoner, still less one who was wounded.

The railway workers, too, talked a great deal about the cruelties inflicted on prisoners, but we never got to see the consequences of such reprisals. On one occasion the special train did stop between two stations after we noticed three corpses tied to a pillar with telephone wire. Their bodies were covered with blood, and they were dressed in their underpants and sailors' striped undershirts. They had no shoes on their feet. A sailor's cap had been pulled over the drooping, blood-stained head of one of them. The caps of the other two were lying beside them. There was no special train of sailors on our side, so they could not be Red Guards and, consequently, could not be prisoners. Who had dealt so brutally with them and why, we never discovered. We untied them and buried them on the railway embankment.

This was the only case that I saw, and I believe profoundly that we would not have treated prisoners in this manner. Because of our sense of discipline we sent all prisoners to staff headquarters and felt no particular animosity toward them. We were fighting against those with the gold epaulets, but they had the same right to defend themselves as we did. True, there was a feeling of class hatred among us, but this had nothing to do with the wild personal hatred that turns a person into a brutal thug and executioner. In comparison with the enemy detachments we had one great advantage: we believed in the power of universal justice and not in personal or class privilege.

The ideologues on the enemy side kept asking themselves: "What motivates such people, mortally tired of war, to face new and cruel sacrifices and privations?" They themselves replied that it was not dedication to soviet power and its ideals but "hunger, unemployment, the vision of a life of idleness and satisfaction, of getting rich through robbery, the impossibility of getting back to one's birthplace by any other means, the habituation of many after four years of war to the soldier's life, as though it were just another trade (so-called 'declassing') and, finally, a greater or lesser degree of class hatred and envy, ingrained over the centuries but whipped up by the most intense propaganda."[30] This was the "materialist" characterization of the first Red Guard units offered by General Denikin, one of the leaders of the robber army. He ascribed to us everything negative that he could observe in his own army, staffed not from "declassed" elements but from the Russian military elite.

Two hundred thousand officers of the tsarist army intended to oppose the same number of Bolsheviks, who by then expressed popular rather than party aspirations.[31] And the most important urban centers were choked with officers in civilian dress. Not only officers but also the elite of the Russian intelligentsia had fled to Rostov and Novocherkassk: "The iron will of the present Russian officer will not be thwarted by any Bolshevik cordon." But such cordons existed more in the imaginations of the refugees themselves than in reality. Denikin noted with sadness that the pavements and cafes of Rostov and Novocherkassk were full of young, healthy officers who had not joined the Volunteer Army. "Because there was no authoritative command and because the officer class was already morally enfeebled, they made bargains with their consciences. Tens and hundreds of thousands struggled to join the army, but because of many different circumstances, including family difficulties and weakness of character, they bided their time, entered peaceful occupations, and became transformed into civilians. Some meekly registered with the Bolshevik commissars, were tortured by the Cheka, and later joined the Red Army."[32]

Although Denikin conceded that the officers of the tsarist army displayed weakness of character, lack of moral integrity, and experienced family difficulties, such factors were not, in his eyes, decisive in their joining the army of the counterrevolution, only in explaining why they loafed around on street corners and in cafes. But his explanation of the Red Guards' motives was exactly the reverse. We could not possibly have a conscience of any sort. How could a worker understand the idea of conscience and what pricks it? No, this was a privilege of the propertied classes . . .

How many officers refused to make deals with their consciences and chose to fight against the militarily inexperienced Red Guard detachments? The same historian of the Volunteer Army notes that by February 1918, in a period of heavy fighting, the capacity of the Volunteer Army had fallen to an extremely low level, to just a few hundred bayonets. Yet when they were forced to retreat from Rostov, some 5,000 joined up. Denikin was delighted that out of 202,000 tsarist officers they had managed to assemble several thousand, for had this not happened, the "Russian people would not be a nation, but dung fertilizing the endless fields of the old continent, doomed to be colonized by newcomers from West and East."[33]

Small consolation . . .

The soviet government had been regarded as an adventure by a handful of plotters that would not last two weeks. Now three months had passed, and still the new government showed no sign of expiring. In fact it was broadening its base and becoming stronger. We had cleared the Don of the Whites, and other detachments had occupied the Ukraine and driven out the Orenburg Cossacks who had risen up in the Urals. Independent Finland had a soviet government. Fighting was going on in Bessarabia, which had been occupied by the Romanians. The Czech Legion, on which General Alekseev placed so much reliance, had declared its neutrality. Foreign military units, mainly the Poles, had been disarmed. The former all-Russian empire, with the exception of territory occupied by Germans and of Ekaterinoslav, was under soviet control.

We had a decree on peace, but there was no army capable of implementing it. We dealt easily with the counterrevolutionary forces but retreated in the face of the onslaught by the regular German army. It wasn't only Red Guard units but also soldiers of the tsarist army who took part in the defense against the latter. The five-million-soldier army had demobilized of its own accord, but nine hundred thousand soldiers remained in the service of the new government, trying to fend off a German army of several millions. In such circumstances there was no alternative to the "obscene" peace of Brest-Litovsk, which Lenin later characterized as follows: "We made big enough fools of ourselves during the Smol'nyi period, although there was nothing shameful in that. How could we think clearly when we were taking on a new task for the first time. We tried this, and tried that. We flowed with the tide, so it was not possible to separate correct elements from the incorrect ones—we needed time for that . . . But the time when chaos and enthusiasm ruled soon passed, and the sign of its passing was the Brest Peace."[34]

On the question of the peace treaty there was not the same unanimity and confidence as in the struggle against the counterrevolutionary army. Although the Red Guard detachments agreed to submit to the orders of the soviet power in the struggle against the Germans, among us were Left SRs who would not go along with this. Our army commander, Sablin, now a general of Stalin, was then a Left SR. Another Left SR was Georgii Gustavovich Bosse, a student of the famous Timiriazev, and now a professor in Moscow.

They had considerable influence on the formation of public opinion. Our forces had decided not to fight the Germans, and were thus compelled to retreat under German fire. Several detachments, however, got involved in battle with Germans and, of course, suffered defeat. They joined us in retreat, bringing to the detachment a three-inch field gun, which was set up on a platform. Our commissar turned out to be an ace artillerist. We headed back for Kharkov without, of course, any reconnaissance. If a railway station was occupied by Germans, we simply turned around and pushed forward after a detour. Sometimes we had to "fight." Once when we were midway between two stations, shells began to explode around the special train, though there were no other signs of an enemy presence. In the distance the sails of a windmill showed up black against the sky, and we decided that this must be a German observation post. Our commissar decided to try out the field gun without its sighting devices. He did not even aim the gun over open sights, simply through the barrel. The windmill vanished from sight. This was the first and last time the gun was fired. The Hungarians surrounded the old man, slapped him on the shoulder, and laughed with joy: "What a terrific aim, and without sighting devices . . ." We went the rest of the way without any shooting.

Armed units going to reinforce the Volunteer Army passed freely across territory occupied by the Germans, yet the Germans fired on us whenever we got close. Red Guards and soldiers coming from the Caucasus formed a front against the Germans near Rostov, but the Volunteer Army did its worst in their rear, regardless of their claim to be fighting the Bolsheviks because they were "German agents." They thus helped the Germans by disarming the very units that were fighting them. Denikin admitted that this was a time when "Russian reality, perverted as never before, dressed up those who had once been robbers and traitors in the cloak of the Russian national idea." Yet he showed his support for these "traitors" who were fighting the Germans by forcibly taking away their cartridges and shells and giving them to the Volunteer Army. Moreover the Volunteer Army gratefully accepted shells and cartridges from the nation's enemy, the Germans. They flung mud at us because of the Treaty of Brest-Litovsk, but they themselves, either willingly or unwillingly, either by their own hands or those of General Krasnov, benefited from German support.[35] The "national" idea thus capitulated to the social one.

We could not prevail against the combined attack of the German army and the counterrevolution. Our salvation came in the form of that "obscene" peace of Brest-Litovsk.

PART TWO

The
Red
Army

Chapter Six

The peace of Brest-Litovsk brought a cessation in the military danger to the young soviet regime, although this would prove to be only a momentary lull. The process of consolidating political power and transforming the economy along socialist lines now occupied the new regime. The process of ad hoc nationalization continued, as workers in individual factories looked to the state to solve their urgent problems of supply and distribution. Trade union organizations debated new forms of labor relations appropriate to socialized industry and determined that the unions and the government should work hand-in-hand to restore production. By midsummer 1918 the regime resolved to systematize this process and decreed a sweeping nationalization of most industrial enterprises, to be administered by branches of the Supreme Economic Council.

Food supplies in the cities reached critically low levels by the spring of 1918, prompting a series of responses, both official and unofficial. Urban dwellers, including workers, streamed out of Petrograd and Moscow and other northern cities, looking for food, employment, and shelter. The Bolshevik regime resolved to supply the cities with food by force if necessary: armed requisition teams were sent out to the countryside to extract surplus grain, prompting fierce resistance from the peasantry under attack.

Trotsky told a workers' meeting in early June 1918: "Our party is for civil war. The civil war rages around the question of bread."

Deteriorating economic conditions, particularly in the cities, began to provoke unrest and protest directed against the Bolshevik regime. When the Constituent Assembly, with its non-Bolshevik majority, was dismissed after its first session in January, Petrograd townspeople took to the streets in protest, and some of them were killed by troops attempting to prevent the demonstration. Leaders of the Constituent Assembly fled to the Volga region, out of the reach of soviet power, and set up a Constituent Assembly there to rival the soviet government. (The government hastily moved to Moscow in February because of the danger posed by the German advance during the peace talks.) Uprisings flared up across Russia against both economic distress and the heavy-handed way in which the Bolsheviks dealt with opposition. The moderate socialist Mensheviks and Right SRs were expelled from the soviets in June for championing this opposition, but strikes and other protests against the regime continued to mount into the summer. The Left SR party, which had shared power with the Bolsheviks after the revolution, broke with the regime in protest of the Brest-Litovsk peace and manifested their opposition in assaults on German diplomats inside Russia. The assassination of the German ambassador Mirbach on 6 July led to a two-day armed confrontation in the streets of Moscow between Left SRs and Bolshevik loyalists.

By July, the regime could blame its growing hard line against dissent—and its economic problems—on an emergency situation beyond its control. Open civil war had broken out once again in May when thirty thousand Czechoslovak troops clashed with soviet forces near the town of Omsk in Siberia. These troops had been prisoners of the Russian army and had volunteered to fight the Germans and Austrians on behalf of their homeland, then *part of the Austrian Empire. In the spring of 1918 they were en route to Vladivostok on the Pacific, in order to ship for America, with the eventual destination of France. Local conflicts along the evacuation route escalated into a major confrontation. Soviet authorities ordered the units disarmed; the Czechoslovaks instead turned back toward the west and quickly captured cities as far west as Kazan, which they occupied on 6 August.*

The Czechoslovak revolt coincided with invasions by Russia's former allies in the north and south, in part to evacuate war supplies, in part (or so the Bolsheviks believed) to crush the revolution. The government responded by calling for a full-scale mobilization of the Red Army. Conscription began first in Moscow and Petrograd and extended next to the regions most directly threatened by the counterrevolutionary forces in Siberia, the Urals, the Don region, and along the Volga. This army, which had recruited 100,000 volunteers in early 1918, grew to 330,000 in August and 800,000 by the end of the year.

The most urgent danger came from the east. Counterrevolutionary troops joined the Czechoslovaks and captured Simbirsk, Lenin's birthplace on the Volga, on 21 July. Kazan fell just two weeks later. Trotsky, now the Red Army commander-in-chief, rushed his new troops east by train and threw them against the advancing forces. In just a few weeks he managed to create a genuine fighting force with the aid of energetic organizational work and ruthless measures against cowards and deserters. Units who fled would have their commanders, their political commissars, and every tenth soldier shot on the spot. These tactics proved successful, and on 10 September a Red Army force of three to four thousand defeated two thousand White occupiers of Kazan. Samara, the Volga city that served as the center of the renegade Constituent Assembly, fell to the Reds on 8 October. The Volga was cleared of forces hostile to the soviet government, and sup-

plies of fuel and food began again to move to the hungry center.

While Red forces were pushing back the Whites in the east, however, counterrevolutionary forces in the south had grown strong enough to advance on soviet-held territory. An army based on former tsarist officers and Kuban Cossacks pushed north out of the Kuban, driving the Reds from the important railway junction of Tikhoretskaia, which linked the Volga to the Black Sea. By the end of August 1918 the Black Sea port of Novorossiisk had fallen to the Whites, and the Kuban, with its rich farmland, was no longer accessible to the Reds' requisition forces.

Soviet
Power
in 1918

After the signing of the Brest peace, my Red Guard unit was ordered back to Moscow and placed at the disposal of the Moscow military commissariat, commanded at that time by Ian Peche. He supervised the uezd military commissariats, whose functions were similar to the former military chief officers.

Neither these uezd military posts or uezd soviets was able to enforce the decrees of soviet power outside the city. Therefore, those places that had party organizations, mainly factory settlements in Moscow uezd, emerged as administrative centers. Our own plant in Tushino served as one such center, and on the basis of the factory and our returning Red Guard unit, we created a regional military commissariat; our center encompassed the territory of several former volosts and served hundreds of settlements.

In our Red Guard unit there were not only workers from our plant, returning to production, but also some "stray" elements: the Hungarian musician–machine gunners and individual volunteers who had joined our unit after its initial formation. These "strays" now stayed on as a platoon within the military commissariat. Commander V. Schreier became the military instructor, but he had no more knowledge than I about the actual work of a military office. His job was to train recruits who had not yet been drafted, so for the time being he and the Hungarians lived in the lap of luxury. They were housed and fed at the commissariat and "worked" as musicians at various parties and gatherings.

This military unit was a pillar of the young soviet power, which in rural areas had no police force or militia of its own. The military commissariat fulfilled duties that did not even belong to it, such as the protection of nationalized property. Later, after the Left SR uprising,[1] we had to establish checkpoints on all roads, checking the passes of all approaching vehicles, seizing weapons, detaining suspicious persons, and so forth. By the autumn of 1918, volost soviets were being set up everywhere, and this reduced the need for a regional military commissariat of the type that had emerged in practice. The job of registering those eligible for military service was transferred to the volost soviet at the Khimki station on the Nikolaevskii railroad.

Around this time we passed the point at which enemies of the new regime had predicted it would fall.[2] We looked forward to celebrating our revolution's anniversary along with the start of the long-awaited world revolution—for the Brest peace had been annulled by the revolution in Germany.

We saw the October revolution as a first stage, a first attempt, and of course mistakes were inevitable. The "world revolution" would teach us how to govern a country and how to organize the economy so that it would satisfy the millions for whose sake revolutions were made. And the more difficulty we encountered on our path, the more hope we placed in the "world" proletariat.

Meanwhile, the Red Army ration[3] was sharply reduced: the ration of bread and groats was cut back, and instead of meat we received Caspian roach or herring.[4] Only on days when I went into Moscow did I eat my fill, and then I had to conceal my good fortune from outsiders. With the help of young Salmyn', who ran the kitchen at the military commissariat, I always managed to find a piece of bread and salted vegetable oil.

The working family lived near starvation. Food could be purchased from local peasants, but at three times the normal price. On the other hand, farther out from Moscow you could buy food or barter for it. But together with their food purchases, the wives of workers brought back dissatisfaction: antiprofiteering detachments caught "speculators" and often took away their last pound of potatoes, bread, or fats.[5] In fact, such anti-profiteer brigades acted outside the laws of soviet power, and they paid no heed to the decree of the Moscow Soviet, which allowed individuals to carry back to town up to fifty-four pounds of grain.

These individual trips were soon transformed into collective journeys for grain for our entire plant. In such cases, half of the grain we acquired went into the storehouse of the soviet and half to the plant. These were not yet the armed food detachments, which acted to requisition "food surpluses" from the peasantry,[6] but only groups of workers from the plant. The plant collective gathered together some money for the journey, as well as manufactured goods and other industrial products to be exchanged for grain. Once even Kalmykov joined one of these trips, and whether because of his gaunt, disheveled figure or because of his usual warmth and his loving heart, several times he successfully acquired a whole wagon full of supplies. He became a food supply "specialist," but he was soon killed somewhere, on this unknown "food supply front."

This "food supply front" could be observed right next to our plant, among the local peasants. In autumn, after the completion of the harvest, hungry wives and children of workers began to dig in the fields with their shovels, to glean the remains of the potato harvest. They had thought that this expedition could be carried out without casualties, that the potatoes would otherwise have been burned or frozen without benefit to anyone. They felt the peasants should not object to this foraging in their fields. The peasants only laughed: "Power may belong to you, the workers, but the potatoes are ours. In order to produce a crop, you have to know how to sow, and this your workers' power does not know how to do." At first this was merely unpleasant talk, but one day the whole village—men, women, and youths—surrounded the gleaners and threatened to beat them up. This was an organized assault, and those who tried to flee were caught. The appearance of a crowd of workers from the plant put an end to the possibility of real bloodshed, but the gleaning of the peasants' fields stopped. The peasants rejoiced at this failure of workers' power . . .

We workers blamed our hunger on the counterrevolution, not on our regime. In the first months we had fought with rebellious Cossacks, with the advancing German army, and with uprisings in Iaroslavl, Rybinsk, and Murom.[7] But these, just like the Left SR rising in Moscow, seemed to be minor episodes. We rank-and-file members of the party and also the government completely failed to foresee the possibility of the formation of a ring of counterrevolutionary troops and a long civil war. In fact, along with the demobilization of the tsarist army, the government was busy with the demobilization of war industries. The Council of People's Commissars (Sovnarkom) was preparing plans for the reduction or elimination of military production. State armaments plants were refitted to produce plows and scythes. The embryo of the future Gosplan worked on the problem of electrification of the whole country and the plan for Volkhovstroi.[8] Many millions of rubles were spent in organizing the extraction of ores and fuel. Nine million poods[9] of cotton were stockpiled for the idle plants of the textile industry, costing many millions of rubles, but less than one-tenth of this was shipped: the civil war halted shipments to the center of both food products and raw materials.

Events unfolded not according to some calculated system of peace, world labor, and world revolution but along the path of world counterrevolution. In April 1918 the Red Army numbered only 106,000 volunteers,[10] but by autumn 299 regiments had been formed from among draftees. Perhaps this would have been enough to hold a front stretching fifteen hundred kilometers, as during the last war, but the front in the civil war was dispersed over the whole of Russia, at times reaching up to eight thousand kilometers. The regiments of the young Red Army were no more experienced than soviet power itself, and at the same time they were scattered over the unbounded expanse of Russia: 5 regiments were stationed in the region around Astrakhan, 22 regiments were fighting in the Kuban against the Volunteer Army of General Denikin, 28 regiments were sent to the Ukraine (around Kursk and Briansk), 38 regiments formed on the German and Finnish fronts, 65 regiments served on the Polish-Latvian front, 97 regiments were sent to the eastern front against the Czechoslovaks, and 44 regiments went to the Don to fight the Cossacks of General Krasnov.

This dry enumeration of Red regiments suggests the anxiety that gripped us. Enemies appeared on all sides, preventing the center from receiving food supplies, raw materials, and fuel for its dying industries. The direct, truthful, and widely understood speech of Lenin at the Sixth Congress of Soviets, like a simple conversation among comrades and friends, produced even greater fear and anxiety.[11] One could not remain a passive observer when the fate of soviet power hung not here in the rear but wherever our troops were sent.

And yet, at a general meeting of the workers at our idle factory, another mood dominated. One year ago there were not enough rifles for the volunteers; now there were not enough volunteers to send to the front. The recent Soviet Congress had called for a draft of 10 percent of all Communists, but our meeting decided to call on volunteers, with the missing numbers to be added at the discretion of the party committee. Many were troubled less from a fear for their skin than by the disorder in the rear, by unemployment and hunger. Many lost heart from the widespread confusion: why and how had it become so difficult to live under our own government? Could we workers and peasants in fact govern ourselves?

A different mood prevailed in the bureau of the military commissars, where the drafted Communists reported. Here dominated a militant and firm conviction that all our difficulties were due to the civil war and that the liquidation of the counterrevolutionary offensive would bring a paradise on earth. The continual flow of arrivals and departures, the lively conversations about news from the fronts, reminded me of the situation in the October days in 1917. We read in the newspapers about the advance of the Don Cossacks to the borders of Tambov and Voronezh provinces, and so all new arrivals were directed to go there, to the south.

A. S. Bubnov issued me a carte blanche, with the unlimited right to travel on any type of transport out of turn and by whatever means it took to reach the headquarters of the Ninth Army on the southern front.[12] It was not all that far to Balashov, but railway transport was quite different from a year ago. Passenger trains did not run on a timetable, they stopped for long periods at large stations in order to make way for freight trains heading for the front and also because locomotives had "fallen ill" on the route.

The carte blanche helped me to travel on any train, be it on the platform or on the roof of a freight car, and after several days I arrived at my destination. The headquarters of the army was just as busy as the military commissariat had been, but with a completely different look about it. People here worked calmly and deliberately; signs on the doors read: "Do not enter without a report" or "Entry forbidden." Those working in the headquarters were well dressed, freshly shaven, they addressed each other by name and patronymic, and this conveyed an impression of politeness and correctness. There was no smell of crude home-grown tobacco in the air, there were no cigarette butts littering the parquet floor . . . A member of the Revolutionary-Military Council, Baryshnikov, dressed like the rest in a military uniform, stood out from the others: the strap on his soldier's blouse was loosely fastened, and he had not yet shaved today. He was interested in news from Moscow, he asked me questions about our district committee, he talked about bread and potatoes, and least of all about what I was interested in. At the end of our conversation he turned to a thick-set and well-fed military man sitting at the next desk with a question: "Comrade army commander, is the position of our troops still unchanged?" I looked at the commander of the Ninth Army, comrade Kniagnitskii, and I saw that he was not the sort of person with whom I could relate as a comrade: we were not birds of a feather.

Having received an affirmative answer, Baryshnikov finally told me about matters at the front: the situation near Povorino was unstable, they were expecting the line to be breached, and he was sending me to the Nizhegorod regiment.

I wasn't at all troubled that I was being sent from army headquarters directly to a regiment and not to division headquarters. I did not ask any questions about what kind of work I was being sent to do: this was understood; I was going not as a commander or commissar but as a member of the party—as a Bolshevik. It seemed that all was quite natural and that Baryshnikov knew best. I would go—and then I would see. While I was dining in the staff canteen, I was given an order appointing me the assistant military commissar of the Nizhegorod regiment. Again—they must have known best, to assign an eighteen-year old kid to conduct political work . . .

While I was making my way to the Povorino station, the regiment had already moved on further, and I had to catch up to it riding on a peasant cart. I wanted to reach them at their next bivouac, but the peasant-carter announced, "This is it—my village," and he would not agree to take me any further. Therefore, it was only the next day that I stumbled upon the rear of a long train of military vehicles and field kitchens, in front of which loomed up platoons and companies of armed Red Army soldiers. The unit marched in good order, as if they were on parade. I rejoiced to see the discipline and order, so different from what I had known in the Red Guard.

I met the regimental commander with his battalion command-ers; he gave an order, and I was offered a horse to ride on. As in army headquarters, here too all the officers addressed each other by name and patronymic; all of them were also smartly dressed. These Red Army soldiers spoke in the old style: the commander of the regiment was dignified by the title of "colonel"; someone else was called "our captain." I quickly realized that the com-manders here were experienced officers from the tsarist army, and it would be difficult for me to relate to them as pals, even if I had wanted to. I tried to start up a conversation with some Red Army soldiers, but they answered me with polite but cool answers. May-be this was because I was a stranger, maybe because I was on horseback while they had to drag themselves along on foot for twenty kilometers.

While I proceeded to the head of the column, located several kilometers ahead, the horizon became shrouded in white, pow-dered with a fine snow. The regiment became wary and tightened up: that night's designated bivouac, a small settlement, was occu-pied by our opponents. We would have to fight for it. I heard an unfamiliar order, the companies stopped, and they reorganized themselves in a quadrangular formation. This was my first expe-rience with this means of defense against cavalry, who could steal up unnoticed in the snowy gloom.

The regimental reconnaissance party patrolled somewhere ahead, and similar protection was placed on the flanks. All this was done crisply, without unnecessary words—I was proud of such a Red Army.

The first shot that rang out stopped the movement of the troops, and the subsequent machine-gun chattering caused the line to scatter. I jumped down from my horse, intending to take a place in the line, but first I had to hand my horse back to the sup-ply depot. Then I heard:

"He's already chickened out—the commissar is skedaddling to the rear."

This was followed with malicious laughter. First I blushed and then turned pale from indignation, but whom to answer? I decid-ed to return. I wanted to tell these men that this was not the first time I had heard the sound of gunfire, that in order to join the line I had to give my horse to somebody, but my neighbors were not in a position to make conversation. Our opponents engaged in loud firing, and it seemed that they were firing not only from the front but also from the flanks. Something crackled from somewhere very close and then from far away. It was hard to know whether this was the cavalry slipping in or the wind mimicking the sound of firing. The Red soldiers replied with a volley of fire, and in the intervals they peered intently into the darkened distance to hear where the sound of firing was coming from, but the sounds of flying bullets could not be heard. Our regiment had machine guns, but from our side there was no firing; I had heard that the Cossacks, for purely psychological pressure, contrived to imitate the sound of machine-gun fire by using wooden rattles. I don't know whether the Red Army soldiers knew about this, but about the cavalry they said:

"We are being led to slaughter. How can we fight with rifles against the Cossacks' sabers? If you live, write to Dasha about how I died for nothing!"

We could see neither our opponents nor their cavalry, but already the conversation sounded like that of the doomed. From the terse, ill-tempered rejoinders, I reluctantly began to realize that this was not the Red Army that I had known.

I said to the soldier nearest me that very recently we had taken Novocherkassk and Rostov almost bare-handed and that no Cossack could have resisted, but he answered,

"I wouldn't know, I can't read . . ." Our conversation was interrupted by the further march of the regiment, and only at the very edge of the village did we enter into a genuine exchange of fire with our retreating opponent.

This very first day with the Red Army, in a regular regiment and not with some partisan unit, showed that my initial impressions about the army had been mistaken. There was not one volunteer in the regiment; they were all young men drafted from the peasantry of Nizhegorod province. Men from the same village stuck together in small groups—this is how they were mobilized, and so they wound up together in this or that platoon. There were very many among them who could not read or could barely read, and at our halting places one could always observe a group of soldiers gathered expectantly around the company scribe: "Write a letter home for me . . ."

They talked among themselves only about their villages, their streams, their sweethearts. They were obsessed with land—they praised the black earth: we could have such lovely fields here, we should build our village here! They were interested only in "my" or "our" village. Red-White, revolution-counterrevolution, nationalization-socialization, all this was for them gibberish, about as interesting to them as a sermon from the church pulpit.

All of this began to make me feel very uncomfortable, very alien: I had nothing to talk about with the Red Army soldiers, and it was even worse with the commanders—former tsarist officers. To think I had come here in a jubilant mood and that I had approached the regiment as if it were something close to me, my own.

For the next several days we advanced, meeting only minor resistance from our opponents, who fell back firing, but did not engage in serious battle. We often had to lie down in the line, and, it would happen, complete our march of twenty or thirty kilometers only late in the evening. After an exchange of fire the Red Army soldiers would always speak of many people killed or wounded, but in official reports the regiment noted only scattered casualties.

There were also discussions about my appearance in the regiment—I was a "white crow," a strange bird. I didn't know why I had become a white crow in the Red Army, in my army. I couldn't understand, I could not explain to myself, why they spoke about me in such ill-tempered and hostile tones. They spoke about their commander as if he were one of them; "ours," they would say, "a Nizhegoroder." Once I heard this scrap of a conversation:

"We don't need to rely on the Cossacks, we have cartridges enough if he doesn't have the sense to beat it!"

This remark so staggered me that, despite my fatigue, I remained awake a long time, asking myself the unanswerable question: what was my crime that the Red Army saw me as an enemy?

If the regimental commanders, those former tsarist officers, had spoken in this way, I could have understood. But to the contrary, they were politely obliging and willingly explained to a "civilian" the things he did not understand. They spoke with me as an outsider, not a friend, but they never demonstrated any ill-will or noticeable hostility. This riddle tormented me all the more because I had not one living soul here with whom I could talk about my experiences, to help find an answer. The more I anguished, the more I withdrew into myself: I could not even talk with a Red soldier without the apprehension that this might be the man who had threatened to kill me without the help of the Cossacks. Lying in the line, firing together with the others, all the while I had to look around me, to see whether or not the barrel of a Red Army rifle was pointed at me.

During daytime exchanges of fire I felt reasonably secure, but usually the battle would begin toward the end of our march, when we were occupying a settlement or a village; with the onset of darkness an animal fear crept into my soul. I was afraid that someone would notice my anxiety, that again someone would cry out, aha, the commissar is a chicken! By now, I had become a coward, and worse than that, I suffered terribly for it. A bullet whistled by. I glanced around in back of me, flattening myself to the earth, digging myself into the snow. I even shut my eyes probably out of this same animal fear.

After a week we approached the Khopyor River, and for the first time the regiment received its baptism of artillery fire in a brutal, sustained fusillade. But as soon as we occupied a settlement the battle stopped, even though the Cossacks had retreated only a little way, just two or three kilometers. Sentries and listening posts were set up as usual—this was the job of the regimental commander. The rest of us all lay down to sleep. The commander spent the night in the same peasant hut as I, since this was the headquarters of the regiment. Early in the morning I was awakened by the telephonist on duty—firing had started on the outskirts of the village and the battalion had called: the battle had begun, and the regimental commander was missing. His orderly said that he and two battalion commanders had left quite a while ago to check on the sentries. What could have happened to them, could they have been wounded?

It turned out that together with two battalion commanders (the commander of one battalion stayed in the regiment), our commander skirted the sentries and ordered the sentry positioned in a ravine to return to camp to sleep; then through this very ravine the commander stole away to the Cossacks.

On this day the regiment went forth not in the morning, as usual, but in the evening, and not forward, but backward, to the rear and then—to disbandment.

After the order to withdraw the regiment, I returned to the division headquarters. I had still said nothing to anyone about my experiences and torments in the Nizhegorod regiment, but I soon received an answer to my riddle, to why they had treated me like an enemy.

The Nizhegorod division, made up of newly mobilized troops and well staffed with former tsarist officers, had surrendered as soon as they arrived at the front. The particular regiment I had joined had just moved to strengthen a neighboring division, and in this way they escaped the fate of the rest of their division. Having learned that the Nizhegorod division had given itself up, this regiment also began to kick up a row. They held rallies with the demand, "Down with the war—long live peace!" resurrecting our slogans of 1917.

The officer ranks of the regiment did not participate in this demonstration; on the orders of a newly arrived commander, the soldiers formed up their units, but they still refused to occupy their positions. The regiment engaged in rallies and meetings for many days in a row, all the speakers from the regiment spoke against the civil war, and only outsiders argued that they should go to the front, that they should defend the revolution against counterrevolution. Finally, when persuasion had failed, the regiment was surrounded by a battalion of sailors, formed into ranks with their commander at the head and stripped of their weapons without opposition. Now without rifles, with the muzzles of machine guns pointing at them, they again refused to obey the order to go to the front. Only under individual interrogation did one unit agree to go to the front, "if everyone goes," but the majority still refused. In this way the regiment was divided into two parts, and from those who still refused, the authorities began to single out every tenth man.

Each of those who was pulled out was shot in front of the others and of course after these executions the regiment adopted a new resolution: to go to the front.

Now I knew. I had joined a regiment that had experienced such events on the eve of my arrival. I began to understand that hostility with which they had met the arrival in their regiment of a Communist, indirectly guilty of the deaths of so many "Nizhegoroders"—friends, acquaintances, relations. But to this day I do not understand why Baryshnikov, an old Bolshevik and experienced man, had not considered it necessary to warn me about where he was sending me, about what awaited me. Possibly, he had decided to take pity on me and on my enthusiasm.

Peasant draftees frequently rallied demanding an end to the war, and some units gave themselves up as prisoners, but having to serve "voluntarily" in the Volunteer Army, they again gave themselves up as prisoners to the Red Army. Such experience spoke louder than agitation, and henceforth these returnees became agitators against surrender.

In our division there were "battle-ready" and "non–battle-ready" units. The difference between them was that the former were composed completely of volunteers—the remainder of the Red Guard; the others completely of draftees—sent to the front without training or political preparation. There were regiments without a single Communist, in others they were scattered individuals and lost in the common mass. These organizational faults were corrected in the process of battle: new units were supplemented with worker-volunteers or with soldiers of the tsarist army who remained in the service of the revolution, and the draftees were distributed among battle-ready units.

In its first year of existence, our young army fought without experienced commanders; the lack was made up in most cases by noncommissioned officers from the old army. Drafted officers began to appear only toward the end of the year. These draftees considered themselves soldiers without epaulets, specialists rather than commanders—counselors of the commissars.[13] Having adjusted to their role as "regimental commanders" rather than "colonels," and taking responsibility for the lives of a thousand soldiers, they served if not from belief, then at least in accordance with the law. And they began to take pride in the victories of their units, in their order and discipline. To recruit such specialists the military introduced new decorations: external distinctions such as epaulets were not permitted, but the chief of the division headquarters could sign himself: "nachshtadiv,"[14] the colonel of the headquarters of such and such division . . .

The commissar of the Fifteenth Division, Evald, had been a worker in a Podol'sk factory, near Moscow, and I was very glad that our division commander, Gusarskii, conducted their relations informally; in difficult situations they conferred as equals. People said that Gusarskii had led an expeditionary force in France in the last war and that he managed to return to Russia in order to offer his services to Kerensky, but not to Kornilov. However, when he returned Lenin and not Kerensky was the head of state; nonetheless, he began to serve the new lawful revolutionary regime . . . It was a rare thing when a colonel of the general staff of the Russian Imperial Army volunteered for the Red Army. Gusarskii felt that confidence was shown to him and he responded likewise. Officers in division headquarters conducted themselves very smartly with him; it was obvious that they valued his opinion not only as the division chief but also as an old officer of the general staff.

The division chief of the Sixteenth Division, Kikvidze, often came to consult with Gusarskii.[15] But Kikvidze was the complete opposite of Gusarskii. Kikvidze spoke with everyone as an intimate, and he spoke with a heavy Georgian accent. He always entered a room in a state of agitation; from the threshold he would gesticulate and shout, but then would congenially shake hands with all who were present. He always railed against Ninth Army headquarters for this or that directive, for the shortages of military supplies; but he never worried about food supplies for his troops— it would be absurd to be in the Don region and go hungry. In his division he was both commander and commissar. He would arrive imposingly, accompanied by a crowd of Dzhigits,[16] who worshipped their commander. To hear them, Kikvidze was the ideal division commander; he never sat around the headquarters, but in battles was always prancing on ahead of his whole division. He had been wounded sixteen times, but never once did he have to stay in the hospital: "They haven't cast the bullet yet that could kill Kikvidze!" Kikvidze himself sometimes said, deliberately and ironically, that he could only be killed by a silver bullet, but behind his irony he believed in this omen. I admired the proud, independent nature and the heroic figure of this Abrek[17] in his shaggy black cap and shaggy felt cloak. But even more I admired his mount, so clean and brilliant, and with such fine legs that my heart stopped beating whenever Kikvidze leaped into the saddle, for fear his legs might break. Horse and master were inseparable.

In Kikvidze's division there was a "regiment" of Dzhigits, a regiment of cavalry from the remains of the old army, and also several infantry units, reassigned from the left flank of the Fifteenth Division. In November and December 1918 we easily gained the settlement of Aleksikovo, and then Uriupinskaia, but every time we approached the Khopyor River, we would fall back to Povorino with many casualties. These systematic failures repeated themselves in a kind of pattern, and we said openly, and even wrote to army headquarters in Moscow, that the opponent was always in the know about the deployment orders from our headquarters: a traitor was ensconced somewhere. Kikvidze deliberately behaved very aloofly when he received a new army order; he would come to consult with Gusarskii and together with their staffs they would work out alternatives. Kikvidze was certain that a copy of the order was already in the hands of our opponent and to carry out an offensive according to the instructions of army headquarters would signify certain defeat. Gusarskii did not object to the army order, nor to the arguments of Kikvidze, but the order was signed, he said, not only by general Kniagnitskii but also by members of the Revolutionary-Military Council; it was imperative that we carry out the order.

"We will carry it out," replied Kikvidze, "but not by the methods and means suggested by army headquarters." Then he stipulated who would go where and when they would go: Kikvidze's cavalry would assist the Fifteenth Division in occupying its position; after this the Fifteenth Division would reinforce the Sixteenth Division. On the next day Kikvidze arrived at our headquarters very satisfied with his successful operation. "The army's order has been carried out ahead of schedule and with minimal losses."

For some reason or another we again dug in on the Khopyor, entrenched under heavy artillery fire. Defying orders from army headquarters, Kikvidze proposed to seize the enemy's battery: we would fall back on the left flank and move forward on the right flank, and his division would surround the enemy from the rear. Gusarskii objected, suggesting we take measures to defend our own battery from the Cossack cavalry. But somehow or other the Fifteenth and Sixteenth divisions coordinated their actions without following the plan of the army staff.

In January 1919 Trotsky came to Balashov, and Gusarskii and Evald were invited to appear before the Ninth Army's Revolutionary-Military Council. Kikvidze received the same invitation, but he replied to us:

"I have sent a telegram: let me take a special train from Povorino for my Dzhigits and machine guns. Without the Dzhigits I never ever go anywhere."

Evald and all those around him laughed loudly, but Gusarskii answered:

"Very well, but I could say a thing or two about the Sixteenth Division . . ."

Evald was a very quiet man, and it seemed to me that he did not know how to let out openly either joy or grief. Our frequent failures on the front in no way disturbed him, or disturbed him no more than an incorrect solution to an arithmetic problem. In this respect he was completely opposite to the Caucasian nature of Kikvidze.

Evald returned from Balashov at night, and I saw him only the next morning, but he was no longer the same quiet, restrained character he had been before his departure. I had a difficult time understanding when he told me that Kikvidze had been right to refuse to go to Balashov. He held out to me a typewritten order of approximately the following contents: "In the name of the Russian Soviet Federated Socialist Republic, the Revolutionary-Military Tribunal of the Ninth Army sentences the division commander of the Fifteenth Division, former colonel of the tsarist army Gusarskii, to the ultimate penalty for his refusal to carry out the orders of the army commander, for independent guerilla-type activities, and for disorganization."

Then Evald described in detail the meeting at the Revolutionary-Military Council. On behalf of the Revolutionary-Military Council of the Republic, Trotsky had laid out the strategic plan for the spring offensive. Kniagnitskii supported the plan in principle, but doubted it could be carried out. The army was uncoordinated; separate divisions advanced randomly, ignoring their orders. Gusarskii, stung by this characterization, defended his past actions. He sharply criticized central army orders. They were difficult to find fault with formally, but blind obedience to these orders inevitably led to the failure to capture their objectives. Only when the division altered the plan of the army staff were they successful. Their opponents seemed to be as well informed about every operation as army headquarters itself. He implied that the responsibility for past failures lay with army headquarters, not with his division. He was accusing no one personally, he did not doubt the integrity of the army commander, but somewhere here there was a nest of espionage.

Trotsky asked point-blank: would the division fulfill army orders without question? Gusarskii said no.

The Revolutionary-Military Council decided to strip Gusarskii of the command of the Fifteenth Division, and they transferred the matter to a tribunal.[18] Evald was released from custody at the insistence of Baryshnikov, who had known him in the Moscow District Committee, but for his edification he was sent over to be commissar in the Fourteenth Division. The Fifteenth Division was ordered to the rear and dissolved, and its commanders and commissars were reassigned. Up to now this had been the best prepared fighting division in the Ninth Army: it had been formed from the remains of Sivers's army from the time of the Red Guard; Sivers had also commanded a so-called special brigade here, and he too was shot for "partisanism," independent actions.[19]

During these days, and not even in the fire of battle, Kikvidze perished: someone had cast his "silver" bullet.[20]

The execution of Gusarskii stunned me as deeply as the behavior of the Nizhegorod regiment. I was completely convinced of Gusarskii's political loyalty and I was sure that a traitor was hidden somewhere in the army. None of us had any objections to the shooting of traitors, but in this case they executed an individual who had been betrayed, in the same way each one of us had been betrayed. We saw this less as a struggle against "partisanism" than the result of mutual hostility between Gusarskii and Kniagnitskii. We also saw in this the desire of the Revolutionary-Military Council of the republic to raise the authority of the army commander, as a former tsarist officer, and to salvage the reputation of an operation that subordinates had dared to condemn.

We remembered the pointless and unjustified downfall of Gusarskii again in autumn 1919, when commander Kniagnitskii and his adjutant quietly got into an automobile and departed to the service of Denikin's advancing troops.[21]

Chapter Seven

In November 1918 the Germans surrendered to the allies in France and German occupying forces withdrew from the areas in south Russia and Ukraine that they had controlled. Having repelled the White armies in Kazan and along the Volga, the Red Army leadership grouped its forces for a reconquest of Ukraine and the Don region.

By late 1918 the Southern Army Group amounted to about one-quarter of the entire Red Army and was divided into five armies. The Eleventh and Twelfth armies were directed toward the North Caucasus, where General Denikin was consolidating his Volunteer Army. Red losses here during the winter of 1918–19 were considerable, and typhus also struck down huge numbers of soldiers.

The Eighth, Ninth, and Tenth Armies, with one hundred thousand infantry and seventeen thousand cavalry, were deployed toward the Don. Against them was a Don Cossack army of fifty thousand under the new ataman, General Krasnov. The Cossack army defended a long front from the Donbass in the west to Tsaritsyn on the Volga in the east. Beginning in January the Red Army advanced all along this front. The greatest successes came in the center, where the Eighth and Ninth armies pushed the Cossack defenders southward and the Reds reconquered much territory for soviet power. The Cossacks put up more resistance on the flanks of the front, in the Donbass and near Tsaritsyn, but their cause was weakened by sporadic anti-White uprisings and desertions from their own ranks. By mid-February 1919 the Don Cossack army had been reduced to fifteen thousand fighters. Ataman Krasnov resigned as leader of the Cossack army, and General Denikin now assumed undisputed control of all White forces in south Russia.

In Siberia at this time White forces enjoyed greater success. An anti-Bolshevik socialist government created in Omsk was overthrown in November 1918 in a military coup led by Admiral A. V. Kolchak. Engaging Red Army troops in a series of skirmishes between the Ural Mountains and the Volga River, Kolchak enjoyed substantial success, but his victories forced him to make a strategic choice. He could seek to link his military forces with Denikin's army in the south, which was regrouping from the Red Army's advance in the winter of 1918–19 or he could direct his forces to the north and break through the Reds to join the British expeditionary force that had landed in Arkhangel in the far north. His army had already been successful in the north and had captured the town of Perm in December 1918. Thus encouraged, he concentrated his troops at that end of the front, hoping perhaps to reach Moscow by the northern route and to beat Denikin to this prize. Kolchak achieved his greatest successes in March and April 1919, just when the Volunteer effort in the south was weakest. But his own army suffered from a lack of experienced officers, and recruits drafted from the Siberian population were not molded into an effective fighting force. By April 1919, a Red Army force under the leadership of Mikhail Frunze launched an attack that would ultimately roll back Kolchak's White forces to the Urals and prevent any merger between the Siberian and South Russian White armies.

On
the Don
Again

Our Fourteenth Division occupied the left flank of the Ninth Army. Across the River Don it linked up with units of the Tenth Army based in Tsaritsyn. Twenty years later this army would become famous because Josef Djugashvili (Stalin) was a member of its Military-Revolutionary Council, but at the time the Tenth Army was renowned because it terrorized the city with mass executions by firing squads and because the guerilla spirit was so acute that the Tenth Army never maintained any kind of liaison with the neighboring Ninth Army: Boris Dumenko's Tenth Army cavalry made a deep raid into the Sal' steppes, which met such forceful White resistance that we had to turn our front to the east in order to protect our own passage across the Don.

Our division occupied the front along the Northern Donets River, and the whole left bank of the Don was exposed: the Tenth Army was afraid to cut itself off from Tsaritsyn. Passage across the Don for one hundred, two hundred, three hundred kilometers was left unprotected; the enemy could easily gain our rear without firing a single shot. We averted disaster only because General Krasnov's army engaged in purely defensive actions. As soon as we had crossed the Khopyor River our advances were met by token opposition, and the division moved forward about ten to fifteen kilometers a day. By early spring 1919 we were on the left bank of the Northern Donets, moving cautiously so that we would not end up in a pocket. We lingered on this border almost half a year, until the autumn retreat of 1919.

My earlier acquaintance with the Don region, when our unit moved only along rail lines, had left in me a vague impression of a rich region. Now, as we marched on foot through the entire Don, through major settlements like Uriupinskaia, Tsimlianskaia, and Konstantinovskaia, I could plainly see that local agriculture here was a world apart from what I had known in central Russia. The average Cossack settlement was not like a Russian village, with thatch-roofed huts, but a town completely different from "towns" such as Volokolamsk, Naro-Fominsk, Zvenigorod, and others.[1] The population of the Don oblast was more than three million people, of which only 1.3 million were the Cossacks, who owned large allotments of excellent land. On average, every Cossack household owned about twenty-six desiatinas of land and fifteen to twenty-two head of cattle, and it is not surprising that 63 percent of the richest households worked their land with the help of hired labor or local peasants—inogorodtsy (non-Cossack peasants living in Cossack towns)—rather than Cossacks.

The Don peasants lived incomparably better than peasants in central Russia, but by comparison with the Cossacks they were all the same poor. Social stratification could be observed even among the Cossacks, but the Cossack poor constituted a tiny minority and played no political role. On the other hand, all the non-Cossack peasants were considered by Cossacks to be Bolsheviks, who they feared would claim an equal division of Cossack lands. In practice, such a precise division did not happen. Among the inogorodtsy were longtime Don peasants, who strived not so much for a division of the land as to achieve for themselves the name of Cossack and the accompanying right to the land; there were also peasant "migrants" from the neighboring province of Tambov, whom the Cossacks scornfully labeled "Bambovites."

In the wake of our military movements came civilian authority in the form of the Revolutionary Committee (Revkom), which usually moved in the rear of the division. Only through the Revkom, and then through locally elected soviets, could we interact with the population, receiving food supplies, forage, and supplies for the division. One of our more difficult tasks was to guard against the unauthorized actions of the espionage units, who galloped their horses to exhaustion and then exchanged their worn-out horses for fresh ones. We regarded such horse-stealing with special sternness; it was the subject of orders to all units and of instructions on political work. In the conflicts that I observed, the Cossacks were upset less by the loss of a good horse than by the idea of thievery itself, by those who took not the horse they had been given but another. But the Cossacks themselves introduced this practice of systematically and legally leaving worn-out and exhausted horses on farmsteads in exchange for well-fed and healthy ones. Once the chair of a village soviet himself offered to exchange broken-down horses in the army train for good ones, but this turned out not to be from the goodness of his heart but for calculated reasons. The horses he wanted to trade had government brands; in other words, they were not his but the "property" of demobilized Cossacks of the old army . . . I cannot remember, during the entire time of our occupation, that we had any other disputes with the population, except about horses.

We were issued strict regulations about our interaction with the local population and also with Cossack prisoners. In cases of arbitrary punishments on our part, the guilty among us were sent to trial, and this was made known to everyone, including the local population. Such incidents usually arose in the heat of battle, but we also took prisoners outside of battle. The solid fronts on both sides of the river precluded the possibility of captivity, but nonetheless the local male population began to grow. Many noncombatant Cossacks retreated alongside their armies, without being actually in their ranks, because of Bolshevik "atrocities." Now they, and even some fighting men, began to filter back. Having thrown away their weapons they first "got lost" around the hamlets, in gullies and ravines, and then after the Red Army had marched by, they returned home. This was a time when there were no prisoner camps; these ex–fighting men were not compelled to join the Red Army, because we did not need more people. Many of them came from the Sal' steppes, and having made a journey of three hundred to five hundred kilometers away from their armies, they willingly entered into conversation with us. They were concerned about their settlements, their villages, about the onset of field work. Because they feared to go about alone and because there were so many of them, they moved along the road in whole files.

We would ask them:

"Hey, farmboy, have you finished fighting?"

And someone always gave the stereotypic answer:

"You really can't hold out against all of Russia!"

Among this crowd I never met a single officer. If any had been present, there was nothing to distinguish them from rank-and-file Cossacks. In the intelligence section of division headquarters I often saw officers come in for questioning, but these were prisoners and not deserters from the ranks, like the Cossacks mentioned above. This staff section was led by one of the assistant division chiefs, also a former tsarist officer. He himself interrogated the officers and prepared summaries of the interrogations. He also received summaries from Army HQ, and he had a special number for his own communiques with Army HQ. In this respect this individual was quite independent from the division chief. He was not a political worker but an intelligence specialist. Even without the permission of the commissar of the division, he received officials from Army HQ, whom he conducted through the front. After questioning here, the captured officers were not yet finished. They were sent to Army HQ, where most were detained in "camp until the end of the civil war." This was the written norm of treatment of captured officers, but in practice there were "deviations from the norm."

Kikvidze had bragged to our Fifteenth Division about how many people he had slashed up in battle, and of course all of them were officers. I knew, from stories people told, that officers were not taken prisoner: an eye for an eye. Once I was sent to a nearby hamlet, occupied by a regiment of our division. On the outskirts of the village I met two young White officers in epaulets, but dressed in unbuckled overcoats. They were guarded by two Red Army men with revolvers in their hands. By the unconcerned look of the prisoners, and the lively conversation between them, I concluded that they were being led to Division HQ for interrogation. I was dressed the same as they, and they looked at me intently: was I one of them? With the same interest I too gazed at the actual "class enemy." But I passed by in silence. I entered the hamlet, and they set off toward the village and our headquarters, but I soon turned back when I heard several shots. The Red Army men returned, saying that they had "exchanged," or terminated, the two golden-epauleted men, captured the night before by the mounted espionage group. Once they had questioned the prisoners, the guards had lied to them that they were sending them off to staff HQ in order to spare them from the thought of death.

Later, in 1921, after the dissolution of the Volunteer Army of Denikin, all officers of this army were required to be registered in the place of their residence. This means that even then there were no special camps. Being taken prisoner did not signify ruin for the officer class as long as capture did not occur in battle. In battle, there was no law except "I am my own master."

Our assignment on the Don was more than its military conquest: our task was to assimilate it to soviet power. This required humane relations with the population and toward our enemies who had laid down their arms. We had to impress this idea in the mind of every Red Army man, in order to break him of the habit of following the unwritten law of soldiers; we had to make him more into a citizen than a soldier. With our advance into the south, with its grape-growing regions, we had encountered problems with drunkenness, and our enemy took advantage of these problems. At Chirskaia station, attacking Cossacks poured the reserves of a distillery into the Don. Local inhabitants managed to stock up on this alcoholic Don water, earnestly importuning the advancing Red Army to partake of it. This scarcely could have been done malevolently, but in the next night's battle the regiment was defeated and had to surrender. After this the division issued strict orders, prohibiting not only drunkenness but even the consumption of alcohol. Once, during the occupation of Tsimlianskaia station, our division chief, Alexander Stepin, returned from several days' march very upset. He was much less talkative than usual, and only after supper he revealed that for the first time in his life he had had to kill a man, and it was one of his own regimental commanders.

On his way to HQ, Stepin had encountered the commander dead drunk, rowdy, shooting into the air, and insulting passing women. He could not manage to take away his gun and he had to shoot him in the full view of the local inhabitants. On the next day this incident was related to me in great detail by my landlady, reacting very negatively to its severity.

"What soldier doesn't drink? And if he harassed us, it is not insulting. It's just the drunkenness that's responsible. He shouldn't have shot the fellow."

For our headquarters, we occupied the large house of a rich wine grower and we dined here at a large table, always with clean napkins and the dinner service of our host. At dinner, the family itself joined us, and the daughter of the house drank a glass of wine, along with everyone at the table. Only Evald and I did not partake of the glasses, and this made us the subject of much teasing; we have but two Bolsheviks, they said, and these two turn out to be monks. There was no one there for whom drinking was not a temptation, but we refused out of principle. Our staff assistant Kozlov made a face, but he drank up his glass of red or white wine only because no one had offered him vodka or cognac—he preferred strong spirits. Those at the table did not simply drink the wine but they relished it, listening to our host comparing the quality of this or that particular wine. It seemed to me that dry wine could never taste good. They drank it not for the taste, but to fortify, to amuse themselves. But after endless discussions about the attributes of this or that wine, I was often tempted to sip a glass.

On the day of our departure the whole family accompanied us, with warm wishes. We had eaten and drunk like conquerors, but upon leaving we paid for all this an unexpectedly large sum. Our host did not know how to oblige us:

"We are sorry you are leaving, because we worry that the next soldiers who come will be different and will sooner or later empty out my cellar. For good people I don't begrudge anything—I will give you some forty-seven-year-old wine as a gift from my grandfather. Only wait a bit" (we were already on horseback)—"it is so buried that it will take a little time to find it . . ."

After such an introduction I decided to violate my principle and to savor the forty-seven-year-old nectar. The winegrower appeared with the bottle, his wife with a tray of tiny glasses, but to me, to the abstainer, they didn't offer a drop . . .

This was not the only time those who housed us wondered what would happen to them after our departure. With my enthusiasm for the fishing rod and hook I encountered many a fisherman. One time, an ancient gray-haired man sat in a boat perched on the river bank holding a fishing rod without a float. The old man began to "babble" more and more, and he started asking me, who were these "bol'shaks," who were the Communists, the Latvians, and the Chinese who would come after the Bolsheviks?[2]

He wanted to know, what was the religion of the Communists,

were they Khlysty, or some other religion?[3] Was it true that in Moscow they issued cards that permitted one to become "engaged" for a certain period stated on the card?

My answers did not satisfy him, and he explained what he had already heard, that the Bolsheviks were not so bad themselves, but "the Chinese are worse than the Yids." The Yids eat rotten pike-fish, but the Chinese even eat possums and frogs. I calmed him, saying that I had only seen Chinese before the revolution, and these Chinese ate the same food as everybody else. I had heard, moreover, that some people eat frogs, but only the very rich; cooked frog legs were reserved for the tsar's table and the like. And Latvians? Latvians were people just like the Russians, they did not eat possums and frogs, some believed in the Orthodox god, some in others, although I myself did not believe in any god, only in human fairness. He asked me about those Latvians who were seven feet tall, with one eye different from other people's, in the middle of the forehead. Unexpectedly, I loudly laughed, and my laughter upset the old man.

"You shouldn't make fun of an old man. If you don't want to speak the truth, then be silent, don't tell lies," he began to reproach me. He was convinced that one could live with Bolsheviks, only you had to "gradually become used to them." When I told him that I was Latvian, he only waved his hand.

"You can tell others these cock-and-bull stories, but I can see that you are not a simple lout. You may be a Kadet, or someone well-born, but you are not a Bolshevik."

So I failed to convince the fisherman that the Bolsheviks would not be followed by people who intended to exterminate the entire Christian race.

The literacy level of the Cossacks was much higher than that of the simple Russian peasants. They frequently would have piles of journals and books in their homes, although no soviet publications. From these journals, including their so-called chronicles, I first became acquainted with the history of the struggle of General Kaledin, with the "ice and steppe" campaigns of early 1918. We did not have anything to contrast to this more or less serious literature. The newspapers and brochures we received for agitational purposes did not answer the questions of the local population on concrete problems. In our papers you could read about the international situation, about the world revolution, about revolution in China, but local interests were described less fully. The papers wrote about organizing communes, collective agriculture according to the "ABCs of Communism" of Bukharin, but local readers wanted to have "instructions" about organizing the commune concerning what they would have to give up of their property, how much they would receive for their labor, and whether there would be such equality that wives and mothers would become community property. The Don newspapers sometimes wrote that in Russia the Bolsheviks had carried out "the socialization of women," and on this question we had to give concrete answers. Our home-grown orators even prepared special talks on this topic, oriented toward the "free love" of Alexandra Kollontai.[4] The audience demanded not abstractions but concrete answers: any erroneous interpretation of Kollontai, or even their own version, was accepted as the rule that would be sooner or later established.

The population came without any special invitation to meetings and rallies in search of answers to the burning questions of the day, but having heard out various "troublemakers" they left still more disoriented. People looked for an authoritative answer, and who could give such an answer better than a commissar? The words of any commissar would be discussed long after he had spoken. References to what the "commissar himself" had said were common occurrences. Often annoyingly there was some unimaginable stupidity, which "the commissar himself" pronounced with aplomb. Once after I delivered a packet of fresh newspapers I lingered too long, spent the night, and was invited to an oral reading of the newspapers. Among the carts was a bonfire of pressed dung, by the light of which someone read the paper. Apparently it was very interesting, because the crowd of listeners kept growing bigger. When I approached, the reader was reading a report about the arrival of the delegation of Sun Yat-sen to Moscow, about the ongoing negotiations between the Russian and Chinese revolutions. His recounting of strange Chinese surnames and names of provinces, and in general, the fact that this was about China, entranced the audience. It was like a fantastic fairy tale. Questions began to rain down, followed by explanations.

The Chinese are good people, first-class, said the reader. It's well known that the tsarist regime kept everyone in darkness and therefore the Chinese are opposite from our people, not completely literate. For this reason they don't speak exactly like us, but you can understand them. For example, they don't say "bread," but "breatt," not "fish" but "fiss"; they call "beans" "soy," but all the same, it's the same "beans." Due to a lack of education, they modify words and instead of "me and you," they say "yours and mine."

He followed this speech with a recitation of Chinese names and surnames, with which he was very well acquainted: Chinese provinces were transformed to Chinese generals, and vice versa. Hubei and General Wu Pei-fu became General Ubeikhui, Sun Yat-sen became Sun-khui in Chai.[5] The listeners were fascinated, and as the saying goes, if you're not interested, don't listen, but don't stop me from telling lies.

Audiences responded to such speakers because they had a ready tongue, they could provide answers to all questions, and they spoke in simple Russian. Newspapers, on the other hand, were written in unfamiliar language. Perhaps my fisherman would have found more satisfactory answers from a conversation with this speaker than from me.

Not all political workers were capable of talking such nonsense, but even the very best could not answer intelligibly about internal politics of the soviet regime and the things that agitated the audience. The land question always occupied the center of attention. Most of the listeners were not in need of land, but feared that under a land partition they would lose what they had. The Cossacks did not object to the rights of inogorodtsy and the Cossack poor to an allotment of land; some of the rich ones advocated dividing their army lands among the poor, but opposed a general redivision. In practice, everybody preferred the old way. The end of the war was not in sight, and everybody lived with the thought— what if the old regime and the old order suddenly return again?

"We don't mind soviet power, under the Kadets it was worse. War, you know."

What happened under the Kadets they knew better than we. Many villages grazed their horses and cattle beyond the Don, in the Sal' steppes, which in many places was a no-man's-land. Both Reds and Whites came here to secure forage and horses; the White Army captured their deserters who were hiding out here. Cossacks showed the receipts issued to them for cattle or forage and threw up their hands.

"What use is this paper? Who will pay it, and when? Better they

should have given us a little money." But not all money was recognized—the currency of the Volunteer Army—"kolokol'chiki,"
was valued as little as "Kerenskies." On the other hand, they valued the paper money of the old government, which we now printed in Moscow as fully legal tender.[6] Meanwhile, the Red Army
received these very same pieces of paper in compensation; only
part of their pay came in Kerenskies. Therefore, for the same money that was worthless in the city, here you could buy whatever you
wanted. The peasants said, "It is more profitable to sell lamb or
chickens for Nicholas rubles than to sell cows and horses for the
other kind."

In the kind of "trench" warfare that we conducted, we stayed
in one place for many months. The rear institutions of the division, including the supply section, were positioned close to the
combat units, so these units received supplies quickly without
having to turn to the local population. Billeted in peasant huts, we
could receive dry rations from the army and have our landlady
prepare them. This was advantageous for us because of what she
would add: milk, sour cream, butter, and eggs. This was advantageous for her because she could sell her products for Nicholas rubles, but chiefly because our rations included sugar, tea, soap, and
herring or dried fish. You couldn't buy these anywhere. Our communal meals at the peasants' table brought all the diners closer
together, and neither we nor they felt as though in an enemy
camp.

At other times we would be in transit and would have to stop
among strangers:

"Old woman, can you fix us something to eat?"

"I don't have anything, the stove is not lit, all I have is some
stewed fruit."

But we knew from experience that first there were always refus-
als; so we held out some Nicholas rubles and asked her to buy
eggs, lard, and potatoes from a neighbor.

"Well, in fact I have some of these, but there is no livestock—
the cattle are grazing far away on the steppe."

Once her suspicions that we would steal her cattle were dis-
pelled, we didn't even have to ask but were offered a rich table full
of food, right up to borsch soup and dumplings, which we wouldn't
even have thought to ask for.

For this reason, whenever I repeated a journey I always tried to stop in those houses where I was known, where without special requests, on the initiative of the landlady, I would find in the morning clean underwear, mended socks, and sewn buttons. I fondly remember the Cossack women of the quiet Don, not so much for the darning of my socks and the motherly concern for an accidental stranger as for their independence in their families. It seemed to me that the women were more cultured than the head of the family. Families lived very amiably, and the members all recognized the authority of the mother; young girls did not suffer from affectations, and soldiers' "grass widows" followed an unwritten law. I don't recall that they saw me as an enemy to fear. On the contrary, very often some grandmother or mother would confide to me how bad it was that her husband was "with the Kadets," and the son served the Reds, that one son was a White, and the other "with Mironov," and what would happen if they met in hand-to-hand combat?[7]

Chapter Eight

February 1919 marked a low point for White forces in south Russia. The Red Army was stretched thin and engaged in pacifying a mistrustful population. Military supplies for the Red Army were difficult to obtain, while the Whites began to receive the first shipments of arms and munitions sent by the British to aid the anti-Bolshevik cause. The White forces gained recruits and confidence, and even though outnumbered by the Reds, they were able to launch successful counterstrikes in late spring 1919.

The Donbass front was the first to crumble for the Reds. Volunteer units, aided psychologically by a handful of British tanks, smashed through the Red defenders, who retreated two hundred miles to Kharkov. In the center, the Ninth Army had already been seriously disrupted by an anti-Bolshevik Cossack rising in its rear. Cossack forces on the upper Don grew into an army of thirty thousand; White pilots who flew over Red lines were greeted with the ringing of church bells in towns that had joined the insurrection. Fighting against these insurgents greatly weakened the morale of the Red Army soldiers sent to fight them. Morale was further shattered in late April when General Vsevolodov, commander of the Ninth Army, sabotaged his orders and crossed over to the Whites.

With weakness in the rear and dissension among the troops, the Reds attempted a counterattack in the direction of Rostov but their forces were rebuffed, and by mid-May the Eighth and Ninth armies were retreating northward in great disorder. By June Denikin and the White armies had won important victories. The Donbass was cleared of Reds, and the east Ukrainian center of Kharkov fell to the Whites on 25 June. A few days later Tsaritsyn, which had been a key to Red control of the Volga, also fell to the Whites. By the end of June the Don territory was completely liberated. Denikin now issued his secret "Moscow Directive" of 3 July, which proclaimed as his final goal "the seizure of the heart of Russia, Moscow." The drive on the center was to proceed from three directions: an assault up the Volga and then an attack on Moscow from the east; a second thrust northward from the Don; and a third offensive from Kharkov along the main rail line to Moscow.

The White cause was strengthened in August by a sweeping raid behind Red lines carried out by Cossack general Mamontov. With a hand-picked Cossack cavalry force of seven or eight thousand, his troops swept through the Red rear, plundering and burning military stores, seizing and sacking the towns of Tambov and Voronezh. After a wild forty days, the raiders slipped back through Red lines, having disrupted and demoralized Red fighters but also having alienated the local population they passed through, rekindling their support for the Reds.

The culmination of the White advance came in October 1919. On 12 October Whites occupied Chernigov, near the northern frontier of Ukraine, and on 13 October they took Orel, on the direct road to Moscow and only 250 miles away.

Retreat

Civil conflicts broke out in the rear of our positions. Prisoners and deserters from the Volunteer Army clashed with partisans and Red Army invalids, all over the issue of land partition. We learned about these disputes from conversations between Cossacks only by chance. In addition, Cossacks protested the local soviet policy of providing transportation for the Red troops, even though these carting duties fell only to those who had fought in the Volunteer Army. Because of their protests, rather than due to actual shortages, we began to run low on food supplies.

Further from the front soviet power was more noticeable: its main task was to transfer food to the starving center. Many years' reserve of grain and other foods soon disappeared from the northern regions of the Don, and this provoked rebellion in the Khopyor district against soviet power as early as April and May of 1919. Behind our lines, some three hundred to four hundred kilometers from the front, in the villages of Veshenskaia and Migulinskaia, soviet power no longer existed. Toward the end of May, White general Sekretev's cavalry broke through to join the rebellion, but the main front to the south still held firm. The rebellion in the rear was an isolated pocket.

The Red Army successfully thwarted the White attempts to force the Donets, even when the Caucasian Army of General Wrangel drove the Tenth Red Army out of the Sal' steppe. But on 1 July 1919 the Whites occupied Tsaritsyn, and our entire left flank from Konstantinovskaia to Kalach, a distance of three hundred kilometers, was exposed. Wrangel's army did not try to force the river, aiming instead for the north. Mamontov broke away to the rear, and on 18 August he occupied Tambov, while we were still sitting on the Donets.[1] Our right flank was shaky because of the retreat of the Thirteenth Army, and we found ourselves in the same location as the Whites. If you consider the uprising in the Khopyor district, then we were actually in the rear of the Whites. Under these circumstances we received an order to retreat along the path we had followed in our spring offensive.

Our plan of retreat was worked out with the same detail and precision that the earlier plan for our offensive had been. The head of the division designated the order of the removal of the supply and combat units and the places and dates of bivouacs. All rear units of the division went in a common train commanded by Peter Chugunov, the chief of the political section of the division. The combat units were led by the division chief, who followed behind at a distance of one or two days' march along with the regimental HQs. We were able to maintain daily contact with him by courier, but only under the conditions established by the "rules of retreat," by which he could find us and we him.

During our half-year occupation of the Don we had accumulated a lot of movable goods, and now we lacked enough transport to move them. We were forced to requisition local conveyances. When we reached Tsimlianskaia we were joined by a medical unit with wounded and sick soldiers. The medical unit also brought with it four carts loaded with four barrels of red wine. The wine provoked objections from many of us temperance activists until the doctor explained that he needed the wine to maintain the cardiac functions of the typhus patients. A glass of wine could substitute for the camphor he did not have.

Before the retreat I had not encountered the typhus epidemic. I thought these typhus-stricken soldiers were an isolated case, but in fact the population was seriously afflicted with typhus. I noticed now that the Cossacks of the villages and hamlets here were quite different from those whom we had met when we came in to the Don. Then everything was blooming and green, now everything was dried up and gray, both from the sun's rays and from our occupation.

Before each designated bivouac we would send forward a billeting officer, who would put a chalk mark on the houses where the units were supposed to spend the night, but on many occasions we slept under the open sky. We encountered hamlets where all the inhabitants were ill with "Spanish flu." There were houses where there was nobody to fetch water for the sick people, and we were greeted with pleas of "drink, drink . . ." Sometimes in an entire family only the children escaped the disease, or else they recovered more quickly than the adults and now they were caring for their sick parents and starving livestock. In such villages the livestock—oxen, sheep, horses, and such—stood famished and uncared for.

This typhus appeared in oases: in one village nearly everyone would be sick, but next door in another there were only isolated cases. The further north we went the more often we encountered the infection; to escape it we did not sleep inside huts but in haystacks or in the farmyards. But with our method of marching, and sleeping without undressing, the lice began to torment us.

Having crossed the Don we received our usual instructions for the next day's march, but this time we were not to continue north, as before, but to the east—to the territory occupied by the Tenth Army. Over the next two days we lost contact with the regimental HQs, and we began to be confused about how we should proceed further. Chugunov advised me to make a detour and go off to the regimental HQ of the Ninth Army. I should request an explanation for our turn to the Volga and find out news about the disposition of the front. I could catch up to the supply train on the following day, at its designated stopping point.

At Army HQ I was greeted with the unpleasant news about Mamontov's raid on Tambov, toward which Baryshnikov had gone, and, it seems, where he had been killed; about the disorganization of the right flank, with which the army had already lost all communication for many days; about the fact that commander Kniagnitskii had left for there and gone over to the Whites. We had been turned toward the Volga because the northern Don was a solid mass of rebellion. With the breakthrough by Sekretev's cavalry there was no assurance that we wouldn't find ourselves in the Whites' own rear. The Fourteenth Infantry Division was the only one that had not lost its fighting effectiveness and that still issued daily reports; now the plan was to name Division Chief Stepin as commander of the Ninth Army in place of the renegade Kniagnitskii.

There was a feeling of utter despair and doubt that the Army HQ could even hold out until morning. Nonetheless, because it was so late, I decided to spend the night and catch up to my division the next morning, in daylight, going straight across country. By noon I had reached the spot of last night's encampment, but our supply train had already moved on.

The main road passed about a verst or two from a hamlet; farther ahead loomed a large village surrounded by green orchards or a wood; in the background gleamed the cupolas of a church. I started off in that direction but then I heard the sound of scattered gunfire. The firing stopped as soon as I got down off my horse. A shepherd approached with a large flock of sheep. He calmly looked my way.

"Hello, uncle. What's that shooting?" I asked.

"Last night the Cossack men rebelled and they're shooting at the Reds."

"And where are the Reds?"

"Who knows? They came last night, they left in the morning, and who knows what's next? So now they are shooting. When will this Christian war end?"

"Have the Reds left the hamlet?"

"I didn't see anything—they didn't pass through the village—maybe they turned back . . ."

This conversation with the old man caused me to reverse my course: perhaps our supply train had been held up in the little hamlet or had turned around if it had been impossible to advance.

Again on my horse, I reached the hamlet without encountering any further shooting. I approached the little settlement, which had the look of "typhus" because of the absence of people.

At the outskirts, at the first house, I saw a living soul—a girl, doing some work in the yard.

"Young girl, could you give me something to drink?"

"I'll bring something at once."

She brought me an earthenware pot of milk.

"Please drink—you haven't drunk it all up yet. Go ahead and drink, the milk is good, it's cold. Or can I bring you some stewed berries?"

Her talkativeness and kindness won me over, and I asked her where the Reds were now.

"I haven't seen them today, but they slept here. Find the village soviet, go to the square, there you'll find out."

We calmly chattered on, and without dismounting from my horse I learned the same thing I had from the old man: the Cossack men had rebelled. The girl was very affable, she seemed ready to talk with me all day long; obviously she liked me. And I liked her cunning, secretive, but smiling eyes.

I was in good humor as I rode to seek out my fellows, and only when I turned into the square did I notice the people who surrounded me, some with rifles, some with drawn sabers. It came like a flash of lightning that they took me for a White because of my proper uniform, cap, and boots and because of the Cossack saddle on my horse.

Just to say something, I asked, "Where's the headquarters?"

"We're not Reds, we're Greens."

But I had already seen that they were not Reds, but either Greens or Whites—for me they were the same. On each of their caps was pinned or stuck a green branch or a broad leaf. I felt someone from behind grab my revolver, which I had completely forgotten about. Someone else pulled my wallet with money and documents from my front shirt pocket. Just at this moment I heard a familiar voice behind me.

"Don't shoot, don't shoot!"

"Aksiutka, why are you fidgeting around here? Go away, quick!"

"You see, I let him down."

My recent pleasant conversation partner, having met my glance, blushed and grew silent.

Someone grabbed my boot. "Get off your horse. Sit on mine."

But his mount had no saddle, and I had never in my life ridden bareback. The Greens, seeing my helplessness, helped me to clamber upon an unsaddled, skinny nag. Someone commented sarcastically, but not maliciously,

"He looks like an infantryman, despite his Cossack saddle . . ."

I was annoyed and furious at my blunder, that I had remembered my revolver when it was already too late, that stupidly I would die like a beast who goes of its own volition to the slaughterhouse.

Our cavalcade left the hamlet and, fording a stream, we approached a thicket of densely grown osiers. Conversation was useless, and I could only stare at the place where they were going to do me in. On my right, holding my horse by the lead, rode a high-cheekboned fat-faced young lout. He was pleased; he had acquired a wallet with Nicholas rubles, and he ingratiatingly tried to talk to me. I did not ask him any questions, and he understood my silence.

"You shouldn't be afraid. We're not Whites, we don't shoot people. We are taking you to our colonel, and there you will find all your pals who spent last night in the village."

I listened silently, but I didn't believe a word. I knew they were leading me away from the hamlet, and that was all. I remembered that I had some pieces of sugar in the pocket of my coat, and I offered some to him.

"Here, now you can drink some tea for me."

He took it, but gave half back.

"They'll have the kettles boiling and we'll be able to brew some tea . . ."

Nonetheless, I didn't look back, I awaited the shots in agony. In front of me, though, was a ray of hope: on the other side of a swampy field were many Cossacks, horses, and the familiar four barrels of red wine.

"Mister colonel, I've caught one more."

This man did not look like a colonel—he had no epaulets and had no green twig anywhere.

"Chase him over to the common herd," answered the colonel.

To confirm my hunch that these were Greens and not Whites, I asked for something to drink, and I was delighted to be offered a whole tankard of wine, which I refused. But there wasn't any water here, and they led me to the "common herd," far from the supply wagons. Here I saw a big crowd of people; some sitting, some lying on their greatcoats, their uniform caps already stripped of their red stars. I saw many familiar faces, but Chugunov's was not one of them. The secretary of the political section, Gengut, came up to me and offered me a place. I asked him about Chugunov and about what had happened that everyone had been captured.

In the evening of the day of my departure for Army HQ, the supply train had stopped for the night while it was still light. The hamlet had turned out to be free of disease, so everyone had been assigned to sleep in various huts. As was standard during our retreat, they had posted no sentries, since the front was somewhere two or three days' march to our rear and there was no reason to expect danger. In this typhus-free village they had decided to put themselves in order; some people changed into clean underwear, some went to bathe in the river, and everyone slept undressed. In the dead of night Gengut had been awakened under the prodding of a rifle muzzle. Chugunov was sleeping in the back room, but apparently had woken from the light and noise. Having seen hostile armed men, he jumped out of the window, still in his underwear. He managed to take with him only his revolver. His white shape in the dark of night was easily seen from afar, and they chased after him, but didn't shoot. Chugunov fired once and then ran further; the Cossacks followed at a great distance, shouting, "Give up!"

By dawn, Chugunov was knee-deep in a quagmire, surrounded by a ring of armed Cossacks, and then he fired his second shot—through his temple. The others were all captured at the same time, without much fuss or opposition. The Cossacks chattered loosely along the way to the field, informing everyone that "your chief commissar" had shot himself.

Gengut was afraid now that, along with the supply wagons, the Greens had seized the correspondence of the political section, with its lists of the Communists in the division. There was no list of the prisoners, and these could assume another surname, but among us were three officers from the administrative staff of the division, including Staff-Captain Kozlov, who recently had been hauled into court for drunkenness. If the officers didn't betray us, then we had nothing to fear. There were many unfamiliar people, soldiers who were not part of our supply train, who were brought in from somewhere over the course of that day. I was not afraid of exposure; my papers had been taken away along with my wallet. I would be just as well off if I called myself Ivanov; I could explain my possession of papers with a different surname by saying I had been assigned to carry the documents of a dead commissar to the political section. Gengut became Chibisov, and all of us other Communists took new surnames.

We were in the midst of a swampy clearing, surrounded by thickets of twigs. The only dry land was where the wagons stood and where the Cossacks gathered. There was also dry land where we slept, but nearer the swamp, which we discovered in our searches for drinking water. The sentries did not hinder us from venturing far from the common herd in order to find pools from which we could draw water in pots, and we made note of this to plan our escape. We didn't have the slightest idea whether we would get bogged down in the marsh before we made it to the thicket nor whether the woods hid a further line of defense beyond the sentries posted around us. With the coming of darkness the first two escapees got away splendidly, and it seemed the rest of us could make our move. But just then gunshots rang out from somewhere. We didn't ascribe any significance to this at first, but then some Cossacks came and demanded to know who had escaped. No one, including the sentries, could answer that question. We were recounted, and the sentries made a large bonfire and announced:

"The colonel has ordered us to hack up anyone who runs away. One person has already been hacked to death, and the other will be brought back to the wagons before morning."

In the darkness I couldn't see the wagons with the wine barrels, but from that direction came the sounds of doleful Cossack songs all night long. With this music in the background we discussed at length all manner of escape plans, but in the end we decided to sleep on it.

The morning sun began to warm us up; from somewhere far off we could hear quickening fire with machine-gun regularity. It had to be us firing, and not Cossacks, because they didn't have machine guns. The firing came closer and we were encouraged. Riderless horses rode out from the clearing; other horses left with riders on them, but paying no attention to the former. The sentries, rifles in hand, were at their posts. We noticed some confusion around the supply wagon, but gradually the firing died down. Several Cossacks approached us, including the fellow who had acquired my wallet, and because of our "acquaintance," he shook my hand and began to speak:

"We-e-l-l . . . , they gave us some heat. Our colonel was killed. Your cavalry is retreating, we suggested they stop fighting us, that they give up their guns, otherwise we won't let them pass. A delegation came to the steppe between us and your cavalry. They were blabbing away, but then someone began to shoot. We saw this, and we too began to fire, the Reds fired at us, and then the fat was in the fire! There were lots of them and few of us. We ran for the woods and they came after us, as far as the river, but then they were afraid to go farther . . .

"The Cossacks are terribly angry! They've decided to divide up the spoils in the wagons and leave only the wine for the troops. Now they plan to take away everything of yours and to leave you nothing in return. Let's exchange boots, how much do you want in trade?"

The prisoners who had been captured during the night had not yet been searched, and nothing had been taken from them. The stuff that was on the carts had disappeared. Now the Cossacks hankered after what we held in our kit bags and also what we held in our pockets.

We considered this an excellent sign: the assault of the cavalry on the rebels could be explained by the fact that our headquarters knew about the capture of the supply wagons, and Stepin was trying to free us. The Cossacks were very uncertain, and therefore they were trying to seize everything they could before it was too late.

We refused to trade or to sell our things. They hadn't fed us, but we had exchanged various small items for bread and lard. Women had come to us, asking if we had any needles, thread, matches, or soap. In this way a regular market grew up around us. And we felt we were the sellers rather than the buyers. We spent a whole day trading, and waiting, and then we heard the sound of gunfire—the sound of our liberation.

On the next day the market appeared again, but now the Cossacks were more demanding. A few people started to sell things, one fellow agreed to exchange boots, and he ended up barefoot. Yesterday's boot buyer again came to me to try to trade. Ingratiatingly, he told me some news: the Reds had already passed by, and the Whites would come no later than tomorrow. They would strip everyone down to their underwear, since this was their custom when they took prisoners.

We realized our situation had taken a turn for the worse because of the Cossacks' altered behavior toward us. They no longer asked, but demanded. Earlier the rebels seemed to number only a few dozen men, but now there were as many armed Cossacks as prisoners. The Cossacks hurried, fearing the Whites would come and seize the booty for themselves. When an agreement to trade didn't materialize, they demanded the stripping of whomever they liked. They chased away their women who tried to buy something from us. Our appearance changed sharply: many of us now went about in Cossack rags, in Cossack hats, in broken-down boots that were useless for marching.

Up to this point I had held out. They couldn't strip me forcibly because I was being hounded by a Cossack who considered me his "catch." Now in order not to be cut off from the general mass of prisoners, I decided I had better transform myself. I didn't want to spend a lifetime in this forest, and I could escape more easily in Cossack garb. My own mother would not recognize me now, and more important, strangers would guess that I was a draftee and not a commissar.

After the killing of the Cossacks' colonel their discipline sharply declined. They were more like a rabble, like the guerrillas that we had been in late 1917, when every man felt himself to be his own commander. The colonel was replaced with an NCO, who began to call out to the Tsaritsyners, Voronezhers, Tambovites—prisoners who were natives of those provinces now occupied by White forces—to leave our group and melt back to their homes. Apparently, there were more "Bambovites" than the Cossacks had expected, and they soon returned them to the common herd. After a while there was a new order—to separate the single men from the married ones. Here was a new problem. Which one to be? Whom would they set free, bachelors or married men? They divided us into two groups, but the married men wanted to be taken for single and the single men for married. Someone started a rumor that they were not going to send us home but shoot us. But which ones? The sentry couldn't keep an eye on everyone, and in the end we again formed a single mass of prisoners.

The agitation of the Cossacks was soon explained. From somewhere far off, and then growing nearer, we heard cries of "hurrah." An even larger crowd than usual gathered around the wine barrels. We learned the reason for the joyous excitement around the wine from the comments of the guards: the commandant of a regiment of the Volunteer Army was engaged in a tasting of Tsimlianskoe wine. The Cossacks discarded their green branches and leaves. On their forage caps appeared the cockade of the old army, a simple white paper or ribbon.

We were roused, and for the first time formed up in two rows, well before the appearance of the commandant. He came toward us accompanied by a dozen of his soldiers and by a whole crowd of Cossacks. The Cossacks marched in front of the officers as if on parade, they strutted as though on stilts, and they saluted jauntily. A loud voice commanded us to attention, but even without the order we stood quieter than the dead. We could have heard a butterfly pass.

Many of the Cossacks had drunk more wine than they should have, but even the commandant, who was sober, took us in with a vacant, sarcastic glance. He began his tour of the ranks without a single word; he would stop silently, look us over, and move on. Everyone he passed was searched: his pockets were turned out, and everything he possessed was taken away. Finally the commandant turned to one of us.

"Yid?" he asked Aronshtam, the brother of the brigade commissar.

"I am a Jew!" he replied.

"Two steps forward. Right face—run!"

Aronshtam turned to the right, but he didn't run. He moved forward a step and looked back. The officer wasn't looking at him, he was going on to the next man. The Cossacks maliciously cried, "Run, you mangy sheep!" But he didn't know where to run, there was a half circle of Cossacks in front of him, Cossacks with rifles pointed. He approached almost to their muzzles, and then fell backward from a shot at point-blank range.

We had thought that they would search for Communists and commissars, but not Jews. I didn't know the nationalities of the prisoners. I didn't know who among us were Jews. I didn't even know the nationality of Gengut—he had light brown hair, Russian eyes, one of which squinted. His surname wasn't Russian, but anyway, now he was Chibisov and not Gengut.

Stunned by the image of Aronshtam's death, I tried not to look at the next shootings of "Yids," which included Russians as well as Jews. Quite close to me they found still another "Yid," the commandant of division headquarters. They did not ask him the standard question: "Yid?" but,

"Orthodox?"

"Orthodox," he answered. He had the typical dark-skinned face of a Tatar.[2]

"Commissar?"

"No, I am not a commissar," answered the Tatar.

"Show me your cross." The Tatar began to unbutton his shirt, but the officer began to mock him.

"Who did you buy it from? How much did it cost?"

He gave the standard order to leave the row. The Tatar side-stepped, many hands pulled him by force, but he refused to run, backing up in mortal fear. Under the blow of a rifle butt he cried out and took to his heels, completely in the opposite direction. The Cossacks only fired at him when he was at some distance. Continuing to run, he seemed to stumble and then ran on, heedless of the fact that the swearing Cossacks were firing bullet after bullet. He ran a little farther and then he fell; we could see him; he gave out a terrifying, sinister wail. Not even women in childbirth wail like this from their pain. The officer continued his tour, shot followed shot, and the Tatar still continued to emit his shrill, heart-rending cries.

At the same time something was happening behind my back. The driver-orderly of our division chief stood behind me, together with a red-haired old man, on a horse with no saddle. Instead of a leg he had a wooden stump, but in his hand he threateningly waved a whip. The orderly's attention was concentrated on the face of the approaching officer, but the redhead cried, "Pay up, or I will tell the captain!" He claimed that on the night before our capture this fellow had spent the night at his hut and had stolen a piece of fatback. The Red Army man had nothing to pay with and tried to prove that he had never slept in a hut and always bivouacked with the wagons, along with the rest of the carters. To escape the lash of the redhead's whip he fell on me; the blood from his smashed nose trickled on me and on my already filthy clothes. The captain was approaching Gengut; after him it would be my turn.

"Yid?" he asked Gengut.

"No, sir!"

"Commissar?"

"No, I am a medical student."

"So you are a Red doctor?"

"No, a medic."

"Move!"

Some Cossack or other also cried "Yid" and beat him with his fists. Another pitched in and Gengut's whole face was covered in blood.

The shooting of the Tatar, the whipping behind my back of the orderly, and the beating of Gengut occurred almost simultaneously. The commotion caused the entourage to hesitate. Gengut wiped off his blood, they passed down the line, and he was left to stand in the row. Although they bloodied him, he showed he was a "student." It is difficult now to describe thoroughly and accurately how I felt as I waited for my turn to be "questioned." I tried to be ready for anything, but they only searched me. The officer moved on. After Gengut, the commandant found no more "Yids" nor commissars in the row. This may have been because the sun was almost setting or perhaps because he was influenced by the cries of terror of the dying Tatar. This amusing spectacle they had organized furnished little satisfaction to the eyewitnesses, but on the other hand the commandant's retinue profited by the pocket-knives, razors, paper, pencils, and odds and ends that they pilfered. Only money and documents were given to the commandant's aide, who followed five paces behind.

When the commandant had moved away, our two rows merged into one and closed up. In single file we moved further, formed into a circle, and were forced to lie down. We were forbidden to sit up and to converse. This hardly mattered: what our souls had just gone through was so foul and so nauseating that we had no words left for talking to our neighbor. Our nervous tension had changed into lethargy.

The guards crowded around three bright bonfires, and whether from the quiet of the night or from our sharpened attentiveness, we heard what they quietly said among themselves.

"There are 260 of them, think how many bullets we'll need . . . ?"

"Let the commandant figure it out. We can always cut them up."

Together we listened to the Cossacks' quiet, calm conversation. We were all so spiritually beaten down that we considered the preceding shootings inevitable, almost predictable. But if they started to use their swords on us, we wouldn't give up so easily! We had become reconciled to the idea of the firing squad, but to die under the saber . . . ?! Inwardly, but only there, a feeble protest gained momentum, and people began to whisper:

"Pass it on: whoever has still got a razor, or a blade, or a knife, or a piece of mirror glass . . . it would be better to cut our own throats . . ."

Such items could not be found. The only sharp thing I had remaining was a needle and thread, stuck in my cap.

Distant heat lightning reinforced our uneasiness. We couldn't sleep during the final moments of our life! Oh, for a last smoke before the end. If we could just catch a glimpse of the sun one more time . . . Nonetheless, we dozed off.

The cold and dampness kept waking us up. It was warm if you slept tight against a comrade, but he would still shiver from the misty rain even though he was asleep. It rained until the dawn broke, but even then the sun didn't manage to warm us. Now a strict guard herded us along to an unknown destination.

We met up with some hay wagons on the road. High up on the hay sat three Cossack women. Pitying us, one of them began to sob, and she kept saying:

"Oi, my dear, and where are they driving you to? The whole station is draped with corpses on gallows . . .

The Cossacks did not react to this, and frowning and silent they led us further along the steppe. They didn't push us and we didn't hurry: perhaps the road led to the gallows. We rested a long time at a descent to a gully and here someone's mind became deranged; he flew off recklessly. The Cossacks at first shouted and didn't shoot. But then they quickly caught up to the escapee—and again our ranks grew smaller by one person.

Before nightfall we reached a large village at Serebriakovo station, where for the first time our names were taken down and we were counted. Some of us were placed in a brick building with a signboard reading "Cooperative"; others were directed across the square to a log shed.

The Cooperative building was already crowded with many prisoners, some of whom were suffering from typhus, and with our arrival there was no place even to turn around. Later in the evening we were joined by some twenty people sent to unload freight, and it became even more crowded. For all these people there was only one tub for drinking water, and it was emptied as soon as it was brought in. We crowded around the door, appealing to Cossacks passing by to bring us some water, and rarely were we refused. But the women, who brought us bread and tomatoes, were forbidden to approach us. The commandant did not allow this.

We crowded around the doors and two windows waiting to be given something to drink. At the shed, where other prisoners had been placed, we noticed some sort of commotion. Under the light of a lantern two long tables were brought in. Would there be an interrogation? A bunch of Cossacks shoved through the lighted open door. Then we heard a mournful cry from one of the women prisoners, and all fell silent.

During our stay on the Northern Donets River, I used to take meals with a poor deacon's widow and her only daughter. Their farm was small: a cow, some domestic fowl, and a garden, whose products they did not have to haul to the market. The old woman was very spritely and talkative, and she interspersed her speech with humor. She melted with pleasure when we showered praise on her borsch, with which she herself was dissatisfied. We had not brought her any local "Circassian beef." But for us even without "beef," with sour cream alone, the soup was delicious.

Quite different from her mother, the daughter was dry, lanky, sort of tedious, she didn't know how to converse the way her mother did. When she was not around her mother would shake her head: "What's to be done—it's the war's fault. In another time she would not languish without anything to do, she would long ago have begun to raise my grandchildren . . ."

The mother herself ran the farm affairs, and we suggested that the daughter find work in our division office. Here she soon learned how to pound on a typewriter, she began to receive Red Army rations, and the mother was even more satisfied with this arrangement than her daughter. When we made ready to leave the district, she, with her mother's agreement, prepared to leave with us.

"Along with the Whites will come my brother, who is serving with the Volunteer Army, and it will turn out badly for me when he finds I have been working for you. Maybe later things will turn out alright somehow, but for now I had better get lost."

We decided to hide from her neighbors the fact that she had retreated with the Reds, saying that she had gone to visit relatives in Tsimlianskaia.

During the month of our wandering on the dusty roads of the

Don she managed to initiate me into the story of her life and to the distinctive ways of the Cossacks. She yearned for, pined for the home she had left behind. At home, with her mother, she had behaved as though dumb, but here she became a completely different person, lively and even more talkative than her mother.

Our division headquarters also employed another young girl as a typist. Small, and frail as a juvenile, she attracted our attention only when we halted. In her company we were always singing and laughing and we enjoyed happy, jesting fun. "The life and soul of the party," we said about her among ourselves.

On the road we had been joined by a third Cossack girl. The one-armed commissar of one regiment, Golubev, asked Chugunov to include in our wagon train his fiancee, riding on her own horse. In order to protect her face from sunburn, she rode with it covered by a white scarf, through which showed her laughing, shining eyes, which became angry when met with the rapt, intense gazes of the men. When we camped for the night, joining the other girls, she was especially distinguished by her outward appearance. Her dainty little mouth and little nose, with trembling nostrils, the fresh white color of her face, and a mass of thick dark hair made her unlike any of the other young girls. You wouldn't believe that this picture of a girl could feed and groom her own horse, that she was accustomed to heavy peasant labor. She could have been a houri or a captive from some Eastern fairy tale, fallen by mistake into our sinful midst. Her beauty made it difficult for me to speak with her as casually as I did with the others.

And now these three Cossack girls had ended up as captives along with us, but they were kept apart, with the captured officers from headquarters. Unlike us, the officers' and women's belongings were not plundered, and now they were being held in the shed.

Our sentry stopped a Cossack passing by, and inquired, as if from boredom:

"Tell me, how are they dividing the spoils—by casting lots?"

"Like always—they do it wholesale, in turns! Whichever girl is free, that one's yours."

"Which one is sweetest?"

"The one is skinny like a tapeworm, the other whore is tasty! She struggled and pissed on herself . . ."

"Hey, what fun! Stand guard for me, I am going to try the commissar-lady."

So when they brought the tables into the shed, a crowd of Cossacks gathered around. A huge number of hands silently seized the girls: they spread two of them on the tables and the third on the floor.

On the next day they were led to the doctor and returned from him with a piece of paper: he certified they were infected with venereal disease. This saved these unfortunates from further degradations.

Former Staff-Captain Kozlov, whom we feared and who was sitting in that same shed as the young women, later told us this story. "When I heard the sickening noises of the Cossacks that evening, waiting their turns, committing their foul deeds on these defenseless women, I decided to avenge them. The next day I avoided the looks of these unhappy women, I felt myself responsible for their shame. If it hadn't been for this incident, perhaps I might have volunteered for the White Army. I used to be secretly haughty: although I served in the Red Army, I was far above the rest of you, I was an officer. But once I witnessed the 'White dream' in the form of this desecration of prisoners, this sanctioned, public rape of women who were Cossacks like themselves, women who only accidentally turned up with the Red Army, I began to abhor this 'White' Army . . ."

I too have often thought about those horrors that those three Cossack women had to experience, when not "Reds"—the enemy— but their own Cossack men, with Orthodox crosses around their necks, committed group atrocities, desecrated defenseless women, "divided the spoils," body and soul, like military plunder. Thank God, I did not have to face those girls again . . .

Chapter Nine

The high point of the White Army advance on Moscow was reached at Orel in mid-October 1919. The line of the White front, from the Volga to the Romanian border in the west, was perilously thin. Victories were achieved only by shifting forces from one section of the front to another, because there were no reserves. And in the rear, the Whites faced growing opposition and social unrest.

One source of opposition was the anarchist leader Nestor Makhno. He had cooperated with the Bolsheviks in the battle for control of Ukraine in the last days of 1918, but turned against the "Commissariats and Chekas," and especially against the discipline Trotsky demanded of his armies. During most of 1919, Makhno's army operated independently, calling on peasants in the Whites' rear to rise up against the "gold epaulets." The further Denikin's army marched toward Moscow, the more freedom Makhno's partisans had for their own maneuvers. In territories that Denikin did control, military dictatorship was in effect. He supported the rights of factory and land owners, stipulating that peasants who seized land must pay a third of the grain harvest to its former owner in addition to taxes for the Volunteer Army. As a Russian nationalist, Denikin failed to reach an accord with the non-Russians in whose lands he operated: Ukrainians, Georgians, Poles, and Caucasians.

In late October the Reds counterattacked at Orel, throwing against the Whites a numerically superior army with a twofold advantage in artillery and machine guns. Orel was abandoned by the Whites when new Red troops threatened to cut their supply lines, and the initiative passed again to the Reds. After three weeks of hard fighting, the Whites began to fall back steadily toward the south. The White cavalry, once formidable, was demoralized, and the new Red cavalry, led by the dashing general Budennyi, harassed the retreating Whites' communications lines almost at will. The Red Army moved for the third time into Ukraine. (The first was just after the October revolution and the second after the Germans withdrew in late 1918.) The Whites' main force withdrew southwestward, toward the Crimea. The Reds meanwhile directed their main assaults on the familiar staging areas of the Don and the Kuban. By early January 1920 Reds had captured the Cossack town of Novocherkassk and were preparing to surround Rostov. The last months of the White regime in Rostov were marked by increasing social disorder, fueled by speculation, economic chaos, and the typhus epidemic that swept through the military and civilian populations.

Prisoner of the Volunteer Army

During the day in our "Cooperative," I could manage to push my way through the crowd of people, but toward evening the floor became covered with both the healthy and the typhus victims, and the only free space was the store shelves. And so I would clamber up. I could lie down there without having to watch out for other people's knees, but the shelves' partitions prevented me from stretching out. Eventually fatigue took its toll, and I would find myself on the floor, heedless of the cuffs and abuse of the people endangered by my fall. Their blows could not counteract my state of dead-tiredness. One morning people were tormented as usual by hunger, but I was worried by an inexplicable thirst, and I waited with great impatience to be taken to work.

They led us out to unload grain. Everyone began to slake their hunger with the cold dry grain, but to me it was like straw. After every sackful, which I carried as if sleepwalking, I ran to get a drink. On the next day, in the afternoon, they sent us to unload flour for the bakery. The prisoners salivated hungrily at the aroma of baking bread; I was interested only in water, but I still did not sense that I was ill. I remember, foggily, that the last sack felt heavier than the others, it bent me down and pushed my nose to the ground.

Then I saw a boundless sea of water, on which I sailed in a frail skiff. The stream raced along, carrying with it tree branches, stumps, shocks of straw, and then whole trees. On all these objects sat familiar people. A girl I had known casually waved her hand at me merrily, she smiled and held out her hand; my sweetheart, about whom I often dreamed, looked at me indifferently and turned away. On a cleanly sawed-off stump, like on the platform of a formal meeting, sat Shmidel', but he didn't pay any attention to me. An entire tree flashed by headlong, and standing on one of its thick boughs was Sapronov. He let out a cry and called to me. My little dugout had no oars and I couldn't move. They all flashed by, leaving me alone. I peered into the waves and saw that everyone had vanished. Only Mazul' alone fought with the stream: he was just on the point of vanishing under the water. My skiff turned over somewhere and now I was sitting on a raft, paddling with both hands. I stretched out my hand to help Mazul': the raft instantaneously overturned and I lay in the bottomless depths. But it was better in these depths than on the raft. I was surrounded by silence, the water wasn't wet, and it enveloped my body like a cloud of warm, soft steam. I desperately wanted a drink of water, and I cried to the invisible Mazul' to hand me a mug. Although I was immersed in water, I could not get any in my mouth.

Someone painfully poked me in the side, asking:

"What are you—German?"

The voice was strange, not Mazul's', it spoke in Russian, and in the same language I implored:

"Just a half mug of water, I need a drink!"

I began to experience the vague sense that my body was filled with something heavy, that I was not lying in water, but no amount of force could open my eyes to look out. They answered me that there was no water, but they had tomatoes. I tasted a pleasant liquid, and then I saw my neighbor with tomatoes in his hands. Everything up to the tomato had turned out to be a pleasant, unforgettable dream. The first and last dream had stuck in my memory like my true past, right up to the color of the water and the intonation of the voices of my friends sailing on it.

My neighbor told me, "We thought that you were German; you were laughing and talking in some other language than ours. Of course, lots of people are saying incomprehensible things; some are commanding a cavalry attack, some are speaking with their mothers, some laugh and cry at the same time."

I lay on the bare, earthen floor; under my head was a thin tuft of rotting straw, at the end of the bed lay a hat with drooping mustaches for brims, like a mushroom, and down-at-the-heel shoes. I was dressed in cotton trousers but without my soldiers' blouse. My undershirt had so discolored that I recognized it only by the buttons my mother had sewn on.

Next to me was a filthy, bare-faced fellow in a soldiers' tunic, wearing drawers the color of my shirt and also barefoot. He was even poorer than me—for he had no hat, but on the other hand he had a soldiers' mess tin, which was being used by all his neighbors. On the other side of me lay a similar person, with a bare belly, along which he bitterly and mechanically scraped his long, dirty fingernails.

Wherever you looked were spread out the bodies of the sick. We lay in the log typhus barracks. Outside, beyond wide-open doors, a sentry patrolled. He didn't let anyone in to us and permitted no one to approach him. Tender-hearted women came up to the barracks and through the bare window openings threw bread, tomatoes, and sometimes fatback. If they were intercepted outside, they put what they had brought on the ground, not permitting anyone to approach them, then they watched from afar at how we picked up the food, and they silently dried their tears with their kerchiefs. They only saw those who had recovered a little and who were able to stand up in the interval before the next onset of recurring typhus. The majority of us could not walk: most lay unconscious, others would jump up and step recklessly over the prone bodies of the others. There was an insufferable stench, which could be smelled from far away. It was not lice, but the air that transmitted the disease—this is what the victims thought, and so did those who were healthy.

Not too far from the barracks we could see a railway embankment with a small bridge, and under it ran a small stream about a centimeter deep. This was our well, but the water in it was yellow and so warm that we could drink it only early in the morning. Each evening we cleared away a little hole, from which in the morning we could scoop up for ourselves the liquid more precious than bread or tomatoes. From here, we could see watermelon fields along the other side of the embankment and a Cossack settlement beyond. The melons and watermelons we saw were poisonous for the sick, you could die from them—or so went the common belief.

Having regained consciousness, typhus patients felt themselves to be completely well. They felt great, practically in a state of bliss; they wanted to speak, to converse, to move about, but their legs failed them. Nonetheless, we would look after those lying down, take off their soiled underclothes, drag them over to another spot, cover up their defecations with earth, take straw from under the dead bodies and place it under the living. In the mornings we would look over the rows of lying bodies, pull out the dead ones, drag them onto the ground, and put them in the shade behind the barrack. In the evening the gravediggers would come for the corpses.

We who had somewhat recovered felt marvelous with gigantic appetites, and we didn't have enough bread to satisfy ourselves. On the other hand, we piled up tomatoes in reserve—we had gotten tired of them. Salt might have helped, but it wasn't provided—salt was dangerous for the sick . . . Therefore we yearned for a piece of fatback—after some fatback even tomatoes tasted good. Judging by the food we devoured, we were not starving, but all our conversations revolved around food, as if this had been a gathering of gluttons and gourmands.

No one knew how long he had been in this barracks; some said two weeks, others said three weeks, no one knew who had been brought in first. The patients lying down remained unconscious, and those who could walk were all occupied in one and the same activity—scratching. We didn't have to search for lice—they were everywhere, there was no escaping them. They multiplied as if in a nursery, they crawled along our shirts and in our shirts, they crawled along the ground and in the straw under our heads. Whoever was strong enough would leave the barracks and shake out the excess lice with whatever strength he had; but the ones that remained would bite day and night. My whole body itched either from stings or from the minor wounds that came from scratching my body. We watched out for the lice of our neighbors. If they began to leave and move elsewhere—that was a sure sign of an imminent death.

Like many others, I was tormented with diarrhea and experienced continual urges to run out into the yard. This running was extremely exhausting, and occasionally I would have to return on all fours, crawling. This diarrhea was not part of our typhus—it came from the warm swill from the little ditch. I was not willing to die, but it was not much better to recover because I would still be a prisoner. Here in the barracks we were on our own, but out there who knew what would happen?

Thus I debated with myself, forcing my way on all fours to pass between the bodies. I saw for the first time the white figure of a nurse walking among the ill. I tried to get up on my feet, but in vain—I was very weak. The nurse poured some kind of powder into my mouth. Soon she pleasantly said good-bye, having explained that she had used up all her medications; she would bring some more the next time. Her appearance brought a breath of life, a contrasting whiff of cleanliness. Before she came it was as if we hadn't noticed the filth, nor the stench, nor the lice.

On her next visit I approached her on two feet, and I praised her powder, with a plea for still one more dose. Without squeamishness, she took my filthy hand, felt the pulse, and discouraged me. She even began to upbraid me:

"Oh no, you don't need camphor. Your heart is working fine. Sleep a little more and don't walk about idly . . ."

"But will they really 'release' me from here? To where? It's so good here, among my own kind."

The news circulated that on Friday there would be a market. My neighbor with the mess tin talked me into going for fatback. We had no money, but we wouldn't have to go begging: people would see we were prisoners, they would call to us and load up our pot. We stole our way under the little bridge as if going for water, from there we escaped into the melon field, and soon we were in the village. The entire village square was full of carts of produce. There was a huge number of carts with wheat, jugs of sour cream, milk, cheese, and butter. We paid scant attention to the numerous carts with vegetables. We walked about and we wondered where all of this had come from: earlier under soviet power the markets were empty, now there were more people selling than buying. Our little pot was nearly full of cottage cheese and sour cream, it was time to go back. There was no bread for sale here; every housewife baked her own. They also didn't have any salt to sell, and it was for this we had risked going to the market. We walked among the carts, looking for fatback, which was always packed in coarse salt . . .

Soon my legs gave out, and my comrade, having left me with the pot at a cart loaded with hay, continued the search for salt or fatback.

Here, where hay was being traded, were very few people, and I didn't pay attention to my surroundings. I began to dip my fingers and to savor my sour cream. Engrossed in this, I didn't notice that someone had approached me on horseback until he demanded that I follow him. Similar riders darted in and out from all sides, checking the documents of the men here. Those who were detained were brought to the courtyard of the village hall. The majority of them were local men who had simply come to the market without their papers. It became clear from the conversation that this was a raid on the Tsaritsyn "commissars," who had scattered about the countryside in small station hamlets and villages.[1]

Me, in worn-out shoes, in cotton trousers, in a Cossack shirt that looked centuries old, they would scarcely take me for a "commissar." No one spoke with me. They fastidiously stood to the side or walked further away. I found room for myself in the full blaze of the sun, waiting in solitude for the interrogation. It was nice and warm. But I wasn't the only one who was warm. I saw how all about me, importantly, businesslike, strode the well-fed lice. Maybe they sensed it was the last day, they were hurrying to leave me in search of a new home, like rats from a sinking ship.

After questioning, the majority of those detained were quietly permitted to leave from the porch; they shook hands with their acquaintances and left by the gate. Occasionally someone was led out through the yard under lock and key.

Finally, from the porch they jabbed a whip in my direction— "Come here." I mentally prepared for the expected interrogation, trying not to forget the name of my mother, father, sister, brothers, and myself: I was Vasilii Petrovich Ivanov, of Moscow province and Moscow uezd, the village of Tushino, a mobilized hussar of the Thirty-eighth postal office . . .

At the door at attention stood two Cossacks; behind the table sat a clerk and a military man in epaulets. The answers I had memorized went in vain, for the officer asked me another question:

"Where did you come from?"

"From the typhus barracks," I answered, confused by the unexpected question.

"Twenty lashes." He spoke this tersely, glancing at me like I was infected with plague.

The Cossack ordered: "About face—march," catching me in the back with a blow of his whip. I left, climbed down from the porch, and headed for the lock-up. The Cossack again flicked me with his whip, directing me to the gate, and hissed without malice,

"Run quicker, you lousy son-of-a-bitch."

I was no fool, and I understood the command "run" had another meaning. I had no strength to run, I could scarcely move my legs, and I hobbled to the gate in the anticipation of another blow from behind. From time to time the Cossack continued to lash, but more often he hissed, "Quicker, quicker . . ." The first blow, under the officer's gaze, had left its trace on my back and a large quantity of typhus-lice in the chancellery. The next ones I didn't feel, but my pursuer with the whip "didn't know," if you please, how to count past ten . . .

Once I was beyond the reach of the whip I began to burn with shame.

"Thank God that none of my pals saw my disgrace. Thanks for not killing me, for 'ten,' and not 'twenty,'" but all the same I also thought:

"So, your black White-guard soul makes fun of your half-dead enemy!"

I swore bitterly at the unexpected ending. But now there was a new problem: how to find the melon field and how to make my way back to the barracks? My friends were already waiting a long time, but for the pot, not for me. I found the path through the field and carefully walked home, escaping the village as quickly as I could . . . I wandered a long way, the village could scarcely be seen, but the railway embankment was not getting any closer. Moving toward me were three figures on horseback. I had nowhere to hide, they would seize me and drag me back again. But they signaled their intention to give up the road, and they themselves went around me by the side of it. I asked how to get to the typhus barracks:

"Turn about back to the station, it is just over there."

Great! How could I "turn about" when I could hardly drag my legs along? The sun was already low on the horizon. The way back was more than a kilometer, I could not get there before dark. My legs gave way and my dry tongue begged for water.

I propped myself on the ground, in order to rest a little, and I tasted the sour cream. The top had crusted over and was covered with a gray dust, and I saw that one "little brute" was grazing there. It had probably been frightened by the whip and had fallen into the sour cream, the nasty scoundrel. I threw it out, wiped the cream off my finger, and at the same time decided to clean the remainder from my shirt. What happened after that is very hard for me to figure out.

I regained consciousness from this next onset of recurring typhus at night. I saw dark windows; from one side, through a glass door, shone a little bit of light. I remembered my dream, how I floundered in dry water, and I believed that something similar was happening now. I began to grope around for the little pot, the source of moisture, but all around me were unfamiliar objects. Sharply and clearly I remembered as if it had just happened how the fat louse crawled along the sour cream and how I had thrown off my shirt. Now I was in the middle of a fantasy. More by scent and by smell than by sight I could tell that I was lying on a clean bed, whose pillowcase smelled differently from the blanket cover; the towel at the head of the bed smelled like freshly ironed linen. I was dressed in clean underwear, at my feet was a soft dressing gown, my head and body were shaven. Nothing hurt, but my head and eyes were bandaged in thick strips of gauze. I couldn't believe that this was real, and not the delirium of my illness. Toward morning, when the patients began to wake up, I pretended to be asleep, and listened to the conversations.

I found out that I was lying among Cossacks and soldiers of the Volunteer Army. With my eyes closed, I agonizingly tried to understand how I had found myself in this marvelous cleanliness and among White Guardists. What would happen, if they discovered I was a "redtop?"[2]

Some nurses came in with thermometers and syringes. Having noticed that I had come to consciousness, they unfastened the cord with the metal nameplate, wrote down the surname Ivanov on their medical chart, and brought me to the dressing station. I found out that I was ill with post-typhus complications—inflammation of the cornea.

Now secretly at night I would pick at my eye to irritate it and to make it worse. I didn't want to get better. What would happen if they got me up again in lice-ridden rags? Just at the thought of this, my body again began to itch, and it seemed that lice were crawling on it once more. It was so nice and clean here.

I lay at the Tsaritsyn evacuation point, equipped by English charity with English medical supplies.[3] They had taken me from the medical train, with a surname, with only a number, but the nurse knew that I had been a prisoner. After a week of perfect bliss they announced that we were being prepared for evacuation. To where? At the stores they handed out a bundle with personal things: inside my trousers they had tucked a cap, old shoes, and a shirt. Trembling, ready to cry, I unwrapped the shirt—it had not been laundered, and after disinfecting it had become rigid, as if it had been starched. With loathing I shook out from it dried, brown grains—the shells of dead insects. The storekeeper laughed maliciously:

"You have produced quite a few critters. If they were alive, they would populate a large city . . ."

I was not the only one like that. Right next to me putting on their rags again were some dozens of prisoners, designated for evacuation. For our trip we were given so much food that we couldn't put it all in our pockets, and we didn't know what to take and what to leave. There was bread, English preserves, dried fish, sugar, and much besides. No one would say where we were going; we lay side by side in a freight car without bunks and ruminated. Night followed day, sometimes during long stops the doors would be opened and the guard would bring us a bucket of hot water. We would ask where we were going.

"To the sea, to drown the lousy lot of you . . ."

But now it was not us who were lice-ridden but he who fidgeted all the time and scratched. We were lightly dressed and we huddled together in a heap to keep out the cold. The closer we drew to the sea, the further south, the colder it became in the car. A cruel, cold wind blew through all the cracks, the doors of the car rattled from the wind as though being beaten. We sat for a long time inside the car wondering when the Novorossiisk northeaster would quiet down.[4]

When we arrived, the sick prisoners were sent to the infirmary for prisoners of war and the remainder were sent to a camp. The infirmary was located in the stone halls of a former barracks with high brick walls. My namesake—another Ivanov—inscribed the names of the patients. He described how nice it was for prisoners in the infirmary and how poor in the camp, from which prisoners were frequently summoned to the counterespionage section and then "written off the books," or shot. In the infirmary everyone was one of us, even the head physician was a prisoner. Only two people—the director, a wartime official named Lipskerov, and the chief clerk Frolov—were Whites.

I was ordered to go to the city to an ophthalmology specialist for eye treatment, and every other day I walked there together with Ivanov. These frequent strolls to the doctor brought us close together, we didn't have to hurry, and we spoke tête-à-tête about a great deal. I found out from him that the Whites were retreating, that the Reds had taken Tsaritsyn. Was this why we had been evacuated? If so, it would have been better to have remained where we were, because it would have been easier to find our way back to our own lines.

Denikin's army was also retreating south; Orel had long since been surrendered to the Reds. The Whites had won victories with the aid of their cavalry, but ever since Trotsky had said, "Proletarians, to horse!" we too fielded a cavalry, and ours beat the Cossacks all hollow. The Red cavalry had captured all the English tanks. The Whites were beating it along the whole front . . .

My mentor warned me not to discuss this news in the ward, because some of the patients, transferred from the camp, were spies of the commandant. The commandant was very dangerous: at the slightest provocation he would send a person to the spit.

"What is this spit?" I asked.

"Over there on the right, beyond the pier, a sandy spit sticks out into the sea—at night they shoot people there. There used to be thousands of prisoners in the camp, but now there are only hundreds. Some were sent to the spit, others to the Volunteer Army."

From the infirmary window one could see the wide expanse of the tranquil sea, the Novorossiisk bay and port. Across the bay could be seen the tall smokestacks of a cement factory.[5] Beyond them were mountains and a bright ribbon of the highway to Gelendzhik and Tuapse.[6] From that direction we heard the sound of artillery, we could see the smoke from the explosion of the shells—the Whites were bombarding the Greens who were hiding in the hills.

"Who are these Greens—the same group who captured me?"

"No, these are our Greens, they are against Denikin and all the Whites."

These conversations drew us closer, and we began to talk even more openly to one another. Nonetheless, I was silent about certain matters, about the fact that I hid under the name of Ivanov, that I was not Russian, but Latvian, that I was not a clerk, but a Communist political worker.

Ivanov was more trusting; he often stopped by the ward when he had no business there. Sometimes he would report the news from the papers—the medical aides had a map in their dormitory, and on it they would mark the progress of the Reds and the Whites. Sometimes he would bring some crude tobacco, and since smoking was prohibited in the ward, we would go into the janitor's room and chatter on without stop. I told him my fear that my eye was no longer discharging and that they would soon send me to the camp. Ivanov calmed me.

"Don't worry, we'll think of something. You've spent a long time in bed, you're very weak. The camp commandant will accept only able-bodied people or complete cripples."

When I first looked at myself in the mirror at the ophthalmologist, I saw my black beard had grown long. I had let it go on purpose, and it made me look much older. In the gray hospital ward my stooped figure looked like that of a starving, thin, bony Hindu. Looking like this, it would have been hard even for my mother to recognize me, not just my friends. Once in the janitor's room a patient had come to me and said, "Hey, uncle, let me have a smoke."

I looked at him and asked, "How old are you?"

"Twenty-seven!"

Well, I thought, if a nineteen-year-old fellow has become "uncle," it means I am really and truly Ivanov, and not Dune.

One time Ivanov stopped by late in the evening and we went to "have a smoke." There he said, "In the morning look at the bay. An English ship loaded with shells is going to dock at the cement plant. The Greens are near to there, very near. If the shells begin to explode, then it will be a bad lookout even for the infirmary—they will put us to a complete rout."

He said all this smiling, completely without a sense of warning. There was something odd, however, in his secretive manner, but he said nothing more.

In the morning I looked out in the direction of the cement factory and saw the black steamer standing there, but I didn't notice anything special. A lifting crane worked rhythmically, continuously: "lift—heave-ho, heave-ho, lift," that was all. Evidently Ivanov had been talking rubbish, turning his wishes and hopes into something else.

The morning passed, the doctor had already made his rounds, and I had stopped paying attention to the bay when an agitated Ivanov ran into the ward, loudly crying: "The steamship is on fire!"

The patients swarmed around the windowsill.

The steamship was too far away from us for us to see what was happening, except that it was surrounded by a huge mass of black smoke. On the shore everything looked deserted now, but on the bay there was animated movement of tugboats and other ships heading out to sea. Finally even the burning steamer was pulled out into the sea. It remained there far on the roadstead, we could see a dome of black smoke, but we heard nothing like an explosion. Maybe they had put the fire out.

Ivanov and I gleefully exchanged glances, but the rest of the ward tensely watched the ship, and someone asserted: "It serves her right, that English ship."

When I found a moment to talk, I asked Ivanov about the details.

"We shall see what we shall see! I only said that the Greens were close to the cement factory . . ."

Soon after this event Ivanov suggested that I help him with the patients, recording the discharge of those who left and the names of those who had died. This work reacquainted me with the doctors and with all the service personnel. They all tried cheerfully to help me, and also to help me improve my appearance. I had to shave and become younger. I threw off my prisoner's uniform and was allowed to choose from the storehouse among the things belonging to those who had died.

Among miscellaneous rubbish lay quite acceptable items of military uniforms. From these riches I chose for myself some soldiers' boots, wide trousers of crummy coarse canvas, a bedraggled cap, and a jacket with elbow-length sleeves. Ivanov was amazed to see me in such clothes, when the storehouse contained soldiers' blouses and pants of my own size, of good quality. I had to explain to him that after the business with the steamship I had gotten into my head the persistent idea that I would join the Greens and that this would be easier to do in civilian clothes than in a Red Army outfit.

He reacted sympathetically to my plan for the future, but advised me not to hurry. Perhaps someone would come, we would select a knowledgeable guide, to go in a bunch would be safer. I visited the city doctor now less often, only once a week, and now I was accompanied not by Ivanov but by Krasotkin—the store-keeper of the infirmary. I could tell from his first words that he knew about my plan to take myself off to the hills.

Krasotkin had been taken prisoner in 1918, after the rout of the Second Caucasian Army.[7] He had survived mass shootings of pris-oners; he himself was maimed during some sort of excesses taken with prisoners. His fingers had been cut off, he was wounded in the forearm, and one hand no longer functioned. He burned with hatred for the Denikin forces and with faith in the justice of our cause and in our victory. He created a fascinating impression: he inspired a warm faith in his political honesty and in his refusal to compromise. He was quite ignorant about what was happening in soviet Russia; he asked about factories without their old bosses, how the division of private estates was coming along. There was much that he didn't want to believe. He wouldn't believe that Moscow and Petrograd had to survive on an eighth of a pound of oatmeal bread, that factories were freezing without fuel; did we have too few forests to compensate for the loss of the coal mines? He rejoiced in the success of the Red Army, but disapproved of the "old-regime" arrangements for the recruitment of former officers into the Red Army: "they will betray us and run to their own kind . . ." I was about to confide in him my true identity, but just then I heard an allegation very strange to my ears:

"The Bolsheviks—that's our regime, but now the Communist-intellectuals are interfering with the worker-Bolsheviks."

I tried to tell him about the party congress, about the change in the party's name from Russian Social-Democratic Workers' party

(Bolshevik) to Russian Communist party (Bolshevik), but he had another explanation for this change.[8] He said that the party was divided into two fractions: Bolsheviks and Communists. The latter had received the majority of votes at the congress and had changed the name of the party to the name of their fraction. He spoke of this with assurance so authoritatively that he "plugged up" my candor.

He advised me not to go to the hills: willing fighters were needed in the city too. And to go over to the Greens was not so simple: behind the cement factory was an entire front, with trenches, pickets, and White listening posts guarding the city. Many people wanted to go to the hills, but there was nothing to do there without weapons. We should wait and go when everything was prepared.

Chapter Ten

The prospects for the White Army by the start of 1920 were bleak but not hopeless. Denikin had withdrawn his army in good order from the Cossack capital, Rostov, and now again gained Cossack support in the effort to liberate their territory from the advancing Reds. In the Don, Denikin was close to railway links and sources of supply, but he was unable to mobilize the Kuban Cossacks to rejoin the struggle. The Whites briefly retook Rostov in March 1920 but were driven out by Budennyi's cavalry. A few days later, Budennyi seized the crucial railway junction at Tikhoretskaia, and the escape route to the Crimea was blocked for the White armies in the Kuban. Their goal became to evacuate troops and material through the Black Sea port of Novorossiisk.

Adding to the Whites' troubles, new partisan bands began to appear all over the northern Caucasus. Calling themselves Greens, these groups united opponents of both Reds and Whites, former Red Army prisoners, and draft-evading Cossacks. Operating under shaky Socialist-Revolutionary leadership, the Greens inflicted serious damage on the retreating Whites and managed to convince many of them to switch sides. The insurgents captured the town of Tuapse to the south of Novorossiisk before internal divisions—between Bolsheviks and others—caused the movement to fragment and dissolve.

Tens of thousands of fugitives made for Novorossiisk in the early months of 1920. The White armies retreated with whatever semblance of order they could muster. Their ranks were swollen by numerous other refugees from battle, disease, and soviet power, including entire Cossack villages, anti-Bolshevik Russians, land owners, politicians, and others who had aided the Whites. All waited in crowded Novorossiisk for a ship to take them to the Crimea or beyond. But there were not enough ships nor coal to fuel the ships that reached the port. Civilians, Cossacks, and White Army soldiers all fought one another for the precious space on board, and there was no room left for military equipment, horses, or for many people. The final ships left the harbor on 26 March 1920, with Denikin and his staff the last to leave. The Bolsheviks entered Novorossiisk that evening, capturing twenty-two thousand soldiers and huge stores of munitions and supplies.

In the Novorossiisk Underground

Soon after this conversation they transferred me to the dormitory of the hospital orderlies, which also accommodated Ivanov, Krasotkin, Shaforostov, the orderly of the chief physician Bondarenko, and five other people besides. We felt ourselves completely at home here. Outside the White Army was retreating toward Rostov and fierce fighting was taking place. It seemed at times that the Red Army would retreat again, but the next day we would expect its arrival. As prisoners, we were powerless to help them.

But we could give a great deal of help to the partisans, the Greens, who fought close by. We could supply them with medicines and bandages from the infirmary; later we would learn how to obtain weapons. At the time of my move to the dormitory we had a different assignment.

The infirmary grounds, surrounded by rectangular brick walls, had a sign at the entry gate "Infirmary of Prisoners of War No. 1," but in December 1919 it primarily housed sick soldiers from the Volunteer Army. In step with the retreat to the south, the Whites also transferred to Novorossiisk many other infirmaries, which were overflowing with the wounded, with typhus cases, and with other patients from the evacuated civilian population. At first we took in only soldiers with typhus, then one ward was designated for officers. At one point we were sent a party of sick women, whom we refused to take because of our lack of female service personnel. Earlier, when only prisoners came, the storeroom was empty. Now it was overflowing with the baggage of the patients. These things were of varying value, but most important for us was every conceivable kind of personal document. Not only service lists passed through our hands but all the military documents of the sick soldiers and officers of the Volunteer Army. Krasotkin told us to collect these soldiers' booklets, marching orders, discharge papers, certificates, passports, and birth certificates. This was easy if the patient died, but even if he recovered, we could appropriate his documents without risk: how would a sick man remember when and where he lost his documents? When I signed in the patients, I also made a list of their possessions that I carried to the storeroom and their value. I was always the first to be informed of the death of a patient, and then it was my duty to go and collect these documents. There were days when I had dozens of possible papers to choose from. In the evenings we would treat the documents with manganese peroxide and would bleach them with lemon juice—the official signatures and stamps would remain untouched.

At first, due to inexperience, the production of my "passport bureau" was not distinguished by great merit. The paper was warped, the cleaned-up part looked different from the spots untouched by the manganese peroxide. Later I learned how to dampen the entire paper, to dry it with a warm iron over a piece of cloth, and soon no one could complain about the quality of my documents.

I had no understanding of the scale of underground work in Novorossiisk at the end of 1919 and the beginning of 1920, but judging by the output of our workshop, our documents alone must have supplied many hundreds of people. There were evenings when the entire room worked as if on an assembly line: someone sorted the documents, someone else burned the ones we didn't need, someone only applied the water, and the next person the manganese peroxide, and so forth, on up to the final drying with the warm iron. On one such day, Krasotkin had brought in a large sack full of documents—the archive of a military chief or commandant of a railway station.

The night before we had been busy with other work. The head physician's orderly had obtained a little vial of cocaine. We mixed its contents half and half with aspirin or piramidon—in order to return the vial to its former appearance. So we retained half of the original amount. In order to "increase" its quantity as much as possible, we divided the powder into packets, like in a pharmacy. We managed to end up with almost one hundred cocaine powders. In exchange for this cocaine, Krasotkin received the bag with the aforementioned documents.

The destination Krasotkin chose for these doctored documents none of us knew nor were interested in, since we already trusted his ideological purity. I was sure that the recipients were our Bolshevik organization, and if Krasotkin chose to distinguish Communists from Bolsheviks, then this was only from ignorance about what was happening on the other side of the front. One day he told us about a meeting with representatives of the Red Army, who had approached the town quite recently, and about news of the soviets. Krasotkin's free movement from the city was made possible because as a storekeeper he had a permanent pass and didn't need a military pass. Going out in his two-wheeled cart for food supplies or medicines, he could meet with whomever he liked, without fear of surveillance.

As for us, our work "in the underground" did not seem especially romantic. We had read in the journal *The Past* about the lives of revolutionaries in the tsarist underground, and our imaginations embellished our dreary reality.[1] At first it was interesting to forge papers and to pass them on to a secret, unknown person, but the work eventually became routine and seemed like simple drudge work. This was not work for a revolutionary: any cook could do it. We became dissatisfied with this kitchen work; we all wanted to engage in "real" revolutionary activity. We wanted to join up with the Greens as soon as possible and to fight the enemy directly, with guns in our hands. Krasotkin tried to quiet our burning passion by telling us how our documents helped this or that Green to live in the city and how representatives of the city organization were able to use our documents to escape to the hills. He left a great deal unexplained, but we could see that he wasn't just telling us fairy tales.

One time we admitted a White Guard who was not ill but had been wounded fighting the Greens. His arm in a sling, he wandered everywhere, like a bloodhound. This suspicious behavior did not inspire our sympathy. He began to drop in even on Quartermaster-Sergeant Shaforostov, and he started to come by our dormitory and chat informally with Krasotkin. I told the latter about my unhappiness with his friendship with a White Guard, warning him that this guard was roaming everywhere, speaking to everyone, and trying to gain people's confidence. He obviously had an ulterior motive. Krasotkin heard me out in disbelief, but he didn't interrupt. Then he said: "Check his documents tomorrow. If you don't find anything suspicious, bring them to me, and then we'll talk."

The next day I looked at the guard's personal documents: a soldier's book, an old military pass with the signatures of a company commander and a medical aide, assigning him to an infirmary. There was nothing else to find. When he had a spare moment, Krasotkin spoke to me. He took the soldier's book, looked it over, and remarked with amusement: "Look carefully, read the surname."

I read and I looked carefully, but I didn't see anything funny. Then he said:

"This is the very identity card that you yourself cleaned of the owner's name, and now you don't recognize your own handiwork! Look at his fingers, at the blue color under his nails: that's from counterespionage. He was grilled with needles under his nails. He is a sailor from the Black Sea fleet. They shot him on the pier instead of the spit, and he managed to fall down in time. The bullet only grazed him in the water. He still had his right arm, and he knew how to dive and swim in the dark. It would have been dangerous to hide in the city, so he came here to the infirmary . . . Now, does it seem to you, that our 'kitchen' is so useless and unnecessary . . . ?"

I blushed from embarrassment, not because of the reprimand but because I had taken the fellow for a White Guard. Krasotkin insisted that no one should know of our conversation, not even the wounded sailor. He believed that Krasotkin alone knew the truth. This sailor thus stayed with us, his arm always in a sling, until the day the Red Army entered Novorossiisk.

After this embarrassment I began to look differently upon our work. I looked for a hidden meaning in every word, I saw revolutionary action in every departure by Krasotkin for food supplies. I used to believe that our watching the spit reflected an unhealthy curiosity since we had no influence over actions there. What did it matter to us what was going on there, I thought earlier, whether someone was walking about, whether they were still digging "trenches"—graves for the nighttime shootings—or whether they had already stopped. Our watching made things neither better nor worse for the victims of the executions. Later, when our organization began to engage in struggle with the counterspies, I began to understand that even our watching had had its logic and significance. The organization could find out the schedule of shootings from these preparatory operations, and it could prepare for the escape of those arrested.

In close contact with comrades, each individual's job became common property, notwithstanding the fact that according to the rules of "conspiracy" no one should know about anything that did not concern one directly. Krasotkin instructed us in "conspiracy" with his words, but in his deeds he didn't always practice what he preached. He completely trusted in each of us—and up until that time none of us had fallen into the hands of the counterespionage. Even the strongest person might not be able to withstand the tortures of the counterspies, might blurt out our secrets and thus kill us all.

"We are working and sleeping peacefully now," said Krasotkin, "but if they arrest me, I advise all of you to anticipate arrest too."

We began to take special precautions toward the possibility of a nighttime visit or raid. At night the gate was locked, and the guards were supposed to come to Krasotkin for the key; we took out several bricks in the walls bordering on two alleys, making in this way a kind of ladder, in order to climb out more quickly. Half of us were to run to one side, half of us to the other. There were nights when we slept in our clothes, and those on duty stayed up all night, watching the street. On those days our room was clean, without a single paper, newspaper, or book. Everything was hidden in the storeroom among the personal property of the patients. If rumors led those in the city to expect a mass search, so did we.

Once Krasotkin advised us:

"Tonight after midnight don't sleep. Don't put out the light, and watch the street. If everything is okay, I'll go to the city for news. I don't know exactly what, but something is supposed to happen tonight."

Toward morning, when usually there was no movement in the city, we heard the clatter of hooves of many riders, tearing along somewhere at a quick pace, and the sound of automobiles; then all was quiet.

Krasotkin returned from the city in joyous excitement and briefly told us what he had heard: during the night three hundred prisoners had escaped from the jail. Later we found out more details.

At the usual hour for taking prisoners out of jail to be shot, a military unit, with two officers, approached the prison. They presented a "genuine" document from counterespionage to release twenty named prisoners. Part of the unit entered the prison yard, the rest remained outside. The prisoners on the list assembled in the building and walked out into the yard. Realizing the prison administrators had accepted the original order without suspicion, the "counterespionage" officer spontaneously decided that he could liberate not just these twenty but all the prisoners. His troops captured and locked up the guards in the prison building, they noiselessly seized the sentries and replaced them with their own soldiers. All of this occurred without any shooting and without any casualties. The danger increased, though, when three hundred liberated prisoners gathered in the yard. They were all exultant, but they were also confused. Their liberation had come totally unexpectedly: many were reluctant to go, and they had to be persuaded. A few simply refused to escape.

We had prepared documents and passes for the escape of twenty men; the remainder had to risk an escape with nothing. They would have to pass through the streets, avoiding police and night patrols. A small group was released from the prison gate and directed to go toward the wine-growing estate of Abrau-Diurso. This was on the opposite side of the city from the cement plant, where the Greens were now engaged. Beyond the city limits, where other Green units were in control, the prisoners would find protection, and the great majority of the escapees managed to be saved. A few men who hadn't paid attention ran home to see their families and to change clothes—the Whites soon fished them out.

This great success in liberating the political prison inspired us to work more actively. Our work was further facilitated by the simultaneous retreat of the White Army and the concentration in Novorossiisk of masses of evacuees who had dragged themselves as far as they could go.

When the White Army, poised in Orel, could hear the sound of all the church bells in holy Moscow, their mood was probably the same as ours was now. But now pushed back to the edge of the sea, this army had lost its moral firmness and its faith in victory. Soldiers combined their unhappiness with the commanders who had brought them to this defeat with attempts to compromise with the victors. With their political capital lost, only those who still held capital in pounds, dollars, and jewels believed they could evacuate a million soldiers and continue to fight. The remainder were dubious and sought to save themselves here. This demoralization opened up the hidden animosities between Don Cossacks and Kuban Cossacks, between draftees and volunteers. Lying in the infirmary mixed up with the prisoners, they openly berated their officers, they recalled how after plundering the local population they had to "divide the spoils" not equally but according to rank. They remembered taunting their prisoners and their expectation of the same fate. They had felt themselves prisoners already long before their evacuation, and now they tried to insinuate themselves as much as they could with the prisoners lying next to them.

"You know, we were drafted, we didn't serve the generals of our own will."

Some of these men were aware that they were mentally betraying everything they had stood for yesterday, but others, through their inability to think things out, expressed themselves completely candidly:

"I'd rather go to any damned place or join with the Greens as long as I didn't have to fall into the hands of the Reds."

I don't know what they were saying in the officers' ward. When I appeared there, all conversation would cease. It wasn't the same as before, when my arrival didn't inhibit them from telling bawdy tales about their intimate past. Apparently now their conversation concerned such burning themes that it wasn't proper for a prisoner to hear it. I assumed that outside the infirmary conversations were even more open, but when Krasotkin reported that he was sending a whole regiment of the Volunteer Army to the Greens and to Abrau-Diurso, we regarded him skeptically:

"Liar!"

"You don't believe it? I will bring them past the infirmary—I personally will ride ahead in a cart . . ."

On the appointed day we heard the sounds of a military march, and we saw soldiers and officers marching smartly in step.

Krasotkin rode in front. He greeted us and then dismounted at the gate of the infirmary, but the "regiment" of the Volunteer Army turned there and followed the cart further. When he returned to us, he told us that for some reason he had managed to hand over only one battalion to the Greens but one with the regimental band. For us he had brought a gift from the Greens—a barrel of white wine.

Until now, everything Krasotkin had told us seemed to us a bluff, and an invention, and we could not believe him until we had seen with our own eyes. We figured it was easier to liberate the prisoners from the political prison, because they faced execution, than to win over a White military unit to the side of the Greens. What we failed to realize was that this was not the same army that had planned to worship in the Kremlin, in that holy shrine of Russia, but an army of men seeking only to save themselves. We understood why you could buy the whole archive of the Volunteer Army in exchange for cocaine: a drug addict doesn't give a damn. Now we realized there was another commodity that was even more valuable than cocaine: the opportunity to join the Greens. This was an opportunity that some officers decided to seize. To prove their good faith, they promised to supply weapons and ammunition, and in this recent case and others, they persuaded their friends and their soldiers to cross over too.

The city underground committee must have been short of manpower if they needed Krasotkin—a prisoner—to run so many errands. The rest of us could get to the city only with a leave pass, and because we were prisoners, we were not supposed to have contact with the city even for conspiratorial reasons. But now that the morale of the enemy was so low, we could find agents among them and protect ourselves and our committee from unnecessary risks.

In this way agents from the White Army carried out our mission of blowing up the Tunnel station, about thirty kilometers from Novorossiisk. They furnished the explosives and undermined the tunnel itself; this service earned them the right to join the Greens. By the beginning of 1920, the Green units had plenty of guns and ammunition. We had long since stopped stealing bandages and medicines from the infirmary; these were dispatched directly from the stores of the Volunteer Army. The joke went around that a certain colonel, negotiating with an emissary from the city, offered on his own initiative to put a machine gun wherever they liked.

As for our "White" chief Lipskerov, nothing depressed him. He walked about as usual, with a wide smile, and he continued to put on weight. The chief clerk Frolov, a man who was irritable by nature, continued to grumble, snuffling through his nose, exploding at the "redtops" even louder than before. But neither one prepared to evacuate. When some Kornilov units arrived in the city, Lipskerov gave us advice on what kind of measures to take if the troops tried to massacre prisoners. The guard was given strict orders; do not admit anyone to the infirmary; keep the gate bolted even in the daytime; and at the first sign of hostile Volunteer soldiers give a prearranged signal. Lipskerov spoke with the sick officers in a similar vein, warning them they could be liable for excesses with the prisoners. To minimize our danger, the sign over the prisoners' infirmary was taken down and in its place we put up a new, brightly painted one: Military Infirmary No. 1.

My work also brought me into contact with Lipskerov: besides registering the sick entrants I also had to keep accounts of the infirmary's military rations. There was nothing complicated in recording the daily arrival and consumption of food supplies. At the end of the month I had to convert ounces to pounds and to check the expenditures against the number of mouths that were fed. However, since my results never tallied with the available reserves of the quartermaster-sergeant, Lipskerov would help me to "make ends meet." I continued as earlier to record everything and to painstakingly work out the results, but Krasotkin only laughed at me: "Never mind, just tell me, I'll bring you whatever you need."

He told me that the warehouses of the quartermaster were overflowing, they handed out everything that was requested without any caviling or checking the number of mouths to feed. There was so much in storage that food supplies were lying under the open sky, and still the English continued to send more in ship after ship. Now that the White Army had their backs to the sea, the English had begun to supply all that had been promised when the army had stood near Moscow. The prisoners' infirmary now enjoyed bed linens and other English hospital linen. In our storeroom lay trunks packed with English food products, including cocoa and dried vegetables. There was more than our cook could cope with. Before discharge, the patients received new English outfits, several pairs of underwear, socks, and excellent boots with leather gaiters. We also outfitted the prisoners in such clothing. But I still preferred my civilian uniform.

By February 1920 the city was overflowing with carts loaded with the property of evacuees, and there was nowhere to put it. Sticking out of the carts were office tables and chairs, wardrobes, and glass cupboards from Rostov and Ekaterinodar. All this seemed absurd: columns of refugees marched along the street on foot, but some cart would be dragging along a useless cupboard. We could see from the window of the infirmary that the entire shore was overloaded with all manner of bag and baggage; day and night the carts hung around, awaiting their turn. And the arriving ships also unloaded as before, leaving empty from the port.

I knew Novorossiisk only as far as the route to the doctor. I wanted to see what was happening in the center and in the bazaar, where there must have been a Babylonian babble. These days every one of us could freely receive a pass—a military document over the signature of Frolov. Earlier when I asked for one he plied me with questions: why, for what purpose? Now he just mumbled something at me and slapped the necessary paper toward me on the table.

I avoided the large and bustling streets, crowded with soldiers, and made my way through back alleys, keeping to myself. I walked along, looking in fascination at the small shops selling goods I had never seen before, such as oysters and olives. I looked at the buyers and sellers, Armenians and Greeks without "Greek" noses. My unprepossessing appearance did not attract any notice, even from the shopkeepers calling for customers. Thus, quietly, I rambled, looking around at this unfamiliar world, until I nearly stumbled into a spit-and-polished officer. I forgot the oysters and olives, and my attention became riveted on this person. I didn't want to pass him; he could suddenly ask for documents and I had only my leave pass. They could still drag me off to counterespionage! I saw that he was in no hurry. He would stop here and there and begin a lively conversation with a shopkeeper, who would look at something held out in the officer's hand. The officer glanced back at me from time to time as if he were waiting for me. To turn back now would attract suspicion—that would be worse. So I decided to walk straight on, while he was talking with the next shopkeeper. Passing him, I noticed that he was showing the proprietor some bracelets and gold rings. I heard him say: "I'll give you gold for pounds or dollars."

The explanation was now quite simple: the officer feared my suspicious demeanor, skulking along as if following him . . .

There were more soldier-sellers in the bazaar than buyers. Sometimes uniformed officers would appear, but the soldiers didn't pay any attention and they didn't salute: brother of mine, they said, we are occupied in the same business, peddling "military trophies."

Bearded Cossacks and soldiers traded from army carts overloaded with these "trophies," which no one wanted to buy. Some peasant woman made off with a mangy sheepskin coat, but the sellers just argued among themselves: they were hurrying for nothing, trading for nothing, perhaps they should charge two times more. They had a whole wagon of all kinds of goods, but the buyers looked through their wares and then left: not suitable. The contents of somebody's great-grandmother's trunk was piled on the cart: all jumbled together were lace, kerchiefs of different colors, a gray and crimson rotted-through silk, meter-long corsets, ladies' cloth dancing slippers covered with silver and gold, hats, and fans.

I glanced once again at the embankment, which looked now like a Gypsy camp, and then I began to return to my prison with a purposeful step. I passed a military man without his epaulets in one of the alleys, on his head was a tall fur army hat with a black badge: a skull and crossbones . . .

I had enough willpower to walk past, but not enough not to turn around and look. At that moment he made the same turn of his head.

It was the familiar dear face of Gengut, which I last remembered covered with blood. I had lost him long ago at the "Cooperative." Could this be him—in the uniform of a White cavalryman?!

I stood dumbfounded, not knowing what to think or what to do, but he was already approaching me with joyously startled eyes:

"Is it . . . you?"

"You're alive, Chibisov?"

"And I thought they buried you long ago already in Serebriako-vo . . ."

It is difficult to convey in words the joy I felt in meeting this man, at whom I had one time paid no attention but who now seemed to me like a blood relation. We had been brought together by the commonality of the past and by the blood of our fallen friends.

When the Volunteer Army created a regiment from among prisoners, he told me, he, as a medical student, was assigned to an infirmary as a medical orderly. None of the doctors there liked his frail and puny figure, nor his intelligence, which was inappropriate in an orderly. The nurses began to whisper: "Yid." He decided in a timely way to enlist as a volunteer in the cavalry division of General Shkuro.[2] For two months they taught him how to tame his horse, to feed it, to ride in the saddle and wave his saber. Now, before being sent to the front, he had received a pass to walk about and take a look at Novorossiisk.

There was so much we wanted to say to each other before we had to part and lose each other again, but the expiration time of his pass was approaching, and we had to hurry. We vowed to memorize each others' addresses and promised that whoever remained alive would take the news to the other's relatives.

I returned to the infirmary, as if drunk from a happiness that no one else could understand and that I couldn't share with anyone. Agitated by this unexpected meeting and by these intensely personal feelings, for some time I became very indifferent to the events around me.

The end of the Volunteer Army was approaching. Steamships sailed away loaded with evacuated people and evacuated property, but many thousands continued to wait their turn on the embankment. Evidently this scenario had exasperated someone; we couldn't hear a word, but from the gestures and the movement along the embankment we concluded a "revolution" had broken out. The steamers were heading away from the battle, bales of bag and baggage were thrown from the deck of a ship. Evidently the deck had been closely packed with people; now some horse or other had found himself a place in this crowd, but then it threw itself overboard and was swimming in the gulf. We tried to guess from our observation point whether the horse had drowned or not, and concluded that there had been a disturbance or rebellion on the ship: there weren't enough places for people fearing for their lives, and at such a time some people were concerned only with finding space for their material wealth.

The last steamer sailed away, and the bay was still. A military squadron floated far out in the sea, but on the embankment as usual there was a crowd of people. We poured out into the city, hoping that the Whites had left and that our side had finally come, but around the city armed soldiers marched as before, hurrying along. Military shells from faraway warships flew by with howls and squeals, but there was no sign of the Reds.

The streets leading up to the embankment were piled high with various sorts of things, and it was hard to tell which there was more of: cupboards and tables or bundles and suitcases. All of this lay about apparently without owners, and for the time being no one paid the least attention to these abandoned riches.

On the next day we saw the same pile of goods, but all of it was now turned upside down, the suitcases opened, the contents strewn about. No one was interested in what was left; hundreds of people scurried about the freight pier, hauling away goods more valuable than the contents of suitcases: cases of English food products. Enterprising merchants obeyed the "law" not to loot, but stood at their doorways, inviting those who entered to "sell" them this or that.

The harbor, which yesterday was deserted, was now covered with many little boats, from which people with boat hooks groped about in the depths: they were hoping to snare something. Others stood on the shore, directing the boaters in their searches . . . Apparently someone had pulled out a suitcase with coins and jewels from the baggage discarded by the mutinying Cossacks. Now these people hoped that the water would yield up still more of this treasure.

Such were the impressions that were imprinted in my memory of the evacuation of the White Army.[3]

We met the Red Army all reoutfitted in new English clothes: the sick Volunteer soldiers, including the hoarding Cossacks, tried to throw off everything military and dress themselves anew. A crowd of Red Army "Budennyi men," cavalry, stopped by the infirmary, looking for horses and for their friends among the prisoners.[4] They were good-natured, and in the thrill of victory they related "heroic" battle episodes. They treated their new prisoners leniently, without hostility: our fight is with the generals and not with you . . . The White soldiers claimed that they had been fooled by the "generals" and they openly and maliciously berated their officers: each one tried to say something specific against them. They remembered that officers were lying here in the infirmary and led the Budennyi men to the officers' ward. In one of the beds they "recognized" a general. We ran to the execution point but were already too late. This was the first and last victim of the first day of the Red Army's capture of the city.

It is possible that some younger "generals," like Shkuro, were indeed hidden among the officers, but I doubt it: the officers were young, not older than thirty-five or forty years. More likely this denunciation was an attempt by some of the Cossacks to do a favor for the new regime and to buy themselves a pardon from death by strangers.

Chapter Eleven

By the start of 1920 the military outcome of the civil war looked fairly certain to favor the Bolsheviks. The Whites were in retreat. A sizeable Volunteer Army force of thirty-five to forty thousand troops had regrouped on the Crimean Peninsula, but there was little possibility that they could use this as a base for an assault on the mainland in the near future. The Whites' best hope was to wait out the Bolshevik regime in hopes of its internal collapse.

The main front was in the west, on the border with Poland. In Poland a military regime led by Josef Pilsudski was attempting to consolidate the newly independent Polish state. Formerly divided among the Russian, Austrian, and German empires, Poland had been economically devastated as one of the main theaters of World War I. The Bolshevik government sought to conclude a peace treaty with the Poles in order to free troops for the final defeat of the Volunteers, but Pilsudski refused to negotiate. In April 1920 the Polish army suddenly attacked the weak Red defenses. Pilsudski's goal was to detach from Russia all the non-Russian territories of the former empire. The Baltic states of Finland, Estonia, Latvia, and Lithuania had already achieved independence. Now the Poles drove into the Ukraine to liberate it as well. Facing little resistance, the Poles occupied Kiev on 6 May 1920.

A new military mobilization was announced inside soviet Rus-

sia, and nationalist as well as class sentiment was tapped to drive out the "Polish lords" from soviet soil. The tide turned by July, and the Red armies began to drive the Poles back, both in the northern districts of Belorussia and in the Ukraine. By August it appeared that the Red forces could turn the defensive war into a revolutionary offensive and carry the socialist revolution to Warsaw itself, in the heart of ethnic Poland, until a decisive Polish counterattack eliminated this possibility. Both sides agreed to negotiate terms of peace in the neutral city of Riga, and the Polish war ended with recognition of the independence of Poland.

With the Polish threat ended, the Reds turned again to the Whites, ensconced in the Crimea. Weakened by desertions and unreliable troops, the Whites could not resist a Red Army assault across the isthmus of Perekop, and the last White armies retreated again. By every means of water transport, the remaining 145,000 troops and family members escaped from their last Russian outpost and dispersed first to Constantinople and then to lives of exile in Europe and America.

Vastly overshadowed by the dramas in Poland and Crimea, Red Army troops continued to consolidate their victories in the territories under their control. The Kuban still stood as a potential base for a White revival, and General Wrangel, the new White commander, hoped to launch an invasion of the Kuban to unite the forces of the two territories. The Kuban seemed promising enough in 1920: the population welcomed the Red Army as a bringer of peace, but as so often happened in the civil war they turned against the regime when peace was followed by soviet requisitioning teams who seized local grain for the distant cities. A new guerrilla army of fifteen to thirty thousand Cossack partisans formed under the leadership of White general Fostikov. General Wrangel landed a couple of parties of soldiers in advance of a broader invasion, and these units caused serious worry to the Red

Ninth Army, occupying a large and unfriendly territory with only twenty-four thousand battle-weary troops. The invasion suffered from a lack of coordination on the side of the Whites, and the Red Army threw in reinforcements against this new danger. By early October 1920 the last of the White armies escaped once and for all from the Kuban territory, some retreating into independent Georgia, others leaving by sea to join the emigration.

On
My Own
Again

I hurried to leave Novorossiisk as soon as possible. I lost all interest in my prison mates and hurried to see those who were closer to me in spirit than Gengut and Krasotkin.

At the beginning of April I found the headquarters of the Fourteenth Infantry Division in Ekaterinodar. Wherever I turned, whomever I asked, nobody knew anything about my friends; they were as completely foreign as in any other part of the Red Army. I heard the name of L. Aronshtam, a brigade commissar whom I barely knew; now he was military commissar of the division. I learned from him that Stepin had died from typhus while serving as commander of the Ninth Army, that Evald had left and nobody had heard a word about him. No matter who I asked about, the answer was always the same: he had fallen ill, he had died. Rarely was anyone reported killed or injured. As for Chugunov, whom I knew to be killed, he knew only that he had disappeared during the retreat. Aronshtam said the same about other workers in headquarters and in the division. I told him of how his younger brother died, but he seemed no more interested in this than in the deaths of any of the others. He asked me two or three petty questions, as if asking about a stranger. My joy at meeting with my sole acquaintance was immediately extinguished.

Why be interested in the past anyway, when ahead of us lay so many new perspectives and plans, so many concerns and joys! In every battalion now there were as many Communists as used to be found in a whole regiment. The political section of the division grew into a huge institution with dozens of organizers, agitators, and instructors. We published our own newspaper, we had our own printing press. The newspaper was printed on paper seized as spoils: sometimes on newsprint, sometimes on yellow wrapping paper. We no longer had to wait two or three months for the Moscow papers to arrive. We had well-tuned permanent contact with combat units and with suppliers of "literature" and other agitational material. Earlier the political section had to seek out Communists in the individual units; now the Communists sought out the political section.

After the war, entry into the Communist party was limited, they did not take just anybody. Besides filling out questionnaires, candidates had to show how well they had mastered the basic principles of soviet policies. We were no longer talking about illiteracy. For illiterates or those who could barely read we organized schools in the regiments with a corps of teachers. And not only the poorly literate studied but also former officers—they had to pass through an examination board, which determined their acceptability for this or that post.

The appearance of the Red Army had changed as well. I encountered regiments fully reoutfitted in uniforms of English origin; the only thing that remained was the Russian greatcoat, which the soldiers did not want to part with: rain would not penetrate it, in the winter it was warm, and at night it was a good blanket. The Red Army stores were filled with English underwear, wool socks, and mittens. The divisional section for supply was overflowing with trophies of war, which nobody needed now in summer: fur-and-leather sleeveless jackets, warm wool underwear, pullovers, and bed linen. It seemed that this could last for many years. We felt a shortage in only one respect: we had barely enough writing paper in the division, only enough for the most important correspondence of the division HQ. All other needs were satisfied by "self-supply."

All intradivisional bookkeeping, and the correspondence of companies and battalions with regimental HQ, of regiments with brigade HQ, and of brigades with division HQ were done on "trophy" paper. The political section organized *subbotniki* to distribute confiscated archives.[1] These distributions went to all units: we picked out sheets with a clean reverse side and cut out an eighth of the sheet without writing. Who would be interested now in the records of Denikin's army after its liquidation? The most valuable historical material was destroyed in this way, burned up after using some part or other of the paper for our current needs. We dreamed about the future, not about the past.

In another departure from past practice the Red Army now included volunteers from among the Don and Kuban Cossacks. We had sent our prisoners back to their homes, but some of them—either because they had seen the light or feared to go home where people knew about their past involvement with the Whites—demanded to be allowed to serve in the Red Army.

There were even more volunteer Cossacks among the cavalry—the "Budennyi men." These included many smallholders; they were recruited along with their horses or were given a horse if they did not have one. The new Budennyi men tried to expunge their guilt for their previous service in the White Army. The "whiter" their soul, the redder they now wanted to become. Just as in 1917 when householders demonstrated their revolutionary zeal by the size of their red ribbons, so now the Cossacks hunted for red shirts, red trousers, or flat fur Kuban hats with red on top. The color of the goods, rather than the quality, determined their value. At meetings, political lessons, or rallies there were none who listened more attentively, or tried harder to understand this world so new to them, than our enemies of yesterday.

Some members of Denikin's army, having failed to be evacuated to the Crimea, preferred to sit out the conflict in small units of Greens along the flats of the Kuban River. These Green detachments represented no danger to our division; only in case of a landing by Wrangel's army were they a potential threat to us.[2] They did not challenge local authorities, and they treated us as friends rather than enemies. Often enough the village soviets claimed neutrality, fearing reprisals from these Greens in the flats: these were their own neighbors, their friends. The flats served as a refuge in case of danger, but most Greens slept at night in their own homes. From some places we heard reports of robberies of soviet cooperatives and market centers; we heard also about murders of soviet bosses passing through and of isolated Red Army members. Because of this, it was dangerous to travel between units of the division or to be billeted in farmsteads located far from one another. Upon a transfer from one regiment to another, Red Army soldiers waited for companions in order to travel more safely.

Once I observed the following scene. We five accidental companions rode along the high road, not far from the rushes, through a safe district. There were no Greens here, so there was nothing to fear. When we approached a farmhouse, we saw several dozen men, with rifles in their hands, run out from the house and hide in the reeds. We were few by comparison with them, and we had been riding so carelessly that they could have taken aim on us all. But they didn't shoot even when we moved closer toward the farmhouse with our guns at the ready. Apparently the farmhouse had served as an observation post for them to watch for approaching groups of Red Army soldiers; they had probably taken us for the advance reconnaissance party of a larger force.

Another incident occurred once when we were on our way to the division HQ at Briukhovetskaia station. Since there were no flats hereabouts, we assumed there were no Greens hiding either, and we casually turned off the road to a small farm, intending to have a drink and a bite to eat. As we turned, a female figure flashed through the farmyard and hid in the house. Was she trying to frighten us? No one else could be seen. As we approached the house, still in formation, we heard the sound of a muffled clap. It did not sound like a gunshot. At the house, hens cackled around us, and the owner opened the door all in tears. At our inquiring glances, she tearfully explained what had just happened. The local Cossacks had brought to her house a wounded man, who had been shot. Warned that we Red Army soldiers were approaching the farm, he thrust his hand in a box filled with bran, stood up out of bed, pulled out his revolver and said good-bye to this world. Because of this occurrence we lost our thirst and our appetite. There was some sort of investigation, the corpse was carried to the village for identification, and we learned that the man whose suicide we had provoked was the commander of the Greens. The echoes of the quieting civil war from time to time let us know it was still there.

The activities of the Greens did not long disturb the peaceful toil of the Cossack villages. An amnesty was proclaimed, which permitted all village and hamlet soviets to take back all their "bandits" as ordinary citizens. The Greens soon dispersed.

Along with the coming of soviet power to the Kuban came obligatory grain deliveries and food supply requisitions by extra-market methods, cooperative trade, and fabulous prices. It was a repeat of the same thing that had happened on the Don a year ago. The Red Army issued strict orders forbidding the requisition of food products from peasants. This was a time when peasants willingly traded milk products, eggs, and bacon for a pinch of tea, matches, or soap. The billeting of Red Army soldiers was not at all burdensome for local families, but on the other hand the "legal" grain requisitions cleaned out their entire grain bins. The dissatisfaction that arose on this score was transformed in some places into open rebellion and led to a refusal to recognize the decrees of local and regional authorities. We knew from the newspapers about the Makhno peasant rebels in the Ukraine and about the Antonov rebellion in Tambov.[3] Now the same thing was beginning in the Kuban. Our division was ordered to battle with the Kuban rebels led by General Fostikov.[4]

By the time we arrived at the area of the rebellion, the units of General Fostikov had managed to fall back and regroup in the hills. We were ordered to disarm the villages, to remove any firearms or other weapons, beginning with hunting rifles and ending with the grandfathers' rusty pistols and hundred-year-old cavalry swords.

During the civil war orders to treat prisoners humanely were often repeated; we were told that once the enemy had given up their weapons and had refused to fight soviet power any longer, they were no longer an enemy. Now, in a secret order of the political section, the same theme returned. The central Cheka published an order, over the signature of Dzerzhinsky, which announced for the information of all political workers that two employees of the Cheka had been shot for beating up prisoners; there was an accompanying explanation of how to conduct oneself with a neutralized foe.[5] But almost simultaneously the Ninth Army published an order proclaiming red terror: all participants of the rebellion in general, and all who had been found with weapons, should be shot without trial on the basis of army order number such and such. Earlier the division tribunal had the right to condemn someone to nothing more than "concentration camp until the end of the civil war." Now, after the civil war, the local tribunal was given the right to execute by shooting without needing the approval of the higher army tribunal. The special section of the division before this had had the right only to arrest and investigate but not to condemn. Now it was authorized to organize the seizure of weapons from participants in the rebellion and to shoot them and to ignore extenuating circumstances. This was meant to instill terror in the population . . .

On arriving in a village, Red Army units would announce a deadline for turning in weapons, enumerated in hours. After resting for the night, the units would proceed further on a forced march to catch up with Fostikov's retreating forces, with whom they never managed to enter in contact. Independent of whether any arms were turned up or not, there were also frequent searches and arrests ordered by local officials. The village Revkom scarcely knew all the participants of the rebellion, and most rebels who were armed had managed to flee. Therefore, the lists for arrest produced by the Revkoms tended to identify local people who had spoken against soviet decrees at some time or other, rather than active participants of the rebellion. This village justice punished people for words rather than deeds. Since the political section did not have time to stay very long in one place, it did not conduct work among the population, except for rallies when it arrived in the village. At these, it announced the deadline for giving up arms and the relevant army order. Only now, for the first time after the war had ended, we began to conduct ourselves as conquerors and to carry out punitive measures. Our actions in the districts of the rebellion differed little from the behavior of the White Army during the civil war itself.

Chapter Twelve

Much of the White Army's staging and preparatory activity had taken place in the fertile Kuban and north Caucasus region. Behind these regions loomed the forbidding mountains of the Caucasus range, with peaks rising to eighteen thousand feet and which was home to tens of scores of mountain tribes who demonstrated a fierce hostility to any external rulers. One of the provinces of this mountain region was Dagestan, which stretched along the Caspian coastline in the east and rose into the mountains in the west.

After the Bolshevik revolution, a succession of governments attempted to establish hegemony over this impassable territory. In spring 1918 the National Committee took control of the region, with military support from former members of tsarist army's "Savage Division" and with political leadership from a Moslem religious leader, Nazhmudin Gotsinskii. This committee was soon replaced by the Military Revolutionary Committee, installed when the Red Eleventh and Twelfth armies marched south from Astrakhan to seize control of the lowland cities of Petrovsk-Port, Derbent, and Temir-Khan-Shura. This government lasted precariously only until summer, when Cossack units retreating from Persia pushed out the Bolsheviks only to find themselves replaced by a nationalist government under the protection of Turkey.

In the spring of 1919 Denikin resolved to use Dagestan as a staging area for his assault on Astrakhan, which commanded the strategic point where the Volga flowed into the Caspian Sea. The White occupiers gradually extended their control throughout the province. But when the military government of Denikin sought to draft the natives into the White Army in August 1919, a wave of resistance rose up against the Russian conquerors. Denikin's forces were cleared out of their mountain garrisons, and fifteen thousand White soldiers were tied down fighting the mountain tribes at the critical moment when Denikin was making his final assault on Moscow.

The Red Army that entered Dagestan was consequently greeted as a liberator, and a new National Communist government was installed with instructions to acknowledge the religious and nationalist sentiments of the native population. But soviet requisition policies and the refusal of some Communists to follow the instructions on tolerance soon led to resistance and rebellion. A new insurgency broke out in August 1920, led by Gotsinskii. The coastal areas remained under soviet control, but the mountain regions proved extraordinarily resistant to pacification. Only when the Red Army occupied Georgia and cut off the rebels' escape and supply routes through the mountains did the movement finally succumb to the Red Army's superior firepower and forces. During the course of 1920 over five thousand Red Army soldiers died in this mountain combat.

The consolidation of power in the core of soviet Russia also proved difficult to achieve. Faced with hostile armies on its borders and a shrinking economic base from which to supply its armies, the soviet regime resorted to increasingly repressive political and economic measures. Opposition parties were outlawed, and dissent among workers was construed as counterrevolutionary support for the Whites. The cities struggled for their existence, as food-producing regions were cut off and peasants resisted soviet food procurement bands. The government response was to strengthen central control over the economy, but this provoked opposition even from among the Communist ranks. Unrest reached a peak in early 1921, with angry meetings and strikes in the major cities and a mutiny in the staunchly radical naval fortress of Kronstadt. This revolt, among sailors who were so intimately linked with the revolution's victory in Petrograd, was quelled only by the massive application of force. The ruling Communist party faced its annual congress in March 1921 in the paradoxical position of having won the battle against the external foe but losing it at home. The Tenth Party Congress consequently adopted two critical decisions. The first was to prohibit public dissent within the party. The second was to loosen control over the economy, starting with restoring to peasants the right to trade freely in grain. The adoption of the New Economic Policy officially marked a new era in the history of the young soviet regime.

Rebellion
in Dagestan

In December 1920 I found myself somehow, with my division, in the homeland of Shamil, hoping to see the land that Lermontov had so picturesquely described in his lyric poetry.[1]

In Dagestan lived 1.2 million people belonging to thirty-four ethnic groups, speaking thirty-four different languages. Common to all was the written language of Avar, but at the same time there were also six other languages used in school. Virtually all these ethnic groups shared the Muslim religion, and the customs and beliefs of old. Apparently, only one group—mountain Jews—was an exception to the general rule, but in most respects they did not differ at all from the other mountain groups: they wore the same sleeveless Circassian tunics, quilted coats, and cartridge pockets, they carried ancient pistols and daggers in their belts, and their women wore the same veils covering their faces. Besides the absence of a common language, the natural features of the area also encouraged the isolation of the tribes populating Dagestan.

In the place of our familiar southern steppes and wide expanses we now encountered high, dark stone heaps, almost without plant cover. Still gloomier and darker, even on bright sunny days, were the gorges, at the bottoms of which ran foaming streams. It seemed there was nowhere here for a person to live, nowhere for fields, orchards, flocks, and pastures. I thought of the Kuban and of the Don, where every Cossack had ten desiatinas of splendid land, but here for a million and more inhabitants there were altogether 450,000 desiatinas of plow land, 700,000 desiatinas of hay meadow, and 1 million desiatinas of mountain pasture. The mountain villagers survived only with imported grain, and their cattle survived only by grazing in leased mountain pastures in Georgia, beyond the high ranges.

In several auls we saw neither sown fields nor gardens.[2] One aul was stuck high in the mountains near bare inaccessible cliffs, and its fields lay somewhere far away. At other auls small enclosures were built on the tiniest slopes of the mountain; behind their walls of loose stones were strips of land one and two meters wide. Every square meter of plowland had been created by hand over countless generations; their fields were not a gift of nature. Many streams ran in the gorges, and somewhere far below you could hear the noise of water. The numerous strips of land in the mountains would wither without water. As in the desert, or in regions of drought, the farmers here brought irrigation channels from far away to their scraps of land. In the Gunib district, for instance, there were 602 desiatinas of irrigated land irrigated by 179 canals, with a total length of 200 kilometers. In the Andizhan district, there were 515 desiatinas of watered land irrigated by artificial canals of a length of 185 kilometers . . . Every handful of land was flooded not only with water but with the laboring sweat of generations of mountain dwellers. Perhaps because the fields here were constructed like houses, made from earth and clay brought in baskets from elsewhere, these mountain plots were valued so highly that Shamil could defend them for sixty years from the encroachment of tsarist Russia. How many years of warfare lay ahead of us? Could one even speak of the "subjugation" of Dagestan if the tsarist government had to maintain here seven thousand troops in military garrisons in nine fortresses even during peacetime, before the war of 1914?

In the chaos of the civil war we did not know what was happening in these mountains. We did not know that here in Denikin's rear a war had raged between the mountain dwellers and the Volunteer Army. This army had been able to hold out in the cities of Petrovsk-Port, Derbent, and in Temir-Khan-Shura, but all the mountain auls and all the Russian fortresses had been captured by partisan units of mountain dwellers. After the White retreat, these units having fought for the independence of Dagestan declared soviet power. The regional Revkom had at its disposal many partisan units of ten or even a hundred soldiers, but their total number was not more than two thousand.

For the mountain dwellers the Volunteer Army of Denikin was the force that had driven them high up in the barren mountains, but soviet power offered the promise of a return to their lost land. Soviet power was "theirs" insofar as mountain men, rather than alien Russians, sat in the institutions of self-government. But whether the Revkom was "theirs" or not, it carried out the orders of the central powers, regardless of the peculiarities of Dagestan. Soviet power promised land but gave forced grain requisitions. The liquidation of the market had deprived Dagestan of grain imports. Subsequently, when free trade was again permitted, ears of corn were as valuable as a piece of lamb of the same weight: there were no imports from Russia, where the market continued to be inoperative.

In September 1920, Said-bey, the grandson of Shamil, returned through Georgia from Turkey, and he raised a rebellion under the green banner of the prophet.[3] For two months the rebels defeated the partisan units of the Revkom and units of the Thirty-second Infantry Division of the Red Army, stationed in several of the fortresses. As in the time of the Denikin occupation, so now the Red Army controlled the cities while the entire region around was in the hands of the rebels. The rebellion had a purely local significance until it began to spread toward Derbent and Baku and northward from Chir-Iurt and Kasav-Iurt, threatening the city of Groznyi and the railroad there. In other words, the transport of oil was at risk.[4] Only then did we have the sense to throw in additional troops: the Thirty-third Infantry Division, a brigade of Moscow military school cadets, and an armored air unit. They were assigned to protect Baku and Groznyi.

Our division was converted into a shock unit for active battle with the rebels, for the occupation of fortresses, and for the liberation of the besieged units of the Thirty-second Division and our partisans. We were completely unequipped for action in mountainous territory: we had no mountain tools nor proper transport. Our horses had been taken out of service, the provision of military and food supplies had been stopped. Now we had to exchange teams of artillery horses for strings of oxen; only in this way could we manage to transport our equipment along the steep roads, which sloped in some places as much as forty-five degrees. It was strange to see a string of donkeys carefully making their way with their assigned load—two loaves of soldiers' bread each . . . Despite the overflowing stores of the quartermaster, combatant units were starving, sometimes going entire days without food. It was feast or famine: only after a battle, when we had conquered an enemy aul, could we (contrary to strict orders) get hold of some dried apricots and dried lamb.

The unfamiliar conditions of fighting in mountainous terrain, whose narrow passages did not permit us to turn around, caused us heavy losses. For a mere two dozen unseen rebel rifles put out of action, many dozens of soldiers on our side were wounded and killed. Because of this, even in reconquered territory, the regiment traveled by putting a large guard on its flanks. They moved as barely visible silhouettes, here falling into a ravine, there again scrambling up on a ridge. The speed of our troops' movement differed little from the speed of movement of an ox team. The circumstances of the fighting reminded me a little of the fight in Moscow in October: you had to anticipate a shot from behind every cliff. The enemy frequently turned out to be not where you expected but somewhere behind or to the side.

The rebels fought with great courage, firing only when they were sure their bullets would not be wasted. Once they had used up their cartridges, they resorted to their daggers. The rebels behaved like guerrillas: every unit had its own supplies, only for themselves. It happened that one unit would haul its rifles with no cartridges, another had many cartridges and few rifles, a third had more machine guns than rifles.

At the beginning of the rebellion the rebel troops were armed with war trophies captured from the defeated units of the Thirty-second Division. Now, thanks to our offensive, the quantity of their supplies declined: they prized every bullet. In the bazaars, rifle cartridges were valued on a par with real money; for this purpose women and children appeared in the Red Army camps, their eyes peering at the ground in search of cartridges that might have been dropped.

The majority of auls were located high in the mountains; individual huts seemed to be swallows' nests rather than human dwellings. We learned to take such natural fortresses by night, when the rebels could not shoot as they chose, when the fighting did not begin until we were close in. Every aul could only be captured by hand-to-hand fighting, and only then when our side had superior numbers.

Bitter fighting took place for Gimry, the home both of Khadzhi-Murat and Shamil.[5] A highway ran along here, which permitted us to bring up artillery and to subject the aul to preliminary bombardment. We did not fire at any specific target, but if even half of our thirteen hundred shells had landed there, there would have been only a heap of ruins in place of the aul. However, Gimry lay in such a narrow shred of land that we landed few direct hits. The regiment stole to the aul of Gergebil' under the cover of darkness and surrounded it from all sides. In the darkness the mountain dwellers could easily break out and hide, but fighting broke out in close alleyways. The battle lasted all morning, and for a whole day huts were taken one by one. For every defender there were dozens of attackers. Only late in the evening the remaining rebels located in the mosque gave themselves up. Besides several hundred prisoners we took nine machine guns with spare cartridges; but in the tight spaces of the aul their daggers were more dangerous for us than machine guns.

Gergebil' was one of the largest auls in Dagestan, and therefore we expected many casualties from among women and children, but it turned out that they had managed, by some unknown route, to escape in time. They even took their cattle with them, although it had seemed to us that not even a dog could have sneaked past our tight ranks. We talked more of this evacuation than about the capture of such an impregnable aul. This evacuation once again confirmed that we still had not adjusted to the peculiarities of the terrain, that even if we knew about crevices in the rock face, we did not know how to take advantage of them.

It turned out that we had to adjust not only to the special features of Dagestan but also to the special policies of soviet power in the Caucasus. It was strange to observe our prisoners, old men with overgrown beards from the collar to the belt, arrayed in thick sheepskin coats from top to toe and armed with revolvers and daggers. We were surprised that the prisoners had kept their weapons: it was not long ago, in the Kuban, that we shot people for burying rusty sabers, but here these active participants in the rebellion retained their weapons!

We did not know that in the custom of the mountain dwellers

it was shameful to appear in public unarmed. "Better without trousers than without a weapon," they said here. "A man without a weapon is a woman with a long beard." We had to come to terms with this new "political literacy." The prisoners were allowed to keep the sheaths of their daggers and the holsters of their revolvers, and having fashioned for themselves wooden daggers as well as wooden revolvers, they proudly marched to the prison of the Revkom . . .

Our Red Army troops unwillingly comprehended this "nationality" policy of soviet power and even more reluctantly accepted the order to treat the prisoners and insurrectionists responsible for cruelties like naughty children. The rebels had taken no prisoners. The corpses of Red Army soldiers had been mutilated beyond recognition, and they had nonetheless fought as courageously as the rebels. The Red Army troops themselves, not waiting for the medical orderlies, had worried about the removal of the wounded, and they had buried the corpses of the dead. It was not as it had been earlier on the Don; there they had thrown the corpses from the road and that was it: they would be buried by whomever and whenever.

The new political literacy obligated us to take into account the population with its many languages, to consider not only the political but also the ethnic friction between individual nationalities and auls. The rebel territory held some auls that were hostile and some peaceful; some recognized the power of the Revkom and others were neutral. Both sides recognized the right of these auls to remain neutral. Such neutrality occurred by oral agreement with chosen, respected elders of the aul. This was enough: no danger would threaten us from these auls. Neither rebels nor Red Army soldiers were permitted to enter them. Even after our victory it was strange to hear them say, "Our aul is neutral—not one Russian soldier entered and we did not let them pass." We had to waste entire days in order to bypass such auls, even when this meant confronting dozens of mountain huts and as many defenders. "What can you do?" swore the commanders. "Such a nationality policy: better to lose a hundred killed than to offend the mountain dwellers."

We had to maneuver and to balance, to think not only about today's problems but also about the problems tomorrow would bring to the implementation of soviet power in the Caucasus. I once observed a colorful, vivid scene as two auls, peaceful toward us, fought between themselves. The villages, located on two mountains, were divided by a deep chasm, but by direct line just a stone's throw away, not more than half a kilometer. The male populations of both villages had poured out onto the streets, crying and yelling in languages mutually incomprehensible to one another, brandishing their bared daggers, ready to cut each other up if it had not been for the natural barrier. Larger than the mountain chasm that separated them was the abyss created by their different tongues and an ancient hatred from the time of their great-grandparents. The slightest excuse—in this case damage done by cattle to some pastureland—was enough to ignite a bloody slaughter.

The Revkom had to deal with this ancient hostility between different nationalities, acting in some places as an impartial arbitrator, in others as judge. The rebels also had to take this hostility into account. In such a complicated mess it was impossible for us to sort things out ourselves, without the help of the Revkom. Without it we could not even understand the nationality policy of soviet power, which contradicted all that we had known before coming to Dagestan. The Red Army, deployed far in the mountains, would remain without food for whole days, but we did not have the right to requisition even one sheep. In Russia trade was prohibited everywhere—here they traded openly not only in mutton and corn but also in cartridges for Russian thirty-caliber rifles. The soviet regime here canceled grain requisitions, raised customs barriers between the borders of separate regions, and waged a struggle against smuggling. You could travel to Baku only with a special pass from the civilian authorities—and nonetheless traders managed to trade gold, women's stockings, and perfumes of foreign origin, obtained in Baku. We did not know where to obtain paper for a simple letter, but in the stationery shop at Temir-Khan-Shura they sold paper of better quality than that used to print our "denznaki," our currency.

Army headquarters issued directives that contradicted the policies of the Revkom, but we in our "partisan" manner, we would not obey such directives if they contradicted "nationality" policy. The Red Army soldiers were surprised and wondered that perhaps if we had had in our territory such a "nationality" policy, we would not have had a peasant uprising . . . ?

The political workers of the division conducted educational

work among the Red Army members and among the local population, explaining that soviet power did not infringe on national independence, the way we said happened under the tsarist regime. However, we ourselves found this nationality policy to be contradictory. If we decided to disobey a directive of army headquarters it was only because the Revkom held for us greater authority.

The members of the Revkom and regional committee of the Communist party—Dzhelaleddin Korkmazov, Said Gabiev, and N. E. Samurskii—nursed and cajoled us political workers in the same way we in turn nursed the Red Army soldiers. They read us lectures on the history of the Caucasus, explaining the peculiarities of its inhabitants, and they told us that to uphold soviet power we had to give up many soviet dogmas. The three above-named men never used the term *dictatorship of the proletariat*. They spoke with great love for their people and defended them from social experiments. It seemed to us that these were "sham" Communists, but in their favor they possessed personal authority, erudition, and high intellectuality. Their chief source of legitimacy was that they spoke in the name of Lenin and the party Central Committee in Moscow. If they did not succeed in changing a particular directive of the military authorities, they would turn to Moscow and receive from there a speedy and favorable answer. An answer from Moscow, from the Central Committee of the party or from the Council of People's Commissars with the signature of Lenin, would resolve all our doubts in favor of the policies of the Revkom. This was the only reason we refused to fulfill orders from the army headquarters.

The capture of Gunib, not far from the pass across the ridge to Georgia, where the leaders of the rebellion were hiding, marked the imminent end of the rebellion. There were a few holdouts—small auls and small detachments of rebels that were not worth the Revkom's energy to fight. In order not to plague the eyes of the mountain dwellers with the grey Russian greatcoats of the Red Army, in order not to insult the national pride of the inhabitants of auls "where not a Russian has ever set foot," the division began to withdraw from the mountain region.

Dagestan had its Communists, proportionally no fewer than in Russia, but most of them lived in the cities. In the entire region, there were twenty-three thousand Communists and candidate members, half of them of the Russian nationality. We joked among ourselves that the Dagestan Communists, like the village dwellers, were divided into soviet, antisoviet, and neutral elements. In part this was true: during the hours of prayer Communists would leave their party meetings to go to the mosque, but they had also honestly fought against the counterrevolutionary Denikin troops, and now against their princes. Such Communists were common among the partisan units that were formed without regard to nationality, where Russians fought side by side with mountain dwellers. The commanders of partisan units were mountain dwellers, and in the majority of units the commissars were Russians. The latter had not been appointed by anyone but they were chosen by the mountain people both as politically "grounded" comrades and for knowing the Russian language. One such commissar was Boris Sheboldaev, wounded in one of the battles.

The Russian Communists were supposed to know the charter and program of the party, but this was not required for local Communists. For them the dictatorship of the proletariat didn't matter at all. This expectation was even taken into account in the subsequent purge of 1921, but nonetheless more than nine thousand of these twenty-three thousand were excluded from the party.[6]

In preparation for the Tenth Party Congress in March 1921 the Revkom was revamped, and we could get down to adding up the victories gained and losses suffered in this unusual war. In three months of fighting the Red Army had lost more than five thousand troops—as many as were lost in the battles with the regular army of Denikin and almost as many as the rebel losses. If despite such heavy losses the Red Army had triumphed, it was because it was no longer the army of 1918. Now it was a strongly united, harmonious collective of platoons, companies, and battalions. Three years ago the division had had only several dozen Communists. Now we had 145 Communist party cells, with 942 Communists and 1,119 candidate members.

At the beginning of the civil war we matched the trained officer cadres of the White Army with Red commanders who at best had been former noncommissioned officers in the Russian army. Now all platoons and companies were led by Red commanders, who had completed the Red commanders' course, or commanders from among the drafted officers of the old tsarist army.

During the war of 1914–17, 202,200 officers served in the 15-million-member Russian army; 48,409 of these officers were recruited to serve in the 3.5-million-member Red Army of 1921. Of 1,396 generals, staff, and senior officers of the general staff of the Russian army, 340 lent their knowledge to the Red Army.[7] The Red Army ranks now held 300,000 Communists—as many as the whole party had had on the eve of its struggle for soviet power. These Communists, once seen by former generals as "insignificant civilians," political members of the armies' Military Revolutionary Councils, now acquired new respect. They were neither civilians nor nursemaids for the teaching of dialectical materialism but strategists with a broader perspective than possessed by our "military specialists." The specialists learned that the commissar of the division was not a spy, but an assistant division commander who could solve tactical and political problems.

The skillful combination of alien elements, organically connected, created a militarily competent army. The Red Army did not feel itself the conqueror of someone else's possessions; on the contrary, it had seized back its own property that had been usurped by the enemy. Therefore it did not have to lament, as General Denikin's followers did, "We did not manage to organize a civil government. There are people in the uezds who should be permanent candidates for penal battalions." The Red Army did not have to complain that "at the front we felt a perpetual lack of officers, although in [Kolchak's] headquarters there were upwards of five thousand officials" or "on the Red side against us works one army headquarters, consisting of three or four divisions and two or three cavalry brigades, but on our side: the headquarters of the commander-in-chief, five army headquarters, eleven headquarters of corps groups, and, it seems, thirty-five headquarters for divisions and individual brigades. Commentary is superfluous."[8]

We also did not have to suffer the situation of General Iudenich, where "the numerical composition of the army was nearly twenty thousand, but the quartermaster was feeding one hundred thousand."[9] We could not have had generals like Mai-Maevskii or the organized embezzlement of public funds, as in Siberia, where the Omsk government of Kolchak received 120 wagons of gold from the Czechs, but soon "lost" it and carried away on their retreat only 28 wagons of valuables.[10] It was not rank-and-file soldiers with their limited perspective but its own organizers and leaders who characterized the Volunteer Army of Denikin in these terms: "The uncontrollable robbery of the population by our military forces, the debauchery and repression by military officials in local areas, the unbelievable corruption of the representatives of power, their open speculation, venality, and, finally, their unrestrained arbitrariness prevailing in their counterintelligence organizations, here were the ulcers of our regime, compelling the population to say: no, this is not the regime that can save Russia."[11]

It was not I, a Communist, but Pavel Miliukov who referred to the monarchist V. V. Shul'gin, attributing the death of the White dream to the fact that the "falcons"—the laudatory name of their forces—did not soar like eagles, as the song goes, but sneaked about like thieves.[12] History and posterity ask less from the poorly literate worker or peasant than from the Russian elite who led the counterrevolution. Therefore, I do not want to write about my illusions as they became shattered by soviet reality. The seamy sides of the White Army monopolized our attention throughout the civil war.

Could one demand from a rank-and-file accomplice in the historical "crime" enacted in October 1917 anything other than a not oversimplified contrast of both fighting sides? I have given here a few snapshots—not paintings—of events, where I myself was a participant—and only that.

We never thought that with the victory over the "White dream" the Red Army of October had concluded its revolutionary tasks. On the contrary, it seemed to us that only now, with the liquidation of the civil war, could we begin the constructive work to achieve the goals of the Russian revolution. We, a half million Communists, did not feel isolated from the 150 million people living in the country. On the contrary, they struggled together with us against the counterrevolution. Their support confirmed for us that the October revolution could not be dismissed as "Blanquism in Tartar sauce."[13]

An ideological enemy of this revolution, a member of the Menshevik party's Central Committee, Iulii Martov, said in 1918:

I can accept the idea that we are an insignificant minority in Russia now. We cannot create much, but we are capable of lighting a path. But I fear that history will not understand us. If soviet power does not endure long, the future historian will look upon it as an unsuccessful, but all the same an honest and heroic attempt to realize socialism. I hope all the same that soviet power will survive sufficiently long enough that the working class can triumph, that in our relations with Bolshevism we will have defended the vital interests of the future working class and of socialism.[14]

But these same vital interests of the working class and of socialism were also defended by the Bolsheviks—without this we would have been just as isolated from the masses as the Mensheviks. We had to stand at the head of these masses, not from somewhere on high, from a birds'-eye position, but in practical work. When the enemy had you by the throat, it was no time for philosophy.

Later, when the army of Denikin stood near Moscow, the same opponents of Bolshevism, in the voice of another Menshevik leader, Fedor Dan, said: "Whatever has been our critical position toward the policies of the Bolshevik government, whatever persecution and repression has been imposed on our party from its side, let all enemies of the Russian revolution know that our party will stand with that government with all its power whenever the issue is the defense of the revolution."[15]

Obviously after two years it had become clearer to see that October had not been Blanquism in Tartar sauce, not merely a heroic episode of the Russian revolution. It had become obvious that there were only two active forces and that impartial observance or philosophical mediation in such a struggle was fruitless.

From our position in the Red Army we looked in front of us, at the enemy; we had little opportunity to glance behind us and to see the bitter soviet reality. We were unwilling to see that at home, in the party, political appointees were replacing elected committees, that the dictatorship of the proletariat was falling into the hands of a dictator; that the soviet constitution and self-government were being replaced by administrative debauchery. It seemed that these transformations were not actions of an enemy but "small defects in the larger mechanism." We more readily explained the huge peasant rebellions that originated after the war as intrigues by enemies of the revolution than by their truer causes.

And so, from the proud tower of the dictatorship of the proletariat we said the hell with national self-determination for Dagestan if it stood in the way of obtaining fuel for our dying Russian industry. From on high we viewed the Dagestan Communists running from party meetings to the call of the muezzin, but we soon had reason to ponder.

At the Tenth Congress of the party Ivan Smilga declared that only 30 percent of the Communists of Kronstadt had fought the rebels. The remainder were either against us or were neutral. Nikolai Bukharin worried about the workers of Moscow and Petersburg who were adopting not Bolshevik but SR resolutions.[16] Why couldn't the Red Army and Red military cadets deal with the rebels? Why did they need to be bolstered by three hundred old men, old Bolsheviks, delegates to the all-Russian party congress, and by Communists from Moscow and Petersburg?[17] This disaffection was something novel, something we had not seen before, and it was difficult for us to understand sitting in the mountains of Dagestan.

In 1921, when letters from Moscow took half a year, when newspapers arrived six or more weeks late, we saw only bits of soviet Russia. We were absorbed in concerns about demobilization, about the transfer to a peacetime footing of the army of several millions, and about the return of those under arms to the "army" of workers.

In this year, with the help of this army of workers, and with colossal expenditure of energy, the country had stockpiled only 60 percent of the grain, 38 percent of oil, and 23 percent of coal, compared with the prewar year of 1914. The remaining branches of industry—metallurgy, steel, and textiles, yielded correspondingly 2.6, 3.7, and 5.1 percent of prewar output.

We saw a huge army and a mass party of the working class but we did not realize that the civil war had caused all of heavy industry to be destroyed. As Lenin said, "If we continue to say *worker*, understanding by this term a proletarian, then this is not true. . . . It is true according to Marx, but Marx did not write about Russia. For over six hundred years this was true, but for contemporary Russia it is untrue . . . the proletariat has disappeared."[18]

But in such a case is not the existing party of a nonexistent class no longer a vanguard but something separate and apart? If Lenin's argument was true, that the victory over the counterrevolution was marked by the disappearance of the class in whose name we triumphed, then had not the slogan of the dictatorship of the proletariat become only a myth? A nonexisting class could not have a vanguard—its own party. Was a regime that rested on a myth merely the mouthpiece of some other actual class? Or was it that without a world revolution we had given birth to a classless, starving collection of people, with silent factories and mills?

When could we expect help from the world revolution? Was it only when the "crayfish whistles"? Amidst these bewildering questions we confronted the end of the civil war, debating, even after the congress, the questions of inner-party democracy and the next stage of the revolution, the New Economic Policy.

But we did not yet raise the question, which Alexander Shliapnikov subsequently posed:

"Another and 'better' working class we will not have, and we need to satisfy the one we do have. . . . By portraying the proletariat in colors that are not its own, comrades look to justify their actions in political maneuvers, and in seeking support from other social strata."[19]

Postscript

As the editors were completing work on this translation they unexpectedly learned, through sources that had been inaccessible to scholars before the dramatic transformation of the Soviet Union, of Dune's posthumous rehabilitation. Following up on this information, Daniel Peris, a graduate student at the University of Illinois, was able to learn that Dune's son, Vladimir, had survived the war and was living in Moscow. In June 1992, Diane Koenker met with him there, and they shared their knowledge about Dune's life. Vladimir's last memory of his father, who had returned to his family only three days before from his Vorkuta imprisonment, was accompanying him to the Red Army mobilization point in June 1941, where Dune reported for duty. Shortly after, Vladimir and his mother fled on foot from Vitebsk (never seeing a German soldier), and they eventually reached safety east of the Volga River. After the war, Ginda returned to Moscow, where she lived until her death in the early 1980s. She never remarried.

Notes

INTRODUCTION

1. Among the best and most comprehensive of these accounts are N. N. Sukhanov, *The Russian Revolution, 1917*, trans. and ed. Joel Carmichael (Princeton, N.J., 1984); Alexander Kerensky, *Russia and History's Turning Point* (New York, 1965), a fuller and more retrospective version of his initial memoir, *The Catastrophe* (New York, 1927); and Anton Ivanovich Denikin, *The Russian Turmoil* (New York, 1922).

2. A party history project, Istpart, initiated the collection of workers' memoirs in the early 1920s. The writer Maxim Gorky headed a project in the 1930s to record the history of individual factories and in the process to encourage workers to record their reminiscences of the revolution. Many were published in Russian in this period.

3. See the collection edited by Victoria E. Bonnell, *The Russian Worker: Life and Labor under the Tsarist Regime* (Berkeley, 1983); and Semen Ivanovich Kanatchikov, *A Radical Worker in Tsarist Russia: The Autobiography of Semen Ivanovich Kanatchikov*, trans. and ed. Reginald E. Zelnik (Stanford, 1986).

4. An English-language account of Sapronov's career is Victoria E. Bonnell's introduction to his memoir *Iz istorii rabochego dvizheniya* (Newtonville, Mass., 1976).

5. Hoover Institution Archive, Boris I. Nicolaevsky Collection, Box 237, folder 5, Box 236, folder 15.

6. These and subsequent biographical details are taken from Dune's papers in the Nicolaevsky Collection, Box 235, folders 1, 2, Box 236, folders 15, 19.

7. E. H. Carr, *Foundations of a Planned Economy, 1926–29*, vol. 2 (London, 1971), 49–50. The originals of some of the Democratic Centralists' declarations are in the Trotsky Archives at Harvard University.

8. The resolution confirming the expulsion is reprinted in "Ob oppozitsii," *Kommunisticheskaia partiia sovetskogo soiuza v rezoliutsiiakh, resheniiakh s"ezdov, konferentsii, i plenumov TsK*, 8th ed. (Moscow, 1970), 4:70–73.

9. Eugenia Ginzburg, *Journey into the Whirlwind*, trans. Paul Stevenson and Max Hayward (New York, 1967). Dune published a chilling account in English of the mass executions at Vorkuta: Ivan Ivanov, "The Vorkuta Massacre," *Modern Review* 2, nos. 5–6 (June 1948): 302–9.

10. His account of this experience can be found in Ivan Ivanov, "Vitebskoe getto," *Sotsialisticheskii vestnik* 32, nos. 1–2 (650) (Jan.–Feb. 1952): 26–27; 651, no. 3 (651) (Mar. 1952): 49–50.

11. Ivan Ivanov, "Russkii Di-Pi vo Frantsii," *Sotsialisticheskii vestnik* 31, nos. 9–10 (647) (Sept.–Oct. 1951): 198–200; no. 11 (648) (Nov. 1951): 220–24.

12. Nicolaevsky Collection, Box 235, folders 1, 8.

13. Conversation between Diane Koenker and Alexander Dallin, project administrator, 7 Nov. 1990.

14. Nicolaevsky Collection, Box 235, folder 2, Box 478, folder 10.

15. Nicolaevsky Collection, Box 236, folder 5. Dune's obituary, by R. A. Abramovich, was printed in *Sotsialisticheskii vestnik* 33, nos. 2–3 (659) (Feb.–Mar. 1953): 51–52.

16. *Sotsial-demokrat*, 28 June 1917.

17. Nicolaevsky Collection, Box 235, folder 1.

18. *Sotsialisticheskii vestnik*, 30, nos. 8–9 (636) (Sept. 1950): 169–70.

19. *Sotsialisticheskii vestnik*, 30 nos. 11–12 (638–39) (Dec. 1950): 219–20.

CHAPTER 1 ★ To Moscow

1. In the battle lines from 1915 to 1918, Latvia suffered immense destruction. Riga, threatened by German occupation from 1915, finally fell to the Kaiser's army on 21 August 1917.

2. *Valenki* are felt boots that come up to the knee.

3. The Provodnik company received some eighteen million rubles in government loans to expedite defense orders during the war years. The figure of fifteen thousand workers refers to the work force of the Provodnik company as a whole. The work force of the Tushino section, where the Dune family was sent, was about thirty-five hundred in 1917.

4. Pereiaslavl'-Zalesskii is a town about 150 kilometers northeast of Moscow in Iaroslavl' province.

5. The revolutionary song "Dubinushka" originated in the 1860s and became popular among boatmen, gangs of manual laborers, and so forth. The song exists in several versions, and its title became a generic term for a type of strongly rhythmic revolutionary song.

6. A *chastushka* is a two-line or four-line rhymed ditty on some topical or humorous theme.

7. Sarts is a somewhat derogatory term for the settled town and village dwellers of Turkestan, most of them Turkic-speaking. See Elizabeth E. Bacon, *Central Asians under Russian Rule: A Study in Culture Change* (Ithaca, N.Y., 1966), 17–18. We are indebted to Alistair McAuley of the University of Essex for help with this reference.

8. The *baogong* system of recruiting labor through subcontractors was widespread throughout China, especially in Shanghai. See Jean Chesneaux, *The Chinese Labor Movement, 1919–1927* (Stanford, 1968), 54–64; and Lewis H. Siegelbaum, "Another Yellow Peril: Chinese Migrants in the Russian Far East and the Russian Reaction Before 1917," *Modern Asian Studies* 12, no. 2 (1978): 307–30.

9. The Treugol'nik rubber works in Petrograd was owned by the Russo-American Joint-Stock Rubber Company and in January 1917 had a work force of 15,338. The Bogatyr factory, which produced rubber footwear, was opened in the village of Bogorodskoe, at the edge of the city of Moscow, in 1911. It had a work force of 2,200 in 1917.

10. Dune is here no doubt referring to his own experiences and attitudes when his father was laid up with lead poisoning (see above).

11. Fedor Ivanovich Shaliapin (1873–1938) was a world-famous opera singer who left soviet Russia in 1922.

12. Ebonite is a hard, vulcanized rubber used as an insulating material. The longer the process of vulcanization, the harder the ebonite produced. Vulcanization is a chemical process that entails heating rubber with sulphur and other ingredients to improve the physical properties of the rubber.

13. In the years after 1905 a craze for detective stories swept through Russia's urban masses. Gems such as *The Daughter of Pinkerton and the Cruel Mother* and *The Detective Murderers: The Duel between Sherlock Holmes and Nat Pinkerton* sold no fewer than twelve million copies in 1908. Although detective stories were referred to, generically, in Russian as "Nick Carters," "Sherlock Holmeses," or, most commonly, "Pinkertons," they were by no means all foreign translations. "Pinkertons" became a generic term for detective fiction in Russia. It derives from the name of the American detective story writer Allen Pinkerton (1819–84), who in real life was Chicago's first detective and also founder in 1850 of the private detective agency that later became famous for its battles against organized

labor. See the excellent book by Jeffrey Brooks *When Russia Learned to Read: Literacy and Popular Literature, 1861–1917* (Princeton, N.J., 1982).

14. Lily Braun (1865–1916), born into a noble family, was a feminist active in the German Social Democratic party who wrote copiously on the emancipation of women. She construed this emancipation as a process that should begin in the present with the establishment of communal households, designed to free women from the double burden of domestic and wage labor. Dune is presumably referring to her autobiography *Memoiren einer Sozialistin: Lehrjahre (Kampfjahre)*, which was published in Munich in two volumes in 1909–11, though he curiously refers to the work as a "novel." See Alfred G. Meyer, *The Feminism and Socialism of Lily Braun* (Bloomington, Ind., 1985); and Jean H. Quataert, *Reluctant Feminists in German Social Democracy, 1885–1917* (Princeton, N.J., 1979), 77–80.

15. Murmansk was founded in September 1916 after the opening of a railway from Petrograd and the creation of a seaport on the Kola Bay of the Barents Sea.

16. The Cossacks served as cavalry in the tsarist army and, when occasion required, were called in as mounted police to suppress civil disturbances. They played a prominent part in the pacification of Latvian insurgents in 1906.

17. The Okhrana was the popular name for the tsarist secret police set up in the wake of the assassination of Alexander II in 1881.

18. Sukharevka was a large open-air market situated in Sukharev Square along the outer ring of boulevards to the north side of Moscow.

19. P. A. Berlin, born in 1877, was a Menshevik economist and historian whose most famous work is *The Russian Bourgeoisie in Ancient and Modern Times*, published in Russian in 1922. He went into emigration, and during the last years of his life Dune corresponded with him. Dune is probably confusing him with V. V. Bervi-Flerovskii (1829–1918), who wrote the classic *Condition of the Working Class in Russia* in 1869.

20. The works referred to are Friedrich Engels's *The Condition of the Working Class in England in 1844* and Sidney Webb's and Beatrice Webb's *History of Trade Unionism* (1894), which was translated by Lenin into Russian and published in 1901.

21. A magneto is an alternator with permanent magnets used to generate current for the ignition of an internal combustion engine.

22. A verst is approximately two-thirds of a mile.

23. Unified Social Democratic organizations, combining both Mensheviks and Bolsheviks, were by no means uncommon in Russia even after 1912. In the spring of 1917 they existed in such major pro-

vincial centers as Perm, Tula, Nizhnii Novgorod, Sormovo, Kolomna, and Iuzovka and were common in the regions of the Urals, Belorussia, the Caucasus, Central Asia, and Siberia. At the beginning of 1917 the Latvian Social Democratic organization in Petrograd was still unified. *Partiinye izvestiia* no. 1, 15 July 1917, 31.

24. An independent nationalist government existed in Latvia from 1920 to 1940.

25. After the outbreak of war vast territories contiguous to the front were placed under the direct authority of the military and Germans and Jews were deported from these areas. The government also expropriated land owned by German nationals and settlers of German descent.

26. Dune is referring to the peace of Brest-Litovsk forced on the soviet government by Germany in March 1918. In February 1918, while the soviet government tried to stall for time, the German army, which had occupied a part of Livonia in September 1917, invaded the whole of the Baltic region, where it remained in occupation until November 1918.

27. By imperial decree of 1 August 1915, eight voluntary field battalions were created whose flags and insignia were allowed to bear Latvian emblems and inscriptions. By 1916 the two brigades, each of four divisions, had a total strength of 130,000. They were known as the Latvian Rifles since they were prohibited by the Russian High Command from having artillery or cavalry. Incidentally, if one takes the territory of what became the Latvian republic, then there were 2.5, not 1.5, million Latvians in 1914.

28. In July 1915 the zemstvos, the organs of local government throughout most of provincial Russia, joined with their urban counterparts to form committees to mobilize the rear to meet the needs of the front. These unions of zemstvos and towns farmed out defense orders from the Ministry of War, saw to their fulfillment, evacuated industrial enterprises, and so forth.

29. An international conference of left socialists met at Zimmerwald in Switzerland on 5–8 September 1915, attended by thirty-eight delegates from eleven countries. Lenin's platform of "revolutionary defeatism" was rejected by the delegates, who accepted a manifesto drawn up by Trotsky that called for a general campaign to force the belligerent governments to come to the negotiating table. Lenin rejected the call for peace with contempt, calling it mere Sunday school chatter. He urged the transformation of the imperialist war into a civil war, arguing that from the point of view of the Russian working class, "a defeat of the tsarist monarchy and its army, which oppressed the Poles, the Ukrainians, and other peoples, would be the lesser evil."

V. I. Lenin, "The Tasks of Revolutionary Social-Democracy in the European War" in *Collected Works* (London, 1964), 21:18. Most Latvians, however, loyally supported the Russian war effort, believing German imperialism to be the greater evil: only the Latvian Social Democracy was a singular exception to this. In speaking of "we," therefore, Dune would appear to be identifying with the majority of his fellow citizens rather than with the socialist minority.

30. The Latvian Rifles, who fought heroically to hold the Daugava line for two years, received precious little help from the Russian High Command. The Siberian rifles consisted in the main of Polish, Ukrainian, Lithuanian, and Latvian deportees.

31. The Grand Duke Nikolai Nikolaevich (1856–1929) was the uncle of Nicholas II; he enjoyed great popularity with the Russian people. In 1905 he had refused Nicholas II's appointment as military dictator and hence paved the way to the semiconstitutional settlement of the October Manifesto. With the outbreak of war in 1914, Nikolai Nikolaevich was appointed commander-in-chief of the Russian forces, but with growing failures at the front Nicholas II decided in August 1915 to dismiss his uncle and assume the supreme command himself. See the portrait of the Grand Duke in Aleksandr Solzhenitsyn, *August 1914*, trans. H. T. Willetts (London, 1989), 767–77.

32. The Empress Alexandra Feodorovna (1872–1918) was born in Germany and brought up at Kensington Palace by her grandmother, Queen Victoria. She married Nicholas II in 1894, and henceforward saw her mission in life as preserving autocracy intact. She detested liberalism and believed fervently in Orthodox Christianity and in the mystical union that bound the tsar to his people. When Nicholas II assumed command of the army in August 1915, Alexandra took over the helm of state. Egged on by Rasputin and supported by her complaisant husband, she proceeded to remove all government ministers of whom she did not approve. She was loathed by the Russian public, who believed her to be leader of a pro-German fifth column within the innermost circle of government.

33. Both Nicholas and Alexandra were deeply religious, and their correspondence—written in English—is replete with references to church services, the gospels, icons, and, not least, to the "man of God," Rasputin. Grigorii Rasputin (1871?–1916) won the good favors of the empress when his hypnotic powers proved to be effective in stanching the bleeding suffered by her hemophiliac son, the tsarevich Alexis. The superstitious tsarina regarded Rasputin as the saintly personification of the loyal Russian people, and he exploited his standing to great effect. Alexandra constantly urged her husband to heed

the advice of Rasputin, and while he generally did so, it is only fair to point out that he was not quite so credulous of this "good, religious, simple-minded Russian" as she. Rasputin was murdered on 29 December 1916 in the palace of Prince F. F. Iusupov.

34. The venerable Count V. B. Fredericks (1838–1927) was minister of the imperial household from the days of Alexander III and probably one of the most faithful servants of the tsar. Nevertheless, as a descendent of a Baltic German family he was identified as a member of the supposed German party of Alexandra. She, incidentally, was referred to as the "Nemka"—the "German woman"—just as Marie Antoinette had once been known as "l' Autrichienne."

35. General V. A. Sukhomlinov (1848–1926) was minister of war from 1909 to 1915 and was held to be responsible for Russia's unpreparedness for war, despite the military reforms he had carried out from 1905 to 1912. He was replaced by General Polivanov in mid-1915. Dune's reference is perplexing since the empress certainly hated Sukhomlinov and it was partly at her instigation that he was arraigned for treason in March 1916.

36. In August 1914 a decree was passed to prohibit alcoholic beverages for the duration of the war. This entailed a very considerable loss of revenue for the treasury since the state enjoyed a monopoly on the production of all spirits. After the ban, peasants turned to making home brew on a massive scale, with a resultant increase in their income.

37. On 23 June 1912 two laws were enacted that dealt with medical insurance for workers in the case of illness or accident. Workers were to contribute between 1 and 3 percent of their monthly wages to a medical insurance fund and the employer would contribute two-thirds of the total sum contributed by the workers. Medical funds (bol'nichnye kassy) were set up in each enterprise to administer benefits, consisting of deputies elected by the workers and representatives of management. The total membership of medical funds in Moscow rose from 21,307 in 1914 to 79,790 in 1917 (of whom 62 percent were men and 38 percent were women), making them by far the largest working-class organizations prior to the February revolution. The Bolsheviks, who were active in the campaign to extend and improve social insurance, used the medical funds as vehicles for political work. Although no medical fund existed at Tushino until 1916, a fund had been set up in the Provodnik plant in Riga in 1913. The administration, however, had fired the elected workers' deputies, thus precipitating a big strike.

38. In fact, T. V. Sapronov was born in 1887, not 1883, so he would have been not quite thirty at the time he came to the Provodnik plant.

39. Sapronov joined the Russian Social Democratic Workers party

only in 1912, although his informal links with the party stretched back to 1905.

40. Sapronov spent his three months exile on the Volga, not in the Tula countryside. See his "Tri mesiatsa na Volge (1916)," *Proletarskaia revoliutsiia*, no. 8 (43) (1925): 216–37.

41. From 1905 to 1907 the Moscow Central Bureau of Trade Unions figured prominently in the city's labor movement, but subsequent efforts to restore the bureau in 1913 and 1914 failed, largely because of police provocation. Sapronov's efforts in the autumn of 1914 met with greater success. The first meeting of representatives of ten unions took place at the end of September 1914, all of them—with one exception—being Bolsheviks. The bureau thus rapidly evolved into a party organ—evidence of the extensive overlapping of party and union functions throughout the war years. According to Sapronov, the Central Bureau was raided on 8 February 1915, but his activities within it had already stopped, for he had fled to St. Petersburg a couple of weeks earlier to escape military call-up. There he stayed until March when he moved to Orel—only to be arrested. He remained in prison until 10 September 1915 and by December was once again engaged in underground political work in Moscow.

42. In the other version of his memoirs Dune explains that seasonal workers were reluctant to join the medical fund, preferring to send their contributions back to the village, since they never knew whether they would be employed at the same factory in the following year.

43. These figures are for the total membership of the construction workers' union in Moscow and not just for the Provodnik plant. According to Sapronov, in January 1917 the illegal union claimed 245 members, of whom only 50 paid their dues.

44. *Printworkers' Voice* was a legal journal published by the Professional Society of Printers in the Moscow Industrial Region. Supported by contributions from printers, the journal first appeared in mid-November 1916.

45. S. I. Polidorov (1882–1932) was a member of the Moscow okrug committee of the Bolshevik party in 1917.

CHAPTER 2 ★ The February Revolution

1. This was Saturday, 25 February 1917. On 23 February strikes and disorders broke out in Petrograd over the bread shortage and the lockout of workers at the Putilov works. Within two days, according to official estimates, 240,000 workers had taken to the streets of the capital. On 25 February Nicholas II ordered General Khabalov to sup-

press the unrest, and the next day there were clashes between troops and demonstrators. On 27 February, however, the garrison in the capital mutinied, and on the same day, the Duma, ignoring an order to prorogue, elected the thirteen-member Provisional Committee. This declared itself the government after Nicholas abdicated on 1 March.

2. The Petrovskaia Farming and Forestry Academy opened in 1865 and was a hotbed of Populist activity from then until 1888. It was located in the village of Petrovskoe-Razumovskoe on the outskirts of the city. Because of its radical connections, the academy was closed in 1894 and replaced by the Moscow Agricultural Academy. It briefly reverted to its original name in 1917.

3. Piter was the popular name for St. Petersburg, whose name had been changed to Petrograd in 1914.

4. Pharaohs was a popular pejorative term for the police.

5. Khodynka Field was on the northwestern outskirts of the city and until the end of the nineteenth century had been a wide expanse of field crossed by streams and gullies. The summer camps of the Moscow garrison were situated there. In 1896 it was the scene of a horrific tragedy when several thousand people were killed or injured as the crowd panicked during a celebration to mark the coronation of Nicholas II. In 1917 the First Reserve Artillery Brigade was stationed there.

6. This policy that was adopted by the labor movement in the course of 1917 was one of industrial unions, that is, all workers in a particular factory or industry were to join a single union, notwithstanding their craft or skill. Initially, however, unions based on trade or craft were common.

7. The Moscow Soviet of Workers' Deputies was formed on 1 March 1917 and met initially in the building of the city duma. From mid-March it convened in the house of the governor-general on Skobelevskaia Square (later Sovetskaia Square), with plenums taking place at the Polytechnic Institute. Beginning on 2 March it published *Izvestiia moskovskogo soveta*. The Executive Committee and Presidium comprised equal numbers of Mensheviks, SRs, and Bolsheviks. The Moscow Soviet of Soldiers' Deputies existed separately. By the beginning of June there were nearly 700 deputies in the Soviet of Workers' Deputies, of whom 536 were workers (including 278 metal workers and 82 textile workers), 54 deputies were nonparty, 172 were Mensheviks, 110 were SRs, and 205 were Bolsheviks. The soviet supported the Provisional Government until September. On 5 September a unified plenum of the two soviets supported the Bolshevik resolution on power. On 19 September Bolsheviks won a majority of places

on the Executive Committee and Presidium, and V. P. Nogin became chair. There was also the Tushino-Guchkovskii Soviet of Workers' and Soldiers' Deputies, which existed in early June and may have sprung up earlier.

8. The temperance movement had first appeared within the Russian Empire in the Baltic provinces in the 1830s. In the last two decades of the nineteenth century a more organized temperance movement appeared that aimed much of its activity at the urban poor and the working class. An official movement sponsored by the government existed alongside an unofficial movement, in which doctors appear to have played a significant part. When the finance minister reorganized the state vodka monopoly in the 1890s he also a launched the *Popechitel'stvo o narodnoi trezvosti* (the Guardianship for Popular Sobriety), which ran a weekly journal, night classes for workers, Sunday schools, lectures, reading rooms, and so forth, designed to provide workers with "healthy alternatives" to the taverns.

9. The SRs were the Socialist Revolutionary party, which emphasized the revolutionary potential of the peasantry and supported the Provisional Government in 1917. The Kadets were the Constitutional Democratic Party, the main liberal party in Russia after 1905.

10. S. Ia. Nadson (1862–87) was a lyric poet somewhat in the mold of Nekrasov, whose tragic vision of the world seemed to bespeak the reactionary times in which he lived. He died very young of tuberculosis.

11. Dune has remembered his Chekhov incorrectly. The "hairdresser" is really a medical assistant (*fel'dsher*) from the short story "The Surgery" (1884). The "disappointed love of poor Lisa" is a reference to N. M. Karamzin's *Poor Lisa* (1792).

CHAPTER 3 ★ Workers' Power

1. War Industries Committees were created by the Ninth Congress of the Association of Industry and Trade in May 1915 to deal with the shortage of munitions. The Central War Industries Committee, located in Petrograd, liaised with the Special Council for the Supply of Munitions in distributing orders to armaments factories. Orders were generally obtained by the Central Committee and distributed by it, but the Moscow Committee, under its chair, P. P. Riabushinskii, could contract directly with the central military departments. The association of the War Industries Committees with the political campaign for a "government of public confidence" caused the government to strip back their powers.

2. City dumas were created by the Municipal Statutes of 1870,

whereby certain bands of taxpayers voted for deputies to a city council (duma) which, in turn, selected an executive board (uprava) and a mayor. After the "counterreform" of 1890, Moscow City Duma had 160 deputies elected for four years. It was responsible for public works, education, public health, welfare, trade, and taxation. In 1913, 63 deputies were factory owners, 32 were merchants, 24 were owners of real estate, and 27 were members of the liberal professions. After the February revolution the restrictive franchise based on taxation was abolished, and elections to the duma based on universal suffrage took place in June 1917.

3. This is probably a reference to the *Letters on Tactics,* written by Lenin between 8 and 13 April and published as a pamphlet. This drew out the tactical implications of the perspectives outlined in the April Theses, for which Lenin had written a draft on 3 April and which were incorporated into the substantial article "The Tasks of the Proletariat in the Present Revolution," which was published in *Pravda* on 7 April. In this Lenin argued that the bourgeois phase of the revolution was over; that no support should be given to the Provisional Government, as a government of land owners and capitalists; and that the task was now to establish a "revolutionary dictatorship of the proletariat and peasantry" by transferring all power to the soviets.

4. August Bebel (1840–1913) was the cofounder, along with Wilhelm Liebknecht, of the German Social Democratic party and its most popular leader for forty years. He was opposed to Bismarck's conception of a unified Germany based on Prussian dominance and spent about five years in prison at various times under the Iron Chancellor. A turner by trade, and self-educated, his most famous work was *Woman and Socialism* (1883). As leader of the Social Democrats he opposed the Revisionists but also kept his distance from the left wing of the party, which stressed the role of extraparliamentary activity.

5. Ferdinand Lassalle (1825–64) was a leading exponent of German socialism, sometime disciple of Marx, and one of the founders of the German labor movement. He was jailed for his activities in the 1848 revolution, but moved toward a more reformist position thereafter. Despite his association with Bismarck in the early 1860s and his conception of a monarchical welfare state, he remained a tireless champion of universal suffrage and workers' rights.

6. It was reported in *Sotsial-demokrat,* 28 June 1917, that the Bolshevik organization at Provodnik had seventeen hundred members. This may be an exaggeration. Another source states that at the beginning of July there were twelve hundred members of the Provodnik branch of the Bolshevik party.

7. V. P. Nogin (1878–1924) was the son of a salesclerk, worked as a

textile worker in his youth, and was largely self-educated. In 1898 he became a Social Democrat. He emigrated to London, where he was appointed agent of *Iskra*, and for his services was made a member of the Central Committee by Lenin in 1903. Beginning in April 1917 he was again a member of the Central Committee but also vice-chair of the Moscow Soviet of Workers' Deputies and chair from 2 October. He was a somewhat "soft" Bolshevik, opposed to a demonstration in July and in favor of maintaining relations with other socialist parties.

8. On 5 July military cadets smashed up the editorial offices of *Pravda* in Petrograd.

9. Dune is terribly confused here. On 4 July news of the events in the capital began to percolate through. A joint session of the Soviets of Workers' and Soldiers' Deputies agreed to ban demonstrations in Moscow by 442 votes to 242, with 6 abstentions. The Bolsheviks quit the session after they lost the vote. The Moscow Committee of the Bolshevik party was split, with leftists such as Bubnov, Lomov, and Stukov, probably in tune with the mood of worker Bolsheviks, calling for the seizure of the post office, the telephone and telegraph exchanges, and so forth. They were ruled out of order by the majority, who reluctantly sanctioned a demonstration to take place that evening. This left the Moscow Committee headquarters and wended its way to the soviet headquarters at Skobelev Square. One unsympathetic source says there were no more than two hundred participants in the demonstration and that they were massively outnumbered by hostile members of the public. In a neat reversal of the famous incident where Trotsky claims to have saved Chernov from the mob at this time, the Menshevik Boris Dvinov claims to have saved the lives of several Bolsheviks in danger of being lynched by the mob by letting them into the soviet building. It was only on 2–3 September that the joint executives of the two soviets agreed to a constitution for the Red Guard and followed this up on the 4th by setting up the Central Staff of the Red Guard, comprising twelve members of the workers' soviet, plus one candidate, and twelve members of the soldiers' soviet. It consisted of seven Bolsheviks, six Mensheviks, six SRs, three Unified Social Democrats, and three nonparty.

10. P. G. Smidovich (1874–1935), of noble birth, was expelled from Moscow University for political activities in 1894. He worked in factories in Belgium and joined the Belgian Workers' party. In 1898 he returned to Russia and became a member of the St. Petersburg Committee. In 1900 he was exiled and acted as an agent for *Iskra* abroad. He returned to Russia in 1903 and was active in the revolutionary movement in the south. In 1905 he took part in an armed uprising in

Moscow. After the February revolution he was a member of the Moscow Committee of the Bolshevik party and of the Presidium of the Executive Committee of the Moscow Soviet.

11. We shall never know the extent to which the Bolsheviks benefited from money provided by the German government for the purpose of bringing about revolution in Russia. From 1915 Alexander Helphand (1867–1924) was the main conduit through which such money was channeled, though he had no direct relations with Lenin. At the beginning of April 1917 the German Foreign Ministry assigned 5 million rubles for political subversion in Russia. After intricate negotiations, in which Helphand played some part, Lenin and other socialists were transported in the famous "sealed train" through Germany to Russia. In the summer of 1917 the Provisional Government published telegrams supposedly proving that money had reached the Bolsheviks in Russia via Scandinavia, but they are inconclusive.

12. A cabinet meeting on the evening of 6 July resolved that "all organizers and leaders of the armed movement against the government be arrested." Alexander Rabinowitch, *Prelude to Revolution: The Petrograd Bolsheviks and the July 1917 Uprising* (Bloomington, Ind., 1968), 217. Lenin, Zinoviev, Kamenev, Lunacharskii, and Trotsky were among those specifically mentioned. Kamenev, Trotsky, and Lunacharskii were imprisoned; Lenin escaped to Finland.

13. Trubnaia Square was so called because of the drain (truba) in the wall of the White City (which was devastated in the fire of 1812), through which the Neglinnaia River flowed underground into a reservoir.

14. A Parabellum was a type of automatic pistol.

15. A "bulldog" was a type of short-barreled revolver.

16. The Dedovskaia mill, like the Provodnik works, was situated in the Zvenigorod uezd, but it was at Guchkovo station, not Golitsyno. The Bolshevik committee at Dedovskaia was, apparently, set up in April and had ninety-two members by June. In elections to the volost' zemstvo in August at Dedovskaia mill the Bolsheviks won 639 votes, the SRs 137, and the Mensheviks 3. According to a report in *Sotsial-demokrat* on 10 August this mill had 3,000 workers, of whom 450 were members of the Bolshevik party.

17. On 27 August 1917 General L. G. Kornilov, supreme commander of the Russian army, received a telegram from Prime Minister Kerensky, removing him from office, whereupon he appealed to military commissars to rise up against the government and convene a constituent assembly.

18. Dune is not quite accurate here. The First Moscow Okrug Con-

ference, which took place on 17 April, was attended by 44 delegates with voting rights. It elected the Moscow Okrug Committee of 11, with 8 from the districts and 3 from Moscow. On 24 May the Okrug Committee decided to make Tushino a separate district, and it was given a vote on the committee. Although the Provodnik party branch was the biggest within the district, it is clear that other party branches existed elsewhere. At the Tushino district conference of the Bolshevik party on 29 July, in addition to the Provodnik delegates there were 4 representatives of the 150 members at Khutarevskaia mill and 3 representatives of the 450 members at Dedovskaia.

19. Often called the "father of Russian Marxism," G. V. Plekhanov (1856–1918) spoke these words at the Second Congress of the RSDWP in 1903. During World War I he adopted a "defensist" position, and after his return to Russia in 1917, he advocated continuance of the war, support for the Provisional Government, and restraint on the part of the soviets.

20. Iu. O. Martov (1873–1923) was perhaps the most outstanding leader of the Mensheviks. In 1917 he was on the left of the party, opposed to the continuation of the war and to the alliance of his party with the Kadets inside the Provisional Government.

21. *Novaia zhizn'* was published from 18 April 1917 to July 1918 by the group Social Democratic Internationalists and Writers. Maxim Gorky was its most prominent collaborator.

22. It was almost certainly earlier than this. The idea of Moscow's initiating an uprising had first been broached by Lenin in September. After 7 October Lenin did not refer to the possibility of Moscow's taking the lead again. The reference here is probably to Lenin's letter written to the Central Committee, the Petrograd committee, and the Moscow committee on 1 October. This was, in fact, the last occasion on which Lenin entertained the possibility of a peaceful seizure of power brought about by the Petrograd and Moscow Soviets' immediately declaring themselves the government. But the debate within the Moscow party about the possibilities of beginning an insurrection in the city took place at the end of September.

23. The Moscow city committee, which had managed to survive during the war, was in charge of Bolshevik activities in the city. At the time of the April conference it was said to be responsible for seven thousand members and by the time of the Sixth Party Congress in August for fifteen thousand. The Moscow oblast' committee was in charge of the party organizations in the thirteen provinces of the Central Industrial Region. By July there were said to be fifty-six organiza-

tions, with forty-five thousand members, subordinate to it. The oblast' committee had a smaller bureau of seven members, which was based in Moscow.

24. Again, this is somewhat misleading. The three Moscow party organizations continued their separate existences. However, on 14 October the bureau of the Moscow oblast' committee, unanimously backing the decision of the Central Committee of 10 October to prepare for an uprising, decided to create a "fighting center" of five, comprising two members of the bureau, two members of the Moscow committee, and one from the Moscow okrug committee. The historian Grunt says that this was a bid by the oblast' committee to bring the city committee to heel. It failed in its purpose. On 22 October the Moscow city committee, without any coordination with the oblast' committee, decided to create its own party center entirely out of its own membership. The next day the oblast' committee insisted that its center have primacy. On 25 October the three party organizations met to solve the conflict. As news of the uprising reached the meeting, it was decided to establish a "fighting center" consisting of seven people. The Moscow okrug committee had one representative, V. I. Solov'ev. T. V. Sapronov was officially merely the deputy representative of the okrug committee.

25. Both sides took up fighting positions on 26 October, with officer cadets occupying the Manege and the city duma building and the Military-Revolutionary Committee strengthening its hold of the Kremlin. The uprising, however, only got underway on the afternoon of the 27th, after the Military-Revolutionary Committee rejected the ultimatum of K. I. Riabtsev, commander of the Moscow Military District (see note 40), to liquidate itself.

26. The Military-Revolutionary Committee was formed at a joint plenum of the Soviets of Workers' and Soldier's Deputies on the evening of 25 October. The decision to create such a body had been taken by the Moscow committee of the Bolshevik party that morning but, initially, Smidovich, in opening the debate in the soviet, did not mention the need for any such body. During a break in the proceedings the Bolshevik fraction met and a resolution was drawn up proposing the formation of a group of seven to support the Military-Revolutionary Committee in Petrograd. The Mensheviks and SRs voted against the proposal, but the Bolshevik resolution was passed. The Mensheviks then decided to join the MRC, with a view to modifying its policies. The MRC had seven members and six candidate members, including eight Bolsheviks, two Mensheviks, and three

United Social Democrats. Subsequently, by coopting many other people and by driving the Mensheviks out, the Bolsheviks ensured that the MRC became an instrument of their own "party fighting center."

27. The first metallic-cartridge bolt-action rifle was invented by Frederic Vetterli in Switzerland 1867. See W. H. B. Smith and Joseph E. Smith, *The Book of Rifles* (Harrisburg, Pa., 1948), 58. We are indebted to Chris Ward for tracking down this reference.

28. Dune suggests that 150 Red Guards went to Moscow. The Bolshevik newspaper *Sotsial-demokrat* reported on 1 November 1917: "The workers of the Provodnik plant have sent 80 Red Guards to Moscow. Those Red Guards who have stayed behind at the plant are demanding that they also be sent to Moscow. Young and old have enrolled in the Red Guard, and those who have enlisted include Menshevik workers."

29. Vindavskii station today is the Rizhskii (Riga) station.

30. The Gorodskoi district soviet (one of the district soviets subordinate to the Moscow Soviet of Workers' Deputies) had its headquarters in Sukharev Square.

31. This building was no longer being used as a tavern. It was the headquarters of the Gorodskoi District Military Revolutionary Committee and the Gorodskoi district committee of the Bolshevik party.

32. Tushintsy meant the group from Tushino.

33. Dune is referring to the old ministry, replaced in the 1950s by the Stalinesque skyscraper on Smolensk Square.

34. This was Sretenskii Monastery.

35. Kitai-gorod was the enclosed area adjacent to the Kremlin. The name probably derives from the Russian word *kit*, which means a bundle of poles used to strengthen the walls before they were made of stone. From the beginning of the eighteenth century, this was the commercial heart of Moscow.

36. These were revolutionary soldiers from the Fifth Army of the northern front who were arrested in the summer of 1917 for their opposition to the war and imprisoned in Dvinsk. At the beginning of September 869 of them were transferred to the Butyrki prison in Moscow, where they called on the soviet to campaign for their release. They were freed on 22 September. There was a Bolshevik cell among the soldiers. They trained Red Guards in the use of arms, and on the evening of 27 October a platoon of 150 Dvintsy under the command of E. N. Sapunov clashed with officers and cadets in Red Square, and Sapunov was killed. The Dvintsy also took part in the battle for the Metropole Hotel.

37. The telephone exchange was taken on the morning of 1 No-

vember by forces under G. A. Usievich (1890–1918), who had returned to Russia with Lenin in April. Until the previous day the Military-Revolutionary Committee had shown every inclination to reach a peaceful settlement with the Committee of Public Safety, and Riabtsev, for his part, had not exactly shown a ruthless determination. It was only after negotiations failed on the night of 30–31 October that the MRC really set about to resolve matters by force.

38. On the morning of 28 October Colonel Riabtsev had spoken to the Military-Revolutionary Committee's commissar in the Kremlin, the Bolshevik ensign O. M. Berzin, saying Moscow was in the hands of the Committee of Public Safety and threatening that if the soldiers guarding the Kremlin did not leave they would be bombarded. Berzin opened the Troitskie Gates, whereupon officer cadets occupied the fortress. Berzin himself was beaten up, and as soldiers of the Fifty-sixth Regiment, who had been guarding it, left they were assaulted and even shot at.

39. The Aleksandr Military School was among the last bastions of resistance. It was disarmed at 4:00 P.M. on 3 November.

40. K. I. Riabtsev (1879–1919) was born the son of a peasant in Kostroma. He entered military service in 1900 and graduated from the Tbilisi Infantry School in 1904 and the Academy of the General Staff in 1912. In July 1917 he became chief of staff of the Moscow Military District and opposed Kornilov. In September he was appointed commander of the Moscow Military District. He was a Right SR and a member of the Committee of Public Safety set up to "struggle decisively against attempts to seize power" by the city duma on the evening of 25 October. On 2 November he was removed from his post by the MRC and left for Kharkov. In June 1919 during the occupation of that city he was arrested and shot by the Whites for having opposed Kornilov in 1917 and for having failed to oppose the Bolsheviks with sufficient vigor.

CHAPTER 4 ★ Rob the Robbers

1. The Red Guards took the Kremlin early on Friday, 3 November, whereas Dune implies Saturday.

2. This would be 6 November.

3. The allusion seems to be to John Reed's classic account of the October revolution *Ten Days that Shook the World*.

4. Four hundred were said to have been buried in the mass grave. The total number of fatalities from the fighting in Moscow may have been as high as one thousand.

5. The Moscow Military-Revolutionary Committee closed down the "bourgeois" press from 26 October to 8 November.

6. The quotation is from Leontii Mechov, "Zapiski dobrovol'tsa," *Beloe delo: letopis' beloi bor'by materialy sobrannye i razrabotannye Baronom P.N. Vrangelem i drugimi,* ed. A. A. von-Lampe (Berlin, 1933), vol. 7.

7. See Karl Marx, *Capital,* vol. 3.

8. In 1703 this country estate on the outskirts of Moscow belonged to Prince D. M. Golitsyn, who erected a palace surrounded by a French park. The palace was demolished at the end of the century. After 1810, when it became the property of Prince N. B. Iusupov, the palace complex was rebuilt to assume the aspect it retains to the present.

9. Northwest of Moscow, this palace was built in the mideighteenth century and, together with its gardens, was reconstructed at the end of the nineteenth. The last owner was Prince E. F. Shakhovskoi.

10. A. V. Lunacharskii (1875–1933) was a Bolshevik propagandist, philosopher, literary and art critic, playwright, and first commissar of enlightenment (education) in the Soviet government.

11. E. V. Gel'tser (1876–1962) became in 1925 the first ballerina to receive the title People's Artist of the Russian Soviet Federated Socialist Republic. R. M. Gliere's ballet *The Red Poppy* was first performed in 1927. It was the first Soviet ballet dedicated to a modern theme. Gel'tser danced the part of the Chinese dancer, Tao Khoa. Gel'tser would have been fifty-one at this time.

12. A. S. Enukidze (1877–1937) was secretary to the Presidium of the All-Russian Central Executive Committee of the soviets for seventeen years beginning in 1918. He directed the daily operations of the Kremlin, overseeing the supply and distribution of food, offices, automobiles, clerical staff, and so forth.

13. A question mark on the manuscript indicates the doubtfulness of this name. Kalnyn' is a common Latvian name and may indicate a member of the Kremlin staff, a fellow Latvian, with whom Dune was on good terms.

CHAPTER 5 ★ The Russian Vendée

1. In his chapter title Dune is attempting to make a connection between the situation in the Don Cossack territory and elsewhere in Russia with an insurrection in France. The Vendée was the name given to the department in western France along the Bay of Biscay, created in 1790. It is the name more familiarly given to the popular in-

surrection against the Convention government from March to December 1793, which pitched an army of soldiers flying the flag of the republic against peasants under the banner of God and king. The Convention saw in it an aristocratic plot to restore the ancien regime and crushed it with horrific brutality. Clearly, Dune sees it this way, too. In fact, the movement cannot be seen as one led by either priests or grands seigneurs, although both played a part. The "Whites," as they were known because of the white cockade they wore, were a motley army of peasants, weavers, and minor country notables desirous not so much to restore the old order as to oppose the new taxes, governmental reorganization, and, above all, the civil constitution of the clergy. The analogy with the White movement in Russia, then, is only a very partial one, the Vendée, in some respects, being more analogous to the popular "Green" movement that pitted the peasants against soviet power. See *A Critical Dictionary of the French Revolution*, trans. A. Goldhammer, ed. F. Furet and M. Ozouf (Cambridge, Mass., 1989); and *Historical Dictionary of the French Revolution, 1789–99*, ed. Samuel F. Scott and Barry Rothaus (London, 1985).

2. Chief executive officer of a Cossack community (voisko).

3. A. M. Kaledin (1861–1918) succeeded General Brusilov as commander of Russia's Eighth Army in May 1916. He clashed with Kerensky and was relieved of his command in May 1917. Returning to his native Don, he was elected ataman in June. He defended Kornilov against Kerensky, although he declined to send troops to support the rebellion. Afterwards Kerensky accused Kaledin of complicity in the latter. At its second meeting at the end of September, the Don krug found Kaledin innocent of the charges and refused to hand him over to Kerensky.

4. This is incorrect. M. V. Alekseev (1857–1918) was a general in both the Imperial Russian Army and the army of the Provisional Government. Having helped bring about the abdication of Nicholas II, he was appointed supreme commander of the army, a post from which he was dismissed in May for his political conservatism. He was succeeded by General Brusilov and then by Kornilov. In the aftermath of the Kornilov rebellion, Kerensky accepted Alekseev's offer to mediate between Kornilov and the Provisional Government. In early November he arrived in Novocherkassk, a small city just north of Rostov-on-Don, where he sought to rally an army against the Bolshevik government. By the end of December, a small force had been organized under the military command of Kornilov, with Alekseev in charge of supplies, recruitment, and diplomacy. Thus was the Volunteer Army born.

5. M. K. Diterikhs, tsarist general staff officer and field command-er, was prominent during the civil war as commander and chief of staff of the Czechoslovak Legion (1918–19), then commander of Kol-chak's forces in western Siberia.

6. The Czechoslovak Legion was recruited by the imperial govern-ment from Czechs and Slovaks living in Russia or captured in battle. By September 1917 the Czech Corps had grown to divisions of thirty thousand, officered mainly by Russians. At the end of October the Czechoslovak National Council in Paris ordered the corps to with-draw from Kiev and maintain strict neutrality in Russian politics. The Treaty of Brest-Litovsk in March 1918 made Russia neutral in the war, but the Czechoslovak National Council remained belligerent. Meanwhile the German occupation of the Ukraine pushed the legion eastward into Siberia, and it was agreed that the troops should be evacuated along the Trans-Siberian railway, to be shipped from Vladi-vostok to France. On 14 May 1918 at Cheliabinsk a dispute broke out between Czechoslovak troops and the local soviet authorities, caus-ing them to side against the Red Army and ally with the SR-backed government in this region.

7. The Kalmyks are one of the peoples of Central Asia whose lan-guage was part of the western Mongolian group of the Altai family and whose religion was lamaist.

8. This letter, written by Alekseev in Novocherkassk on 8 Novem-ber, was published in *Beloe delo* (Berlin, 1926), vol. 1.

9. General A. I. Denikin (1872–1947) was commander of the west-ern front during the July offensive, Russia's last military effort in World War I. He became chief commander of the Volunteer Army, then commander-in-chief of the Armed Forces of Southern Russia, and was ultimately recognized by the Whites as Supreme Ruler of Russia before resigning that position to General Wrangel. Here and elsewhere Dune quotes from A. I. Denikin, *Ocherki russkoi smuty* (Paris, 1922), vol. 2. Its English translation is *The Russian Turmoil.*

10. This non-Cossack regiment passed a resolution in No-vocherkassk on 1 December refusing to recognize the authority of Kaledin's Don government. Two days later, it was disarmed with the assistance of Alekseev's officers, putting up no resistance.

11. On 9 December the Military-Revolutionary Committee in Rostov, encouraged by sailors' support and counting on local Bolshe-vik regiments and Red Guards, announced that it would not recognize the authority of the Don government. Only on 15 December did Kale-din finally subjugate the city.

12. N. I. Muralov (1877–1937) played a key role in the insurrection

that brought Moscow under Bolshevik rule. He was commander of the Moscow Military District in 1917–18 and later a member of the Revolutionary War Council.

13. The system of commissars and commanders did not come properly into operation until March, after Trotsky took command of the Red Army and sanctioned the recruitment of former tsarist officers and generals. These so-called "military specialists" were watched over by two political commissars—an institution established by the Provisional Government—so that at every level the war effort was directed by a three-person revolutionary military council. According to the principle of dual command, orders were to be obeyed only if they bore the signatures of both officer and commissar.

14. V. A. Antonov-Ovseenko (1884–1938), as a prominent member of the Military-Revolutionary Committee, played an important part in the Bolshevik seizure of power in Petrograd. In the new government he was one of three members of the Committee for Military and Naval Affairs. Various assignments followed, including command of troops against Kaledin's Cossacks and the forces of the Ukrainian Rada.

15. Iu. V. Sablin (1897–1937), as a Left SR member of the Executive Committee of the Moscow Soviet, played a vital part in the struggle that brought Bolshevik power to Moscow. On 14 December he was appointed chief of the First Moscow Revolutionary Detachment, which was sent to Kharkov to assist Antonov-Ovseenko. His force of 1,500 was one of three armies under the latter that defeated Kaledin and captured Rostov-on-Don and Novocherkassk. He opposed the Treaty of Brest-Litovsk and was implicated in the Left SR uprising against the Bolsheviks in July. However, he was given amnesty in November. Still barely twenty, he went on to become commander of various infantry and cavalry forces against the Whites and the Kronstadt rebels.

16. Esaul was the title of a Cossack captain. V. M. Chernetsov led a partisan unit of about 150, which was formed on 13 December 1917 in connection with the Bolshevik uprising in Rostov. Chernetsov had led a partisan detachment that had operated behind German lines during the war. In 1917 he commanded a Cossack unit to repress striking miners in the Donbass. This detachment was the main force at Kaledin's disposal.

17. Colonel E. F. Semiletov (1872–1919) returned from the front to the Don in 1917 as a lieutenant-colonel and in December formed a detachment from young officers and students to fight the Bolsheviks. Many of Chernetsov's partisans joined this detachment after their

leader was killed. Semiletov was promoted to general in 1919 and died of typhus in the same year.

18. It is not certain that A. N. Ponomarev (1897–1954) (if this is he: Peter Kenez gives his initials as A. V. Ponomarev) was ever a general. A. M. Nazarov was elected provisional ataman after Kaledin's suicide on 12 February 1918, an appointment confirmed five days later. On 19 February, however, the Sixth Don Cossack regiment refused to fight the Reds. When the Military-Revolutionary Committee took Novocherkassk on 25 February, Nazarov was arrested and later executed.

19. This conference took place in Novocherkassk on 11–12 January 1918. The inogorodnye were reluctant to fight the Bolsheviks because they feared that fighting would facilitate a Cossack dictatorship. The Bolshevik delegates interrupted the speeches of Kaledin and M. P. Bogaevskii with shouts of "executioners!" and "down with counter-revolutionaries." Although they passed the resolution hostile to the Volunteer Army, which Dune mentions, as a result of Cossack concessions, however, including the promise of three million desiatinas of land for the inogorodnye and a general amnesty, the majority of delegates conditionally accepted the necessity of fighting against the Bolsheviks.

20. F. G. Podtelkov (1886–1918), cavalry sergeant-major of the Sixth Don Guards' Battery, was elected chair of the Don Cossack Military-Revolutionary Committee in January 1918 and then chair of the Council of People's Commissars of the Don Soviet Republic at the First Congress of Soviets of the Don in April. On 10 May he was captured by Cossacks and executed.

21. V. S. Golubov was a Left SR Cossack leader, a brave fighter and adventurer whose principal aim was to become ataman. In January 1918 he deserted Kaledin and joined up with Podtelkov's pro-Bolshevik forces. It was he who led the troops that occupied Novocherkassk. It is not clear whether this is the same person as the N. M. Golubov (1881–1918) cited in another source, which says that he was a Cossack cavalry lieutenant with a remarkable record of bravery during World War I who became a Bolshevik in 1917. He fought against the forces of Kaledin, but at the end of March fell out with the Bolsheviks. On 29 March 1918 he was shot by Cossacks for his part in the destruction of Chernetsov's partisans. This roughly corresponds with Dune's account of Golubov's fate, but he may have confused two people of the same name.

22. Strictly speaking this was not yet the Second Special Army but the Fifth Soviet Army. R. F. Sivers (1892–1918) helped found the Bolshevik newspaper of the Twelfth Army, *Trench Truth* (*Okopnaia*

pravda), in 1917 and was jailed for his part in the July Days of that year. In November 1917 he was ordered to command a detachment to the Ukraine and on 24 February led the capture of Rostov from the Whites. In November he was seriously wounded and died shortly afterwards.

23. A desiatina is approximately 2.7 acres.

24. Dune's account exaggerates Bolshevik sensitivity to Cossack sentiment. Even before the occupation of Novocherkassk on 25 February, Sablin had announced to krug representatives: "Cossackdom as a separate and privileged estate should be eliminated." Peter Kenez, *Civil War in South Russia, 1918* (Berkeley, 1971), 121.

25. The battle at Likhaia, which Dune goes on to describe and which saw Chernetsov's partisans inflict serious casualties on Sablin's troops, took place on 31 January 1918.

26. This is a pun. The Russian word translated as "damnable" is *likhoi*, a word meaning "evil." Its feminine form, *likhaia*, was also the name of the station.

27. This was Chernetsov's last victory. On 3 February he and a hundred partisans were surrounded and forced to surrender. At nightfall he attacked Podtelkov, the Red commander, with his bare hands; in the confusion many of his partisans escaped, but Chernetsov was killed on the spot.

28. F. F. Abramov (1870–1963), after a long career in the tsarist army, in 1918 returned to his native Don, where he commanded the northern group of partisans. He was later inspector of Don cavalry.

29. Sivers had entered Rostov on 23 February. Sablin could have taken Novocherkassk on the same day, but he waited for the troops of the Military-Revolutionary Committee under Golubov to take the city. This they did on 25 February. Although Golubov was allowed to lead the occupation of Novocherkassk, the Bolsheviks never fully trusted him, keeping him out of Rostov, the center of power. Golubov did not carry out the Military-Revolutionary Committee's order to pursue Popov's army after it fled Novocherkassk, and instead captured M. P. Bogaevskii, close friend and assistant of Kaledin. In early April he turned against the Bolsheviks and toured villages around Novocherkassk to enlist volunteers. He had to flee after the Bolsheviks sent a detachment after him on 7 April. A few days later, he became one of the first victims of rebellious anti-Bolshevik Cossacks, who had not forgiven his earlier treachery.

30. Denikin, *Ocherki russkoi smuty*, 2:205.

31. It is not clear from where Dune gets this figure of 200,000 officers of the tsarist army (below he gives a figure of 202,000). Peter

Kenez reckons that at the end of 1916 there were 145,916 officers. See "A Profile of the Pre-Revolutionary Officer Corps," *California Slavic Studies* 7 (1973): 145.

32. Denikin, *Ocherki russkoi smuty*, 2:205.

33. Ibid., 2:199.

34. Speech at the Ninth Congress of the Russian Communist party, March 1920, printed in V. I. Lenin, *Polnoe sobranie sochinenii* (Moscow, 1963), 40:254.

35. P. N. Krasnov (1869–1945), commander of the Third Cavalry Corps from August 1917, was assigned the responsibility by Kerensky of retaking Petrograd after the Bolshevik seizure of power. Active in the Volunteer Army, he was made ataman by the new provisional Don government in May 1918.

CHAPTER 6 ★ Soviet Power in 1918

1. On 6 July 1918, Left Socialist-Revolutionaries assassinated the German ambassador to Russia, Count Mirbach, to demonstrate their opposition to the Brest-Litovsk peace and to any cooperation with "German imperialism." In the ensuing confusion, some Left SRs seized Dzerzhinskii and Latsis, the two leaders of the Cheka. Bolsheviks would charge, with scant foundation, that this was an attempt to seize power in order to continue a guerrilla war against Germany. The attempted coup was easily defeated the next day by loyal soviet troops. See Lutz Häfner, "The Assassination of Count Mirbach and the 'July Uprising' of the Left Socialist Revolutionaries in Moscow, 1918," *Russian Review* 50, no. 3 (July 1991): 324–44.

2. Opponents of the Bolshevik seizure of power in October 1917 had widely claimed the new government would not endure more than a year.

3. The "Red Army ration" was a synonym for the highest ration category, issued to Red Army soldiers and selectively to their families and to essential skilled workers. In the autumn of 1918, manual workers were entitled to two pounds of bread, intellectual workers one pound, and nonworkers one-half pound.

4. The Caspian roach is a small flat fish found in the Caspian Sea; it is usually dried, as a result of which it becomes even flatter.

5. Authorized by the Sovnarkom in January 1918 in order to ensure the transport of foodstuffs and to fight speculators, anti-profiteering detachments of five to ten people were posted in cities, at railway stations and jetties, and on major highways.

6. In response to the food supply crisis, central and local governments enacted a series of emergency measures to establish a "food

supply dictatorship." These included the formation of antiprofiteering brigades and armed food supply detachments.

7. In July 1918 counterrevolutionary assaults were attempted in three cities to the north and east of Moscow. Iaroslavl, north of Moscow on the Volga River, was seized on 6 July by a surprise attack of conspirators from the League for the Regeneration and Freedom of Russia, led by the former terrorist and later confidant of Kerensky, Boris Savinkov. Savinkov's forces held out for two weeks before the town was retaken by Bolshevik troops. In connection with this, the league seized the town of Murom, east of Moscow, on 8 July and held it for two days. They also launched an unsuccessful assault on Rybinsk, near Iaroslavl, on 7 July.

8. The state planning agency, Gosplan, was created in April 1921 to continue work on central planning that had been begun by several state agencies from even before the February revolution. Volkhovstroi was a planned hydroelectric station to be built on the Volkhov River north of Petrograd. It was completed in 1926.

9. A pood equals thirty-six pounds.

10. This is probably an error on Dune's part. More recent Soviet accounts, based on archival research, put the figure at just under two hundred thousand.

11. Lenin gave two speeches to the Sixth All-Russian Special Congress of Soviets, 6–9 November 1918, which were printed in full in *Pravda* on 9 and 10 November and *Izvestiia* on 9 November. In both speeches Lenin named Western imperialism as the major enemy of the revolution. "We know," he concluded the speech marking the anniversary of the October revolution, "that the beasts of imperialism are stronger than we are, they can commit on us and our country great violence, brutality, and torture, but they cannot defeat the international revolution. They are full of savage hatred, and therefore we say to ourselves, let come what may, but every worker and peasant of Russia should fulfill his duty and go to die, if this is necessary to save the revolution. We say, let come what may, but whatever calamities the imperialists may yet bring, they will still not save themselves. Imperialism will perish, and the international socialist revolution, despite them, will triumph!" *Polnoe sobranie sochineniia,* 37:152.

12. The Ninth Army was created by order of the Revolutionary-Military Council of the southern front on 3 October 1918, assembled from units of the Povorino and Balashov-Kamyshin sectors of the southern front. From October to December 1918 it engaged in battle with the Don Cossack army in the region of Povorino, Elan, and Balashov. Its first commander was A. I. Egorov (1883–1939), who was replaced on 24 November 1918 by P. E. Kniagnitskii.

13. Bolshevik leaders were divided over the use of former tsarist officers, but the commissar of war, Trotsky, was a strong supporter of employing both former officers and former noncommissioned officers (NCOs) as Red commanders. By November 1918, over 22,000 former officers and 128,000 former NCOs were mobilized, and during the entire period of the civil war some 48,000 former officers and 128,000 former NCOs served as commanders in the Red Army. The loyalty of such commanders was to be secured by the presence of military commissars, representing the interests of the proletarian state and the party. The "military specialists"—the commanders—were to be in charge of military-operational work, but all orders had to be countersigned by the commissar.

14. The full Russian term is "nachal'nik shtaba divizii." Abbreviations such as these became part of the popular language during this period, but in this book, except for here, all have been rendered in their full rather than abbreviated form.

15. Vasilii Isidorovich Kikvidze (1895–1919), born to the family of a lower-level Georgian bureaucrat, completed gymnasium and served in World War I as a "privileged volunteer." He belonged to the Left SRs in 1917–18. In November 1917 he was elected to the Military-Revolutionary Committee for the southwest front and at the end of December led a special unit against troops of the Ukrainian Central Rada. He fought throughout early 1918 with the nascent Red Army, and in May 1918 formed the division that he led, named the Sixteenth Infantry Division, in October. According to official sources, he was severely wounded in an assault on a small Cossack village (later renamed the Kikvidze village, Volgagrad oblast) on 11 January 1919, and died on the 12th (see below). The Sixteenth Division was renamed the Sixteenth Kikvidze Division in his honor.

16. Dzhigits are Caucasian horsemen.

17. An Abrek is a Caucasian mountain bandit.

18. Trotsky's account of this decision is reported in a letter to the Bolshevik Central Committee of March 1919. In it, Trotsky rails against "comradely discipline" of the sort Gusarskii and Kikvidze represented. In Trotsky's account, both Gusarskii and his successor for twelve days, Mikhail Vasil'evich Sluvis, "wilfully disobeyed an order and disrupted a well-conceived operation and, in self-justification, started at conference meetings to accuse the Army Command of breach of faith. . . . I had both Divisional Commanders arrested. Five Commissars, Party members, came to see me to give explanations and to obtain protection. I handed them over to the courts for abandoning their posts without permission. Gusarskii was shot on the orders of the tribunal to which I had handed him over. After this the

foregatherings of divisional commanders and commissars came to a stop. The Ninth Army immediately went over to the attack. This moment was a turning-point in the history of the Ninth Army. As regards their at-homes and tea-party sessions my attitude not only to the divisional commanders (who were, probably, not acting from any evil motives), but also to the Commissar-Party members was not a 'comradely' one." *The Trotsky Papers, 1917–1922* (The Hague, 1964), 333.

19. From summer 1918, Sivers commanded the First Ukrainian Special Brigade. Officially, he died of wounds in Moscow on 2 December 1918 and was buried in the Field of Mars in Petrograd.

20. Official sources claim that Kikvidze died at enemy hands, but the date of his death is the same as that of the meeting where Trotsky's tribunal condemned Gusarskii. Dune seems to imply Kikvidze either was executed too or committed suicide.

21. Dune's allegation here is puzzling. Kniagnitskii remained in the service of the Red Army until 1938, when he disappeared along with other members of the army command structure. However, his activities between June 1919, when he left the command of the Ninth Army, and November 1919, when he assumed command of the smaller Fifty-eighth Infantry Division, are unaccounted for. Perhaps he could have defected to the Whites and then changed his loyalty again in November, to be rewarded with a lesser command. His successor in the Ninth Army, N. D. Vsevolodov, commanded just ten days before going over to the Whites. Perhaps Dune heard this report and assumed the commander was still Kniagnitskii, or perhaps Kniagnitskii had indeed preceded Vsevolodov as a turncoat.

CHAPTER 7 ★ On the Don Again

1. These were small manufacturing towns in the Moscow region. Agricultural pursuits here were usually secondary.

2. A "bol'shak" was a peasant head of household.

3. The Khlysty were a Christian sect whose religious celebrations involved frenzied dancing and sometimes sexual orgies.

4. Alexandra Kollontai (1872–1952) was a Bolshevik and a feminist. She was the first woman in the soviet government, the first commissar of social welfare, but she was better known for her conflicts with Lenin about sexual freedom and the role of workers in the socialist regime. Kollontai believed that after the revolution the bourgeois institution of marriage would disappear, that free sexual unions would come to prevail. The role of the state would be to provide communal child-raising and housekeeping services, not to police family

life. This state was best organized at the point of production, and she supported the Workers' Opposition in 1921. Her ideas on sexual liberation received fictional development in *Love of Worker Bees* (1923). Later, Kollontai was virtually exiled from Russia in a series of diplomatic posts.

5. The play on words here in Russian is intended to be obscene.

6. Given the change in government in 1917 and the number of different governments in the territories under White rule, there were no stable and acceptable monetary instruments during this period. Rubles issued by the tsarist government, "Nicholas rubles," continued to circulate. Denikin's Volunteer Army printed its own paper ruble currency nicknamed, for unknown reasons, "kolokol'chiki," "little bells," perhaps because of the color of the flower of the same name. The Provisional Government's notes were known as Kerenskies, after its last prime minister.

7. Filipp Kuz'mich Mironov (1872–1921) was a Red Army commander of Cossack origin. He was arrested in 1919 for disobeying orders and sentenced to be shot and then was pardoned by the All-Russian Soviet Executive Committee. But having been appointed unit inspector of the cavalry in the Red Army early in 1921, he was arrested by the Don Cheka on the basis of a denunciation and shot in Moscow's Butyrki Prison.

CHAPTER 8 ★ Retreat

1. The "Mamontov raid" lasted from 10 August until 19 September 1919. The White general Konstantin Konstaninovich Mamontov (1869–1920) broke through the Soviet Eighth and Ninth armies with six thousand cavalry, three thousand infantry, twelve field guns, seven armored trains, and three armored cars. Seizing Tambov on 18 August, they were able to disrupt transport and terrorize the population. Finally surrounded by Red troops on 18 September, a portion of Mamontov's group was able to evade their pursuers and rejoin the Volunteer Army. The episode revealed the tactical importance of cavalry in the civil war.

2. "Tatar" was a common term for Turkic and Persian inhabitants of the empire, who were almost exclusively Moslems.

CHAPTER 9 ★ Prisoner of the Volunteer Army

1. The Tsaritsyn commissars were the former political leaders of Tsaritsyn (later Stalingrad and Volgagrad), gateway to the Caucasus

and an important strategic objective. Successfully defended by the Red Army in 1918, it fell to the Whites on 30 June 1919.

2. A "redtop" is a variety of mushroom and a derogatory name for a Red Army soldier.

3. Tsaritsyn was recaptured by the Red Army on 3 January 1920.

4. Novorossiisk is located on the Black Sea, linked by direct rail with Tsaritsyn.

5. This cement factory is possibly the one that provides the setting for the proletarian novel *Cement* (1925) by Fedor Gladkov, whose action is set in this period of the winding-down of the civil war.

6. Gelendzhik was a coastal town about 36 kilometers from Novorossiisk, and the town of Tuapse was 130 kilometers away.

7. The Red Army of the Northern Caucasus, led by a Latvian, Karl Kalnin, was trapped between the Volunteer Army and the German army's occupying forces in July 1918, despite superior numbers. The decisive defeat at the railway junction Tikhoretskaia on 14 July cut off the Red Army units from one another and strengthened the Volunteer Army's links with its rear.

8. At the Seventh Party Congress in March 1918, the Bolshevik party voted to change its official name from the Russian Social-Democratic Workers' party (Bolshevik) to the Russian Communist party. The purpose of the name change was to symbolize a complete break with the reformist Social-Democratic parties of Western Europe.

CHAPTER 10   ★   In the Novorossiisk Underground

1. *The Past (Byloe)* was a journal devoted to the history of the revolutionary movement in Russia. The first series, published abroad between 1900 and 1904, concentrated on the 1860s and 1880s. A new series was published in Russia in 1906 and 1907, which included memoirs and articles about the revolutionary movement up to 1905–7.

2. General Andrei Grigor'evich Shkuro (1887–1947) was a White Army lieutenant-general from a Cossack family. He was notorious for his severe cruelty and lack of discipline, which was extreme even for the White leadership. His men wore a skull and crossbones and wolf's head insignia on their uniform and were known as Shkuro's Wolves. After the civil war, Shkuro emigrated and served with Hitler's army in World War II. He was returned to the USSR in 1945 and was later executed.

3. Novorossiisk was captured by the Red Army on 27 March 1920. Units of the White Don Army managed to escape by sea to the Crimean peninsula, others escaped further south to Tuapse.

4. Semen Mikhailovich Budennyi (1883–1973) had become the symbol of the Red Cavalry. A tsarist cavalryman from a family of poor non-Cossack peasants in the Don region, he worked his way up through the Red Army cavalry ranks, becoming commander-in-chief of the Cavalry Army. He remained a favorite of Stalin's and was buried with full honors in the Kremlin Wall.

CHAPTER 11 ★ On My Own Again

1. *Subbotniki* were days of organized work, usually on a Saturday, which in Russian is *subbota*. The practice began in the cities during the civil war to mobilize workers to help unload freight cars and distribute needed food supplies.

2. The remnants of the White Army regrouped in the Crimea under the leadership of General Baron Peter Wrangel. Their planned counteroffensive failed after initial success, and although Wrangel came close to recapturing Ekaterinodar, the capital of the Kuban, the Crimean peninsula fell to the Reds on 11 November 1920. Wrangel and some 145,000 people fled from the Crimea to Constantinople, marking the virtual end of the White movement.

3. Nestor Makhno (1889–1934) was a poor Ukrainian peasant, radicalized in prison and converted to anarchism. He began to gain fame as a partisan chieftain in 1918, and despite his anarchism at first worked closely with the Bolsheviks. But he also defended insurgent peasants against soviet power in the Ukraine and was dismissed by the Red Army. At this point he raised his own army, harassing both Reds and Whites. At its height, Makhno's army included forty or fifty thousand troops, captured the major town of Ekaterinoslav (later Dnepropetrovsk) in October 1919, and proclaimed a "regime of anarchy." Driving out the Whites, his army continued to engage in guerrilla operations, contributing to the final defeat of Wrangel. But his disagreements with soviet power continued, and in August 1921 he and the remnants of his army were forced to escape to Romania.

Aleksandr Stepanovich Antonov (1888–1922) had less of a political program. A nominal Socialist-Revolutionary, by 1919 he had organized a terrorist band in Tambov province composed of Red Army deserters and local peasants. A widespread uprising against soviet grain requisitioning broke out in the province in August 1920, and fierce partisan warfare spread throughout Tambov province and parts of neighboring Saratov and Penza provinces until April 1921. At the height of the movement, between January and April, Antonov's army numbered about twenty thousand. The uprising was finally quelled by the injection of large forces of reliable Red cavalry and the abolition of the loathsome requisitions policy. Small pockets of resistance held out until late 1921. Then a fugitive from soviet power, Antonov was discovered and shot in June 1922.

4. Fostikov was a White Army general who had escaped to the foothills of the Caucasus Mountains after the breakup of the White Army. Here he formed a partisan force he named the Army for the Regeneration of Russia. By early summer 1920, he had a force of fifteen to thirty thousand fighters, almost all Cossacks. Isolated and with no means of communication, he was unable to link up with Wrangel's assault on the Kuban and retreated into Georgia with the remnants of his army in October 1920. In November, he joined Wrangel's army in its last defense of the Crimea. The Ninth Red Army, to which Dune was assigned, numbered at this time twenty-four thousand.

5. The Cheka, whose nickname comes from the first two initials of its official title, Extraordinary Commission for the Struggle with Counterrevolution and Sabotage, was created on 20 December 1917 under the leadership of a Polish Bolshevik, Feliks Dzerzhinskii (1877–1926). From small beginnings, the secret police organization eventually developed wide powers and autonomy. The secret police of Stalin's terror, the GPU and NKVD, and the more recent KGB, evolved from this commission, and in recent times KGB officers still proudly called themselves Chekists.

CHAPTER 12: REBELLION IN DAGESTAN

1. Shamil (1797–1871) was the leader of a "holy war" against Russian expansion by the Dagestan and Chechen mountain people. Educated by Muslim clerics, Shamil was named imam in 1834, and relying on the support of the free peasantry and the clergy, he enjoyed great success against tsarist troops. His movement was finally defeated in 1859. Shamil and his family were exiled to central Russia.

Mikhail Lermontov (1814–41) was a poet and novelist, a major figure in nineteenth-century Russian literature. Extensive travel in the Caucasus first with his family and later in the army provided Lermontov with exotic settings for his verse and his novel *A Hero of Our Time*. A number of his poems, including "Izmail-Bei" (1830) and "Khadzhi-Abrek" (1833) portray sympathetically the Islamic mountain tribes and their fierce resistance to Russian power.

2. An aul is a Caucasian mountain village.

3. The "green banner" was that of the prophet Mohammed. One of the leaders of the rebellion was the Muslim cleric Imam Gotsinskii.

4. Oil was shipped by rail from the oil center of Baku, on the Caspian Sea, through the north Caucasus city of Groznyi (later the capital of the Chechen-Ingush Autonomous Republic), and from there west and north to Russia.

5. Khadzhi-Murat (1790s–1852) was a family member of the Avar khanate; he joined Shamil's rebellion and became a trusted adviser and brave fighter. He broke with Shamil in 1851, went over to the Russian army, and was killed in battle. He is the subject of a short story by Leo Tolstoy as well as of a Lermontov poem.

6. In June 1921, the party's Central Committee resolved that the party should be cleansed, or purged, of all undesirable elements. Ostensibly the motive was to expunge the opportunists and moral undesirables who had flooded the party: drunkenness, careerism, religious belief, laziness, and corruption were commonly cited grounds for purging, but disagreement with the party's political line was also sufficient cause for ejection. By the end of 1921, a quarter of the total membership of the party had been removed, so the Dagestan purge was relatively more sweeping.

7. Dune's figures are drawn from standard compilations of the time, but some are misleading and others are open to question. Fifteen million soldiers served in the Russian Imperial Army from 1914 to 1918, but after losses, the size of the army in 1917 was about 7.3 million. The size of the officer corps was approximately 130,000 to 145,000, with casualties of 107,000. The Red Army by late 1920 numbered approximately 5 million; of these, roughly 48,500 were officers recruited from the tsarist army. Most accounts agree that 300,000 Communists served in the Red Army, although this number fluctuated substantially during the civil war.

8. Dune is quoting from White general Baron Aleksei Pavlovich Budberg, who was chief of the general staff of the White admiral Kolchak in Siberia. These comments are from his diary, published in *Arkhiv russkoi revoliutsii* 15 (1924): 291.

9. General N. N. Iudenich was a White commander on the northwest front. In 1919 his attack on Petrograd narrowly failed.

10. A White commander, Vladimir Zenonovich Mai-Maevskii (1867–1920) was notorious for his drinking bouts, orgies, and for the terror and lawlessness that reigned in territories under his control. His soldiers, whom he permitted wide latitude in looting and plundering, were said to adore him. He was dismissed as commander-in-chief of the White Army by Denikin in December 1919.

11. K. N. Sokolov was a Kadet politician. These remarks presumably come from his memoir of the civil war, *Pravlenie generala Denikina* (Sofia, 1921).

12. Pavel N. Miliukov (1859–1943) was a major Kadet leader, former history professor, and first minister of foreign affairs in the Provisional Government in 1917. He wrote a number of reflective works on the revolution from his exile in Western Europe. These words are from his *Rossiia na perelome* (Paris, 1927), 2:207.

Vasilii Vital'evich Shul'gin, a conservative nationalist leader in the tsarist dumas and notorious anti-Semite, was an important political actor in Denikin's administration.

13. Louis Auguste Blanqui was a French utopian communist and revolutionary in 1848 who advocated revolutionary conspiracy over popular movements. The Bolsheviks in October and afterward were very sensitive to the accusation of Blanquism dressed in Eastern "Tartar" clothing.

14. Dune does not identify the source of this quotation but it is possibly recorded in the proceedings of one of four all-Russian congresses of soviets held in 1918.

15. Cited from the stenographic report of the Seventh Congress of Soviets of the Russian Soviet Federated Socialist Republic, 9 December 1919, *Sed'moi vserossiiskii s"ezd sovetov rabochikh, krest'ianskikh, krasnoarmeiskikh i kazachikh deputatov. Stenograficheskii otchet (5–9 dekabria 1919 g.)* (Moscow, 1920), 19.

16. Ivan Smilga was a hard-line Communist who argued that the 70 percent of Communists who did not actively oppose the Kronstadt rebellion should be disciplined. Nikolai Bukharin, later a critic of Stalin, was a left-wing Bolshevik in 1917, but the events of the civil war helped to transform his position. Both men, and all party leaders, worried in early 1921 that the party had lost its base of proletarian support. The discussion referred to here is from *Desiatyi s"ezd RKP(b), mart 1921 g. Stenograficheskii otchet* (Moscow, 1963), 253, 224–25.

17. Dune is misleading here, exaggerating the weakness of soviet power. In fact, General Tukhachevskii mobilized fifty thousand hand-picked troops against the hapless rebels. This was very much a military operation. But when the initial assault on Kronstadt was repulsed, delegates to the party congress volunteered to assist the army.

18. *Odinnadtsatyi s"ezd RKP(b), mart-aprel' 1922 g. Stenograficheskii otchet* (Moscow, 1961), 37–38.

19. Alexander Shliapnikov (1884–1937?) was one of the leaders of the Workers' Opposition, which had its origins among Communist trade unionists in 1919. They criticized the party for becoming too bureaucratic in its economic administration and for depriving workers of a role in industrial management. Shliapnikov in particular advocated an equal sharing of power among party, trade unions, and so-

viets. This criticism had so intensified by March 1921 that the Tenth Party Congress voted to curb the opposition by muzzling all party dissent. These words are from *Odinnadtsatyi s"ezd RKP(b)*, 104.

Suggestions for
Further Reading

Berkman, Alexander. *The Bolshevik Myth (Diary 1920–1922)*. New York, 1925.

Bonnell, Victoria E., ed. *The Russian Worker: Life and Labor under the Tsarist Regime*. Berkeley, 1983.

Brinkley, G. A. *The Volunteer Army and Allied Intervention in South Russia, 1917–21*. South Bend, Ind., 1966.

Carr, E. H. *The Bolshevik Revolution, 1917–1923*. 3 vols. London, 1953.

Chamberlin, William Henry. *The Russian Revolution*. 2 vols. Princeton, N.J., 1987.

Daniels, Robert V. *The Conscience of the Revolution*. Cambridge, Mass., 1960.

Denikin, Anton Ivanovich. *The Russian Turmoil*. New York, 1922.

Erickson, John. *The Soviet High Command: A Military-Political History, 1918–1941*. London, 1962.

Ferro, Marc. *The Bolshevik Revolution: A Social History of the Russian Revolution*. Translated by Norman Stone. London, 1980.

Figes, Orlando. *Peasant Russia, Civil War: The Volga Countryside in Revolution (1917–1921)*. Oxford, 1989.

Footman, David. *Civil War in Russia*. New York, 1962.

Frankel, Edith Rogovin, Jonathan Frankel, and Baruch Knei-Paz, eds. *Revolution in Russia: Reassessments of 1917*. Cambridge, 1992.

Kanatchikov, Semen I. *A Radical Worker in Tsarist Russia: The Autobiography of Semen Ivanovich Kanatchikov*. Edited and translated by Reginald E. Zelnik. Stanford, 1986.

Kenez, Peter. *Civil War in South Russia, 1918*. Berkeley, 1971.

———. *Civil War in South Russia, 1919–1920*. Berkeley, 1977.

Kerensky, Alexander. *Russia and History's Turning Point*. New York, 1965.

Koenker, Diane. *Moscow Workers and the 1917 Revolution*. Princeton, N.J., 1981.

Koenker, Diane P., William G. Rosenberg, and Ronald Grigor Suny, eds. *Party, State, and Society in the Russian Civil War: Explorations in Social History.* Bloomington, Ind., 1989.

Lih, Lars. *Bread and Authority in Russia, 1914–1921.* Berkeley, 1990.

Lincoln, W. Bruce. *Red Victory: A History of the Russian Civil War.* New York, 1989.

Lockhart, R. H. Bruce. *Memoirs of a British Agent.* London, 1932.

Luckett, Richard. *The White Generals.* New York, 1971.

McAuley, Mary. *Bread and Justice: State and Society in Petrograd, 1917–1922.* Oxford, 1991.

Mawdsley, Evan. *The Russian Civil War.* Winchester, Mass., 1987.

Rabinowitch, Alexander. *The Bolsheviks Come to Power.* New York, 1976.

———. *Prelude to Revolution: The Petrograd Bolsheviks and the July 1917 Uprising.* Bloomington, Ind., 1968.

Radkey, Oliver H. *The Unknown Civil War in Soviet Russia: A Study of the Green Movement in the Tambov Region, 1920–1921.* Stanford, 1976.

Rigby, T. H. *Lenin's Government: Sovnarkom, 1917–1922.* Cambridge, 1979.

Schapiro, Leonard. *The Origin of the Communist Autocracy.* 2d ed. Cambridge, Mass., 1977.

Serge, Victor. *Conquered City.* Translated by Richard Greeman. Garden City, N.Y., 1978.

Shklovsky, Viktor. *A Sentimental Journey: Memoirs, 1917–1922.* Translated by Richard Sheldon. Ithaca, N.Y., 1970.

Smith, S. A. *Red Petrograd: Revolution in the Factories, 1917–1918.* Cambridge, 1983.

Sukhanov, N. N. *The Russian Revolution, 1917.* Translated and edited by Joel Carmichael. Princeton, N.J., 1984.

Von Hagen, Mark. *Soldiers in the Proletarian Dictatorship: The Red Army and the Soviet Socialist State, 1917–1930.* Ithaca, N.Y., 1990.

Wade, Rex. *Red Guards and Workers' Militias in the Russian Revolution.* Stanford, 1984.

Works by Eduard Dune
(pseudonym Ivan Ivanov)

"Vorkutskaia tragediia." *Sotsialisticheskii vestnik* 28, nos. 4–5 (607–8) (20 May 1948): 93–96.

"The Vorkuta Massacre." *Modern Review* 2, nos. 5–6 (June 1948): 302–9.

"Vorkuta." *Sotsialisticheskii vestnik* 28, nos. 8–9 (611–12) (27 Sept. 1948): 159–60; 29, no. 3 (618) (25 Mar. 1949): 50–51; 29, no. 5 (620) (27 May 1949): 87–88.

"Russkii narod v okkupirovannykh oblastiakh i 'Vlasovtsy.'" *Sotsialisticheskii vestnik* 28, no. 11 (614) (30 Nov. 1948): 212–13.

"Pis'mo." *Sotsialisticheskii vestnik* 29, no. 5 (620) (27 May 1949): 96.

"SSSR i 'diktatura proletariata.'" *Sotsialisticheskii vestnik* 30, nos. 8–9 (636) (Sept. 1950): 169–70.

"Pis'mo v redaktsiiu." *Sotsialisticheskii vestnik* 30, nos. 11–12 (638–39) (Dec. 1950): 219–20.

"Ubiistvo Kirova." *Sotsialisticheskii vestnik* 31, no. 3 (642) (Mar. 1951): 67–70.

"Russkii Di-Pi vo Frantsii." *Sotsialisticheskii vestnik* 31, nos. 9–10 (647) (Sept.–Oct. 1951): 198–200; 31, no. 11 (648) (Nov. 1951): 220–24.

"Vitebskoe getto." *Sotsialisticheskii vestnik* 32, nos. 1–2 (650) (Jan.–Feb. 1952): 26–27; 32, no. 3 (651) (Mar. 1952): 49–50.

"Trudoden' kolkhoznika i ego nachal'nika." *Sotsialisticheskii vestnik* 32, no. 3 (651) (Mar. 1952): 43–45.

I-v. "Smert' Alliluevoi." *Na rubezhe*, no. 4–5 (Sept. 1952).

Reference
Bibliography

Abramovich, Rafael. "Pamiati E. M. Dune." *Sotsialisticheskii vestnik* 33, no. 2–3 (Feb.–Mar. 1953): 51–52.

Anikeev, V. V. "Svedeniia o bol'shevistskikh organizatsiiakh s marta do dekabria 1917 g." *Voprosy istorii KPSS* 2 (1958): 126–93.

Benvenuti, Francesco. *The Bolsheviks and the Red Army, 1918–1922.* Cambridge, 1988.

Bilmanis, Alfred. *A History of Latvia.* Princeton, N.J., 1951.

Braunthal, Julius. *History of the International.* Translated by Henry Collins and Kenneth Mitchell. New York, 1967.

Bubnov, A., S. Kamenev, and R. Eidemann, eds. *Grazhdanskaia voina 1918–1921 gg.* Moscow, 1928.

Budberg, Aleksei. "Dnevnik." *Arkhiv russkoi revoliutsii.* 12 (1923): 197–290; 13 (1923): 197–312; 14 (1923): 225–314; 15 (1924): 254–345.

Desiatyi s"ezd RKP(b), mart 1921 g. Stenograficheskii otchet. Moscow, 1963.

Direktivy komandovaniia frontov krasnoi armii (1917–1922 gg.). 4 vols. Moscow, 1970.

Dvinov, Boris. *Moskovskii sovet rabochikh deputatov, 1917–1922.* Interuniversity Project on the History of the Menshevik Movement, no. 1. New York, 1961.

Geroi grazhdanskoi voiny. Moscow, 1974.

Geroi oktiabria: biografii aktivnykh uchastnikov oktiabr'skogo vooruzhennogo vosstaniia. 2 vols. Leningrad, 1976.

Grazhdanskaia voina i voennaia interventsiia v SSSR. Entsiklopediia. Moscow, 1983.

Grunt, A. Ia. *Moskva 1917–i: revoliutsiia i kontrrevoliutsiia.* Moscow, 1976.

Häfner, Lutz. "The Assassination of Count Mirbach and the 'July Uprising' of the Left Socialist Revolutionaries in Moscow, 1918." *Russian Review* 50, no. 3 (July 1991): 324–44.

Haimson, Leopold H., ed. *The Mensheviks: From the Revolution of 1917 to the Second World War.* Chicago, 1974.

Istoriia rabochikh Moskvy 1917–1945 gg. Moscow, 1983.

Iz istorii grazhdanskoi voiny i interventsii 1917–1922 gg. Moscow, 1974.

Kakurin, N. *Kak srazhalas' revoliutsiia.* Moscow, 1925.

Kommunisticheskaia partiia sovetskogo soiuza v rezoliutsiiakh, resheniiakh s"ezdov, konferentsii, i plenumov TsK. 8th ed. Moscow, 1970.

Kostomarov, Grigorii D. *Iz istorii moskovskoi rabochei krasnoi gvardii.* Moscow, 1930.

Krastyn', Ia. P. "Rabochee dvizhenie v Latvii v gody novogo revoliutsionnogo pod"ema." *Bol'shevistskaia pechat' i rabochii klass Rossii.* Moscow, 1965.

Kuznetsov, I., and A. Shumakov. *Bol'shevistskaia pechat' Moskvy.* Moscow, 1968.

Letopis' geroicheskikh dnei. Moscow, 1973.

Miliukov, Pavel N. *Rossiia na perelome.* 2 vols. Paris, 1927.

Milligan, Sandra. "The Petrograd Bolsheviks and Social Insurance, 1914–1917." *Soviet Studies* 20, no. 3 (1969): 369–74.

Modern Encyclopedia of Russian and Soviet History. 54 vols. Gulf Breeze, Fla., 1976–90.

Moskva. Entsiklopediia. Moscow, 1980.

Moskva-oktiabr'-revoliutsiia: dokumenty i vospominanii. Moscow, 1987.

Naida, S. F., et. al., eds. *Istoriia grazhdanskoi voiny v SSSR 1917–1922 gg.* Moscow, 1959.

Ocherki istorii moskovskoi organizatsii KPSS. Moscow, 1979.

Odinnadtsatyi s"ezd RKP(b), mart–aprel' 1922 g. Stenograficheskii otchet. Moscow, 1961.

Oktiabr' v Moskve. Moscow, 1967.

Rossiia v mirovoi voine (v tsifrakh). Moscow, 1925.

Russkie narodnie pesni. Moscow, 1957.

Sapronov, T. V. *Iz istorii rabochego dvizheniya.* Edited by Victoria E. Bonnell. Newtonville, Mass., 1976.

———. "Tri mesiatsa na Volge (1916)." *Proletarskaia revoliutsiia,* no. 8 (43) (1925): 216–37.

Sed'moi vserossiiskii s"ezd sovetov rabochikh, krest'ianskikh, krasnoarmeiskikh i kazachikh deputatov. Stenograficheskii otchet (5–9 dekabria 1919 g.). Moscow, 1920.

Sidorov, A. L. *Ekonomicheskoe polozhenie Rossii gody pervoi mirovoi voiny.* Moscow, 1973.

Skrylov, A. I., and G. V. Gubarev, eds. *Kazachii slovar'-spravochnik.* Cleveland, 1966.

Sokolov, K. N. *Pravlenie generala Denikina.* Sofia, 1921.

Soratniki: Biografii aktivnykh uchastnikov revoliutsionnoi dvizhenii v Moskve i moskovskoi oblasti. Moscow, 1985.

Sovetskaia istoricheskaia entsiklopediia. 16 vols. Moscow, 1961–76.

Starikov, Sergei, and Roy Medvedev. *Philip Mironov and the Russian Civil War.* Translated by Guy Daniels. New York, 1978.

Stewart, George. *The White Armies of Russia.* New York, 1933.

Trotsky, Leon. *The Trotsky Papers, 1917–1922.* The Hague, 1964.

von-Lampe, A. A., ed. *Beloe delo: letopis' beloi bor'by materialy sobrannye i razrabotannye Baronom P.N. Vrangelem i drugimi.* 7 vols. Berlin, 1926–33.

Vsia Moskva. Moscow, 1927

Index

Orenburg Cossacks, 112
Ostozhenka Street, 73
Ostrovitianov, Konstantin Vasil'evich
(1892–1969), 37, 40

The Past, 191, 261
Pavlovskii settlement garrison, 53, 58,
59, 73
Peace formulas, 21, 75
Peasants: attitude toward revolution,
37, 50; attitude toward work, 9, 11;
as Bolshevik supporters, 56; in Don
region, 102, 140; and food supply,
122, 123; and land, 10, 83; and
medical fund, 240; and October
revolution, 80; political demands
of, 54; in Red Army, 128, 129, 132;
and workers' club, 40, 41; workers,
at Provodnik, 6
Peche, Ian Iakovlevich (1881–1942),
121
People's Commissariat of Enlighten-
ment, 84
Pereiaslavl'-Zalesskii, 234
Peris, Daniel, 231
Perm, 138
Persianovka, 108, 109
Petrograd: labor unrest in, 27; name
change of, 241; in protest over
Constituent Assembly, 118
Petrograd Soviet, 28, 45
Petrovskaia Farming and Forestry
Academy, 241
Petrovsk-Port, 213, 218
Pharoahs, 241
Pilsudski, Jozef (1867–1935), 203
Pinkertons, 235
Plekhanov, Georgii Valentinovich
(1856–1918), 56, 246
Podtelkov, Fedor Grigor'evich (1886–
1918), 101, 108, 254
Poland: independence of, 91; soldiers
of, 94, 112; at war with soviet
Russia, 203, 204
Police: in February revolution, 31, 32,
34, 241. *See also* Cheka; Okhrana;
Pharoahs
Polidorov, Stepan Ivanovich (1882–
1932), 24, 25, 37, 240
Polivanov, General Aleksei An-
dreevich, 239

Ponomarev, Andrei Nikolaevich
(1897–1954), 101, 254
Popov, General Petr Kharitonovich
(1868–1960), 255
Povorino, 126, 134
Pravda, 244
Presnia district, 52
Press: bourgeois, 80, 250; communist,
146
Printers, 240
Printworkers' Voice, 24, 240
Prisoners: condition of, 166; in
Dagestan, 221, 222; escape from
Novorossiisk, 194; treatment by
Cheka, 211; treatment by Greens,
158–62; treatment by Reds, 71, 72,
109, 110, 141–43, 211, 212;
treatment by Whites, 109, 163–65,
182, 185, 192; in Volunteer Army
hospital, 181
Private ownership, 76
Provisional Government, 43–45; origin
of, 28, 241; popular attitudes
toward, 48, 57
Provodnik plant: Bolshevik branch in,
243, 246; ebonite department in,
15; evacuation of, 5, 6; factory
committee in, 37, 38, 48, 51; in
February revolution, 36, 38; in July
days, 53; medical fund in, 239;
militia in, 36, 37, 51; after October
revolution, 80, 86; Red Guard in,
55, 60, 61, 96, 121, 122; war orders
at, 234; work conditions in, 6;
workers' control commission in, 47
Public order: after February revolution, 49; after October revolution,
80, 81
Putilov works, 240
Putnyn', 96, 106

Railway transport, 103; in 1918, 100,
125; workers, 99, 102, 109
Rasputin, Grigorii Efimovich (?1871–
1916), 238, 239
Raw materials, 47
Red Army: armored air unit, 219;
Army of the Northern Caucasus,
261; attitudes toward soviet power,
228; billeting, 143, 144, 148, 154,
155, 158, 167, 211; cavalry, 172,